Facts On File Encyclopedia of

Black Women

IN AMERICA

Religion and Community

Encyclopedia of
Black Women in America

Facts On File Encyclopedia of

Black Women

IN AMERICA

Religion and Community

Darlene Clark Hine, Editor

Kathleen Thompson, Associate Editor

☑® Facts On File, Inc.

Facts On File Encyclopedia of Black Women in America: Religion and Community

Facts On File, Inc.
11 Penn Plaza
New York NY 10001

Library of Congress Cataloging-in-Publication Data

Facts on File encyclopedia of Black women in America / Darlene Clark
    Hine, editor ; Kathleen Thompson, associate editor.
                p.   cm.
        Includes bibliographical references and index.
    Contents: v. 1. The early years, 1619–1899 — v. 2. Literature —
v. 3. Dance, sports, and visual arts — v. 4. Business and professions —
    v. 5. Music — v. 6. Education — v. 7. Religion and community —
        v. 8. Law and government — v. 9. Theater arts and
entertainment — v. 10. Social activism — v. 11. Science, health, and
                            medicine.
            ISBN 0-8160-3424-9 (set : alk. paper)
            ISBN 0-8160-3434-6 (Religion and Community)
    1. Afro-American women—Biography—Encyclopedias. I. Hine,
            Darlene Clark. II. Thompson, Kathleen.
                    E185.96.F2   1996
        920.72'08996073—dc20   96-33268

Facts On File books are available at special discounts when purchased in bulk quantities for businesses, associations, institutions or sales promotions. Please call our Special Sales Department in New York at 212/967-8800 or 800/322-8755.

Text design by Cathy Rincon
Cover design by Smart Graphics

Printed in the United States of America

RRD FOF 10 9 8 7 6 5 4 3 2 1

This book is printed on acid-free paper.

Contents

How to Use This Volume

SCOPE OF THE VOLUME

The *Religion and Community* volume includes entries on individuals and organizations in the following subject areas: club work, community service, organized religion, and social work.

RELATED OCCUPATIONS

Professionals in related occupations covered in other volumes of this encyclopedia include the following: journalists (*Business and Professions*), labor organizers (*Social Activism*), medical professionals (*Science, Health, and Medicine*), social activists (*Social Activism*), and teachers (*Education*).

HOW TO USE THIS VOLUME

The introduction to this volume presents an overview of the history of black women in the fields of religion and community service. A chronology following the biographical entries lists important events in the history of black women in black churches, benefit societies, and clubs.

Individuals and organizations are presented in alphabetically arranged entries. If you are looking for an individual or organization that does not have an entry in this volume, please check the alphabetically arranged list of entries for all eleven volumes of this encyclopedia that appears at the end of this book, in addition to each of the tables of contents of the other volumes in the series.

Names of individuals and organizations for which there are entries in this or other volumes of the encyclopedia are printed in boldface. Check the contents list at the back of this book to find the volume where a particular entry can be bound.

Introduction

In 1984, a black woman named **Leontine T. C. Kelly** stood and looked out on the city of San Francisco. In that area, there were 400 United Methodist churches with 100,000 members—black and white—and she had just been chosen their bishop. She would decide what minister would best serve which congregation. She would ordain young ministers beginning their service to the church. She would settle arguments, soothe feelings, and make decisions that would affect those 400 congregations in profound ways.

Leontine Kelly was not alone as she looked out on her bishopric. Behind her stood a free black woman born in 1783 who would not stop preaching no matter who tried to thwart her. There was an American woman called "God's image carved in ebony" who led revival meetings all over England, Scotland, India, and West Africa. There was a young woman of twenty-one who stood before a black Baptist convention in 1900 and spoke on "How the Sisters Are Hindered from Helping." And there were millions of other preachers, missionaries, nuns, deaconesses, church secretaries, choir leaders, and faithful church members.

At the same time, in Washington, D.C., another woman carried out the mission of black women. As **Dorothy Irene Height** sat in the president's office of the **National Council of Negro Women** (NCNW), hundreds of awards and honorary degrees

Dorothy Height has devoted over half a century to the cause of equality and human rights for all people. As the head of the National Council of Negro Women, she walks in the footsteps of centuries of black women fighting for a just American society.

attested to her leadership. But the greatest honor was in knowing that she sustained the tradition of black women in eighteenth-century Philadelphia who formed benevolent societies to help the free black community survive. She walked in the footsteps of the women of the Ladies Literary Society of New York who, in 1837, helped fund an antislavery journal. Her achieve-

1

ments glowed with the fire of women who, in 1892, fought for a place in the **World's Columbian Exposition's** Woman's Building.

All these women are part of the history of religion and community in African-American society.

ROOTS IN THE SLAVE COMMUNITY

Religion and community have always been closely interwoven in black America, as they were in Africa. And, as in Africa, women have played many roles.

The slaves brought to America came from a number of different African cultures. In some of those cultures, women had been merchants and traders. In some, they had been priestesses. They had played musical instruments in some places and had been singers in others. Most seem to have been storytellers to one degree or another.

The roles of women in the slave community echoed the roles they had played in the African cultures from which they came. And, under the tremendous pressures of slavery, many limits on women's roles, of necessity, broke down. Where there was a need, it was filled by anyone who had the skills, or the courage, to fill it. Those who could heal healed. Those who could lead led. And those who could preach . . . well, that was more problematic.

Most enslaved Africans brought to the Americas came from the west coast of Africa, in the area that ranges from Senegambia in the north to Angola in the south. From this area, they brought two major religious traditions. One was Islam. Followers of that religion came from Ghana, Mali, and Songhay, all of which had ties

with northern African Islamic countries. The other was the folk-based tradition that combined elements from many areas in West Africa.

Many of the slaves who ended up in North America went first to the Caribbean, where the African religious traditions met up and mingled with Roman Catholicism. Strong evidence of the nature of these traditions is found in the Caribbean religions that "Africanized" Christianity, such as santería in Cuba, shango in Trinidad, and cumina in Jamaica. There are also strains of African religions in the folk beliefs and stories, as well as the music, of African Americans throughout North and South America.

When Christianity was introduced into the slave community in North America, it came with its own rules . . . and roles. In the Northern colonies, slaves were encouraged and often required to attend the same churches their masters attended. They were also often given religious instruction. These African Americans participated in the life of the church, but they did not in any significant way form it. It mattered little in these churches what roles black women might once have played in Africa. The possibilities for women in these churches were already clearly defined and limited.

In the South, the situation was different. African Americans were introduced to Christianity primarily by missionaries from Britain—the Society for the Propagation of the Gospel in Foreign Parts—not by their owners. Most slaveholders believed that Christian slaves would be more likely to think they were equal to their masters and cause trouble. They usually tolerated, but did not encourage Christian conversion. As a result, Christian slaves worshiped separately from their masters.

The first exclusively black churches were in the South and were Baptist. The Bluestone African Baptist Church on the Byrd plantation in Mecklenburg, Virginia, was formed in 1758. The Silver Bluff Baptist Church was founded in Silver Bluff, South Carolina, in 1773. Other churches were founded in 1776, 1780, and 1785 in Petersburg, Richmond, and Williamsburg, Virginia.

A study by Mechal Sobel of African-Baptist churches during that time reveals that women were deaconesses, members of separate women's committees, and delegates to meetings. They were not, however, allowed to preach.

Most of these churches existed for only a few decades. Then, after Nat Turner's rebellion in 1831, laws began to be passed in the South forbidding black Christians from worshiping without the presence of "respectable" whites. The fear was that another Nat Turner would arise, believing, as he had, that God had appointed him to fight slavery. Black churches did not surface again in the South until after the Civil War.

During these years, some slaveholders took their house slaves to services in white churches. There, African Americans were seated separately, often in balconies. Sometimes, slaveholders allowed white ministers to hold services in the slave quarters. However, to a large degree, religious activity went underground. Prayer meetings were held in secret in the slave quarters or, when surveillance was stricter, in caves and forest clearings. These meetings were often led by women.

The slaveholders were right to fear Christianity. Although it has sometimes functioned to keep African Americans from rebelling, it has just as often been the source of their strength to resist. And the church, whether it existed in a brush arbor or a great stone edifice, has been the organizational basis of the struggle for justice.

African Islam was still in evidence at this time. There are records in biographical narratives of Islamic practices among slaves. A black man named Omar ibn Seid, of South Carolina, wrote in Arabic script and quoted from the Koran. However, the tribal religions of West Africa were seen more and more either as influences on Christianity, rather than active religions in their own right, or as underground religions, such as vodun, or voodoo.

Black women were key figures in the underground religions. The most famous of the voodoo leaders, for example, was **Marie Laveau**. By 1830, she was exceptionally wealthy and powerful because of her influence in both the black and white communities.

There were a few black Roman Catholics during the eighteenth century, and their numbers began to rise with the immigration of Catholics from Haiti. Among these was **Elizabeth Lange**, who founded the first religious community of black women in America, the **Oblate Sisters of Providence**, near Baltimore, Maryland. There were also a number of black Catholic communities in Louisiana and Florida. One of the world's oldest black Catholic churches was founded in St. Augustine, Florida, in 1829.

In the late 1700s, black churches began to arise in the North as part of a conscious move toward separatism by free black Christians. The majority of black Christians in the North were Methodists. That denomination had welcomed and actively recruited black members. A crucial moment in the spiritual life of founder John Wesley had been shared with a black fellow-worshiper, an Englishwoman known to us only as

Betty. When Wesley came to North America, he sought out and baptized slaves, including a number of black women. The Methodist Church condemned slavery for most of the eighteenth century.

However, black church members were not treated as equals in white churches. Around the turn of the century, African Americans tired of the discrimination they experienced and began to form their own churches.

First, they formed separate, individual churches, such as the Bethel African Methodist Church in Philadelphia, founded in 1794, and the Joy Street Baptist Church in Boston, founded in 1805. Then, in 1816, the African Methodist Episcopal (AME) Church was founded. It was not a single place of worship, but a denomination, an organization of churches. Soon after, the African Methodist Episcopal Zion Church became the second major black Methodist denomination. After the Civil War, both these churches successfully recruited members in the South. Then, the Methodist Episcopal Church, South, encouraged the founding of the Colored (later Christian) Methodist Episcopal Church.

The role black women played in these and later Protestant denominations was based on that of women in white Protestant churches. Women were a crucial part of the white Christian church, but their place in it was strictly defined.

The African-American community adapted this structure in a way that gave women a great deal of influence and participation. According to Cheryl Townsend Gilkes in *Black Women in America*, there are four basic pillars of the Afro-Christian tradition—preaching, prayer, music, and testimony. Women have been responsible for three of these—prayer, music, and

testimony. Preaching, officially, was left to men. This satisfied the white Christians who had power over black worship. Later, it satisfied the black men who believed their manhood depended on the maintenance of traditional gender roles. Black women worked around it.

From the beginning, black women served in the ministry of music as choir members, choir directors, and organists. As early as 1828, the St. Thomas Episcopal Church in Philadelphia hired a young woman, Ann Appo, as church organist, a job that thousands of black women have filled with devotion and creativity ever since. Black women also wrote many of the best-known and best-loved songs in the hymnbooks. The church provided black women with their most consistent musical outlet. Whatever restrictions were put on them in other places, they could always make music in church.

Testimony has included both standing and speaking in church and teaching the gospel to young people. It has also included visitation to the homes of members and potential members. Black women have taken the major role in all these areas.

Black women also served as missionaries, but their roles were usually limited. The wives of male missionaries were called "assistant missionaries" and were expected to work with women and children. They received little or no pay and less credit. A single woman was also classified as an assistant missionary and given reduced pay and responsibility. Nonetheless, in 1830, women made up 49 percent of the American Protestant missionary force overseas. By 1880, that number had increased to 57 percent.

In the third province open to women—prayer—black women developed an eloquence that rivaled and often surpassed the preacher's. They frequently prayed before the sermon in the regular church service. In addition, they held prayer meetings in their homes. Some developed groups of loyal followers for their prayer ministries. Sophie Murray and Elizabeth Cole, of the Philadelphia Bethel African Methodist Church, were both reported to be evangelists of the congregation who "held many glorious prayer meetings [where] many souls were brought to saving knowledge."

Preaching, however, remained a male preserve. **Jarena Lee**, the first woman to petition for the right to preach in the AME Church, was refused. But she was given permission to hold prayer meetings in her house. For some time she did. Then, moved by a firm belief that she was called by God and that His power was greater than that of her religious brethren, she went out on her own. She was one of many black women to do so.

THE PREACHING WOMEN

In 1849, Jarena Lee published a "spiritual autobiography" that told of her more than three decades of traveling and preaching the Christian gospel. According to that document, she first asked to be allowed to preach in 1809, when she was twenty-six years old, at the Bethel African Methodist Church of Philadelphia. Her request was flatly refused. At that time, women were not accepted as preachers by either white or black denominations. The first woman to be ordained would be Antoinette Brown, a white women ordained by the Congregationalists in 1853.

Lee renewed her request in about 1816 to the newly organized AME Church organization, led by bishop Richard Allen. She was again refused, but it was then that Allen granted permission for the private prayer meetings. Not long after, Lee felt that she must speak in a public church service when the minister of Bethel Church "appeared to lose the spirit." Her sermon was so powerful that Allen commended her. From there, she went on to travel the northeastern region of the country, preaching as she went along.

Lee was soon joined by other AME women. **Zilpha Elaw** was moved to preach by her belief that Jesus had appeared to her in a vision. However, she did not act until thirteen years later, in 1817, when she went into a trance at a religious revival. Convinced that she had been sanctified by God, she began to preach, or "exhort." She continued to preach in her own area, around Burlington, New Jersey, until after her husband died. Then, in about 1825, she became a traveling preacher. She spoke against slavery and racism while preaching in the South, as well as Washington, D.C., and Maryland. Later, she preached in England.

Lee and Elaw both challenged convention by insisting that they, and other women, had rights in the eyes of God that were not being recognized by their brothers in the church. Behind their determination to change things for black women was a certainty that they believed came from divine inspiration.

To describe **Rebecca Cox Jackson**, another nineteenth-century preacher, writer Alice Walker coined the term "womanist." In the 1830s and 1840s, Jackson traveled from town to town and church to church, preaching her own personal vision of God. But she also spoke of the importance of unity among black people. And she insisted that churches had to deal with the fundamental questions of black life—civil rights, families, education, and the possibilities for better jobs.

In 1868, **Amanda Berry Smith** also felt herself sanctified by God. She was a member of an African Methodist Church. However, she was attending a service at a Methodist church, led by John Inskip, a well-known white preacher, when she felt herself blessed. She said of the experience, "I wanted to shout 'Glory to Jesus!' but Satan said, 'Now, if you make a noise they will put you out.' I was the only colored person there and I had a very keen sense of propriety." By the end of the service, she felt that God had not only covered her with peace and power but had cured her of her fear of white people.

The following year, after her husband's death, she began conducting revivals. She spent most of her preaching career "exhorting" white audiences, particularly in the National Camp Meeting Movement, a Holiness crusade within the Methodist Episcopal Church. Beginning in 1878, she spent twelve years preaching in England, Scotland, India, and West Africa. Of her preaching in India, Methodist Episcopal bishop J. M. Thoburn said, "She possessed a clearness of vision which I have found seldom equalled. . . . During the seventeen years that I have lived in Calcutta, I have known many famous strangers to visit the city, but I have never known anyone who could draw and hold so large an audience as Mrs. Smith."

Smith spent a number of years in Africa, particularly Liberia. Then, in 1890, weakened by illness, she returned home. In her later years, she settled in Chicago and began to raise money to open an orphanage and industrial school for black children. In 1899, the school opened. Smith expanded it over the years and ran it entirely without government funding. In 1913, seriously ill, she was forced to retire at the age of 76.

The focus on economic and civic welfare revealed by the lives of these women preachers has been a continuing one in the black church. The emphasis has been so strong that it is almost impossible to separate the history of the church from that of social welfare movements, political activism, and community organizing.

And this, not preaching, is the area in which women have been most active. They have been the fund-raisers and caretakers. They have founded orphanages and homes for the aged. They have run kindergartens and day-care centers. They have established schools and crusaded for moral reform.

Among the most striking examples of the work of black churchwomen is the mutual benefit society. Thousands of these organizations, and their successors, have literally ensured the survival of the black community and its members over the centuries.

MUTUAL BENEFIT SOCIETY

As a rule, mutual benefit societies, like most other black institutions, came from the church. But sometimes it was the other way around, with the mutual benefit society, an institution nearly as basic as the family, taking the lead. The African Methodist Episcopal Church, for example, evolved from the Free African Society, a mutual assistance organization founded in 1787 by the free black citizens of Philadelphia to provide their community the rudiments of social welfare.

In 1793, the welfare functions of the Free African Society were absorbed by the Female Benevolent Society of St. Thomas, one of hundreds of such societies organized by free black women in antebellum cities. By

The Independent Order of St. Luke was founded in 1867 by an ex-slave, Mary Prout. By 1899, the order had fallen on hard times and might have ceased to exist had it not been for Maggie Lena Walker. Under her leadership, by 1920 the Order of St. Luke had more than 100,000 members in twenty-eight states and had created the St. Luke Penny Savings Bank, a weekly newspaper, and a department store, and generally had become a collective force to reckon with in Richmond, Virginia, where the organization was headquartered. Pictured here is its office staff. (NATIONAL PARK SERVICE)

1838, there were 119 mutual aid societies in Philadelphia alone, more than half of which were female associations, and women made up nearly two-thirds of the membership of all benefit societies.

Some of the earliest established female societies in Philadelphia were the Benevolent Daughters (1796), the Daughters of Africa (1812), the American Female Bond Benevolent Society of Bethel (1817), the Female Benezet (1818), and the Daughters of Aaron (1819).

In general, benefit societies collected dues, which they distributed among their members to relieve the sick and to bury the dead. Just as often, especially in church-related societies, their activities embraced a larger commitment to community uplift and moral reform. This was the case with the Female Wesleyan Association of Baltimore and New York City's Abyssinian Benevolent Daughters of Esther. Another New York society, the African Dorcas Association, was founded in 1827 to provide clothing for black schoolchildren. These were all church-related women's organizations dedicated to improving the welfare of African-American people.

The Colored Female Charitable Society of Boston (1832) pledged itself to "mitigate [the] sufferings" of widows and orphans. The African Female Benevolent Society of Newport, Rhode Island, sponsored that city's school for black children from 1809 until 1842 when Newport finally opened a public school. In neighboring Massachusetts, the Colored Female Religious and Moral Society of Salem (for dues of 52 cents per year) offered weekly prayer, religious conversation, profitable reading, and friendly advice, along with sickness and death benefits to members who would "resolve to be charitably watchful over each other" and not "commit any scandalous sin, or walk unruly."

The 1846 charter of the New Orleans Colored Female Benevolent Society of Louisiana, in addition to providing insurance benefits, called for the "suppression of vice and inculcation of virtue among the colored class." The Female Lundy Society in Albany and its sister institution in Cincinnati, both founded in the 1840s, combined antislavery with social welfare.

With the rapid expansion in the number and variety of black organizations, especially after 1830, it was difficult to place labels on the moral reform movements, political protest groups, mutual benefit societies, secret lodges, insurance associations, credit unions, orphanages, schools, library companies, and literary societies. There was both a division of labor and a melding of functions in order to serve the all-encompassing purpose of racial deliverance.

This distinctive mission widened into a war for survival after emancipation. Self-help and racial solidarity coincided with the advancing career of Jim Crow. As four mil-lion former slaves sought institutional support, voluntary associations among black women multiplied by the thousands.

At the turn of the twentieth century, W. E. B. DuBois's pioneering studies in sociology uncovered so many mutual aid societies that he found it "impractical to catalog them." Among women in the black belt of Alabama, DuBois concluded, "The woman who is not a member of one of these [benevolent societies] is pitied and considered rather out of date."

In Petersburg, Virginia, DuBois gave up after listing twenty-two mutual benefit societies, at least half of which were women's associations such as the Sisters of Friendship, the Ladies Union, the Ladies Working Club, the Daughters of Zion, the Daughters of Bethlehem, the Loving Sisters, and the Sisters of Rebeccah. It was in nearby Richmond, however, that the mutual benefit society among black women assumed its highest stage of development in a century-long evolution from folk networks among female slaves to national organizations among professional women.

By the close of Reconstruction, black women in Richmond had organized twenty-five "female benevolent orders." The most important among these was the Independent Order of St. Luke, which had expanded to Richmond from Baltimore, where it had been founded in 1867 by a former slave, **Mary Ann Prout**. By 1899, the order had fallen on hard times, and might have expired had it not come under the leadership of **Maggie Lena Walker**.

Born in Richmond in 1867, Walker had been active in the Order of St. Luke since the age of fourteen, while also teaching in Richmond's public schools. The organization became the instrument of her vision for community development. By 1920, under her leadership, it had more than 100,000 members in twenty-eight states. It had created the St. Luke Penny Savings Bank, a weekly newspaper called the *St. Luke Herald*, and a department store, the St. Luke Emporium.

Walker and St. Luke women funded scholarships, helped found a school for delinquent girls, fought for women's suffrage, protested racial disfranchisement, denounced lynching, and took the lead in the 1904 boycott against Richmond's segregated streetcars. The Order of St. Luke symbolized a major transition in the evolution of African-American institutions. By the turn of the twentieth century, many of the functions of the benefit society increasingly passed into hands of black insurance companies, savings banks, settlement houses, hospitals, civil rights organizations, and government agencies.

However, just as many of these functions passed into the caring hands of black clubwomen who, as descendants of the mutual aid tradition, continued to offer substance and hope in the vast spaces where modern institutions seldom reached. The connection between the Daughters of Africa and the **National Association of Colored Women** (NACW) may not have been direct, but it was clear. And it ran through the Independent Order of St. Luke and thousands of earlier such societies that also lifted as they climbed.

THE CLUBWOMEN

"Lifting as We Climb" was the motto of the black women's club movement, which had its roots in the women's church groups and

"Lifting as We Climb" was the motto of the black women's club movement. No one personified this commitment more than Margaret Murray Washington. She is pictured here (seated) with the Tuskegee Women's Club. (LIBRARY OF CONGRESS)

benevolent societies. It grew out of the literary societies that had, besides discussing the latest poems of **Frances E. W. Harper**, promoted social improvement and the advancement of the race. However, toward the end of the nineteenth century, it took on a character of its own.

The club movement developed in Northern cities such as Boston and Philadelphia. In these cities, free black women were enthusiastic participants in the many church and community groups formed to provide the services they could not expect from a white government. They were also aware of their position as the black elite. Often coming from families that had been free for generations, they had many more resources, financial and educational, than the average black woman in the United States.

These club members were from the black middle class and upper classes. However, their class was defined more by their education than their wealth. The members of the Bethel Literary and Historical Association in Washington, D.C., for example, were almost all teachers. The **Woman's Loyal Union**, in New York, was founded by a teacher and a journalist. The Woman's Era Club of Boston was founded by a journalist who had also served on the U.S. Sanitation Commission.

Although some of these women were the wives of prosperous business and professional men, a great many were not. They were not idle women trying to find ways to spend their time. They were busy women trying to find ways to improve the status of black women and black people in general in this country.

The clubs founded schools and raised funds for hospitals, orphanages, and homes for the aged just as their white counterparts did. But there was a special consciousness behind their efforts, an awareness that they were serving their own people—and that no one else was going to.

Boston, New York, and Washington, D.C., were the hub of what would become the national club movement. Washington, in particular, was the home of many of the black elite. Its Bethel Literary and Historical Society provided a forum, as well, for the intellectual elite. The great women leaders and speakers of the day spoke to its members. In 1892, members of the Bethel group came together with others in Washington to form the Colored Woman's League of Washington, D.C.

In that same year, New York and Boston clubs were formed after a testimonial dinner held in New York to honor **Ida B. Wells-Barnett**, an equal rights crusader and antilynching activist, brought women leaders together. New York women, including **Victoria Earle Matthews** and Maritcha Lyons,

formed the Woman's Loyal Union. Boston women, including **Josephine St. Pierre Ruffin**, her daughter **Florida Ruffin Ridley**, and **Maria Louise Baldwin**, founded the Woman's Era Club.

Three things then happened within a few years to ignite the national movement. One of them involved exclusion by white women. One involved slander from a white man. And one involved a sense of the ridiculous.

During the early 1890s, the World Columbian Exposition in Chicago was being organized. It was proclaimed the most important and spectacular world's fair ever held. Under pressure from suffragists, the United States Congress had agreed to the establishment of a Woman's Building at the fair. The suffragists, however, were not put in charge of the building. That job went to Mrs. Potter Palmer, the socially prominent wife of one of the fair's financial backers. When she put together her "Board of Lady Managers," suffragists were conspicuously absent—and so were black women.

A group of Chicago women confronted the Lady Managers, but their petition for participation in the building was rejected. According to Palmer, black women were not included in the planning of the building because they had no national organization to represent them. The Colored Women's League of Washington, D.C., tried to organize a national convention of black women's clubs in time to qualify but wasn't successful.

In the end, the Lady Managers accepted a proposal from **Fannie Barrier Williams**, wife of a prominent black attorney in Chicago. She was appointed a clerk in charge of exhibit installations, and a New York black women's club put together an exhibit that was accepted.

In the meantime, the Colored Women's League continued its quest for a national organization. It sent out an announcement in the *Woman's Era*, the monthly magazine of the Boston Woman's Era club, which was circulated widely and had become a publication used by clubs around the country. In their announcement they asked for delegates from other clubs to join with them as a national black women's organization at the National Council of Women convention in 1895. A few responded and became the National Colored Women's League . . . but not the women of the Woman's Era Club.

That was the first log laid on the fire. The second occurred that same year. James W. Jacks, a member of the Missouri Press Association, took it upon himself to straighten out an Englishwoman named Florence Belgarnie, an admirer of Ida B. Wells. Jacks wrote a letter to Belgarnie explaining that she was wrong to give her support to such a person. He accused black women of having "no sense of virtue and of being altogether without characters." He went further, saying that black women were "prostitutes, thieves, and liars."

Foolish as this charge may seem today, black women of that time were forced to take it seriously. After the Civil War, the white South set out to try to justify the actions it had taken during slavery. White men had forced themselves sexually on black women all during slavery. Their justification was the lie that black women had no moral virtue to protect. If they, as white men, had raped, harassed, and exploited "good" women, then certainly they would have been guilty of great evil, but black women weren't "good," so it didn't make any difference. This was the lie that Jacks repeated in his letter.

The letter was circulated among clubs around the country. When Josephine Ruffin saw it, she wrote "A Call: Let Us Confer Together." She declared that black women must come together "to teach an ignorant and suspicious world that our aims and interests are identical with those of all good aspiring women." She also sounded the note that would become the theme of the national club movement. She said that black women must spread this message "not by noisy protestations of what we are not, but by a dignified showing of what we are and hope to become."

Ruffin went on to say that changing the image of black women had to be accomplished collectively, because the character and accomplishments of individual women were seen as exceptions. "Because all refutation has been tried by individual work," she wrote, "the charge has never been crushed."

Ruffin's call was answered when 104 women from twenty clubs came together at a conference in Boston and formed the National Federation of Afro-American Women. Later, the membership included thirty-six clubs from twelve states. It did not include, however, the National Colored Women's League.

Two major efforts had been made to consolidate the ever-growing black women's club movement. Two "national" organizations now existed. In fact, they both held their national conventions in Washington, D.C., in July of 1896. Members of one "national" organization were running into members of the other "national" organization on the street as they journeyed to their respective meeting rooms. And everybody decided it was all a little silly. A committee was formed to work out the differences between the two groups and, that same year, they merged to form the National Association of Colored Women.

This was the first strong, unified national black organization, preceding the **National Association for the Advancement of Colored People** (NAACP) by almost fifteen years. It would serve the community for four decades.

The members of the National Association of Colored Women believed that the black community was always judged by its "lowest" members. To gain respect for themselves, they felt they would have to make every black person worthy of respect, an impossible job for any population. The belief that it could and must be done by African Americans was the source of two aspects of the club movement and the rising middle class in general. First, it inspired tremendous service to the community. Second, it often led to an adoption of white middle-class values and culture.

In service to the community, the black women's club movement was unparalleled. Individual clubs and regional federations addressed themselves to the particular problems in their areas. For almost all of them, this began with care for the aged.

In the late nineteenth and early twentieth centuries, there were many former slaves who had no pensions, savings, or families to care for them. The women's clubs founded homes where these African Americans who had already suffered terribly could have some comfort in their old age. The clubs raised money to pay for the homes and their maintenance.

Next in order of priority was medical care. In that time of Jim Crow, hospitals were usually segregated, and the colored hospitals or colored departments of white hospitals were often horribly underfinanced. The women's clubs raised money to try to bring care up to a minimal level of quality. They also founded clinics and hospitals.

Then there were the children to take care of. Women's clubs founded or subsidized children's homes all over the country. They also opened day nurseries and kindergartens. These were very common, since they could be operated in a church basement or a member's home, with largely volunteer staffs.

Finally, the women's clubs operated community centers. A typical center would offer a day nursery, kindergarten, library, clubs

Ida B. Wells-Barnett brought her four-month-old son, Charles Aked Barnett, to the 1896 meeting at which the National Association of Colored Women was formed. They were such a ubiquitous presence that he was voted "baby of the association." This photo was taken a few months later. (THE JOSEPH REGENSTEIN LIBRARY, THE UNIVERSITY OF CHICAGO)

for boys and girls, evening classes for working adults, music programs, and social gatherings. Often, job placement offices and rooms for lodging were also available.

All these services were operated and paid for by the black community. A very similar program was proposed half a century later by another club—the **Black Panther Party**.

The women's club movement fostered the same pride in self-reliance and self-determination that would re-emerge in the 1970s with the Black Power movement. But it was also defensive, motivated by a need to prove itself to the white population. This defensive posture sometimes limited its effectiveness. A very different attitude was shown in another arena. There, the final appeal was to a higher power than white society.

HOW THE WOMEN ARE HINDERED FROM HELPING

While they worked to form a national club movement, many of these same women were battling on another front. By the last decades of the 19th century, the division of labor within black churches had become well established. Men were in the pulpit and organizational meeting room. Women were everywhere else. They formed by far the majority of worshipers at Sunday services. They filled the choir. They raised money to keep the church going and to give to mission work. They visited the sick, gave food to the hungry, and counseled the troubled.

And yet, black men continued to imitate the male-dominated structure of the white church. Indeed, they often went further,

guarding their position in the church so zealously that it is impossible not to ask why.

One conceivable answer is that the church was so central to the black community. African Americans were ruled by a government in which they had no power and no real participation. That government ignored their needs and paid scant attention to their welfare. The black church functioned, in a way, as an alternative form of government. Those who led it were leaders of the black community at large. Men were extremely unlikely to give up any of their leadership positions simply because those positions were the only ones available.

In the largest black denomination, the AME Church, women carried on the struggle begun by such early preaching women as Jarena Lee and Zilpha Elaw. The church had made a concession to the influence of women in 1868 when it created the position of stewardess. These women, chosen by the minister of each church, were officially allowed to render service to the church.

This was far from enough for the women of the AME Church. Many of them still wanted to preach, and they *did* preach. In spite of the church's failure to recognize them, they became traveling evangelists, as well as missionaries. And while the church denied them, individual ministers were often more than ready to invite them to carry on revivals in their churches because the women were so effective. Finally, in 1884, the General Conference of the AME Church agreed to license women preachers.

These preachers, however, were not ministers of the gospel. They were not ordained. They could not administer sacraments. And they were not allowed to have churches.

Four years later, at the 1888 General Conference, the women were back. This time, the men were forced to deal with the fact that one of their number, Bishop Henry McNeal Turner, had ordained a woman, Sarah A. H. of North Carolina, without the sanction of the church. Turner was reprimanded, and the conference again absolutely forbade ordaining women.

AME Church women, however, continued to preach and to fight for a stronger, recognized position in the church. In fact, in 1888, **Sarah E. Gorham**, at the age of fifty-six, won the right to serve as a missionary in Africa. She was the first woman appointed by the AME to serve in a foreign field. She established the Sarah Gorham Mission School in Magbele, Sierra Leone.

In 1900, the men again tried to pacify the women by creating the position of deaconess. It was not nearly enough to satisfy those who were looking for full participation. For one thing, unlike deacon, deaconess was not an ordained position. Women would not be ordained in the AME Church for another forty-eight years.

However, the 1890s saw the formation of women's missionary societies. These were opposed by the male hierarchy, but the women carried on in spite of that. **Sara J. Hatcher Duncan**, in 1897, became general superintendent of the Women's Home and Foreign Missionary Society of the AME Church, making her one of the most influential women to that date in the black church.

The situation for black women in predominantly white denominations was complicated by a move for black self-determination. This was particularly true in the Baptist Church. Church leaders made it clear that the right to govern themselves, for which they were all fighting, was to be restricted to men. Besides barring women from the pulpit and the boardroom, black

Baptist men often segregated them in worship services and forbade them to organize separate women's societies. When black male church leaders sought greater power over their own churches, it was not surprising that they refused to share it with women.

Regional associations of black Baptist Churches began to form in the 1880s. These associations, called conventions, were forces for racial advancement both within the church and outside it. But they were almost entirely in the hands of the official leaders of black Baptist churches—the men. Women, however, did not sit back and watch. They formed their own conventions.

The women's conventions of the Baptist Church at first focused on those areas considered appropriate for women. One of these was higher education. Because Southern states did not provide public education for black students on the high school or college level, higher education was a critical issue for churchwomen, as it was for clubwomen. Many of the black Baptist women's conventions, in fact, were founded specifically to fill this need. There were the Baptist Women's Educational Convention of Kentucky, for example, and the Women's Baptist Educational and Missionary Convention of South Carolina.

These women's conventions raised and controlled their own money. They allowed involvement to men only as honorary members. And they were seen as a threat by men, who tried to outlaw them or to put male officers at their helms.

Of course, the women fought. Inspired by the woman's rights fervor of the time, they argued, agitated, and wrote about women's position in the church. Mary V. Cook, a professor at the State University of Louis-

A twenty-one-year-old Nannie Helen Burroughs (pictured here on the far left) gave an electrifying speech at the 1900 National Baptist Convention meeting entitled "How the Women Are Hindered from Helping." It led to the formation of a separate Women's Convention, which had almost one million members by 1903. (LIBRARY OF CONGRESS)

ville, a school owned by black Baptists, wrote about how ministers and male laymen locked women's societies out of the churches, literally. Mary Broughton, another teacher and leader, told of physical threats against the women.

In 1895, the men's conventions joined together to form the National Baptist Convention (NBC). In 1900, at a meeting of the convention, **Nannie Helen Burroughs** stood up to speak. She was twenty-one years old at the time. Her speech was entitled "How

the Women Are Hindered from Helping" and it was based on the scriptural reference, "Ye entered not in yourselves, and them that were entering in ye hindered."

Burroughs spoke with passion and eloquence and, with the help of two men—Mary Cook's husband and Burroughs's own boss at the time—the women won the right to form their own auxiliary to the NBC, the Women's Convention (WC). Burroughs became corresponding secretary and, during her first year in office, delivered more than 200 speeches and wrote more than 9,000 letters. By 1903, she reported, the WC had almost one million members.

Burroughs remained corresponding secretary and the major organizer of the WC until 1948. In that year, she became president and remained so until her death in 1960. Under her leadership, the WC worked against lynching, segregation, employment discrimination, and African colonialism. Its members fought for fair housing, better education and health care, and urban revitalization. The WC was a strong supporter of the NAACP and many of its leaders were also leaders in the NACW and, later, the National Council of Negro Women.

These changes in the position of women in the established churches were intensified by a new movement in African American religion at about this time—a new movement and new churches.

THE SANCTIFIED CHURCHES

To understand what happened to the black church at the beginning of the twentieth century, it's important to understand what happened to the community at large. When the century turned, 90 percent of African Americans still lived in the South. As late as 1910, 80 percent lived in rural areas.

Here's a picture of the place of worship of the average African American of that time. It's a small church in a small town, or in the countryside, in the South. It has its own preacher and a loyal, hard-working congregation. It's probably either Baptist or one of the black Methodist denominations—AME, AME Zion, or CME.

Suddenly, the picture changes. Following World War I, there is a migration of African Americans from the rural South to the urban North. Populations, and congregations, in those small Southern towns shrink. Now, churches have to share preachers because each one cannot support its own. The regular preacher is there one Sunday a month or maybe two. The other Sundays, there are prayer meetings, musical programs, maybe a traveling evangelist. There are church suppers and choir practices. The emphasis has shifted from preaching to prayer, music, and testimony.

In the North, there is a change as well. All those Southern workers coming north found themselves getting lost in the large mainstream churches. They were used to having positions of leadership and responsibility. They were used to a church that directly filled their spiritual needs and often helped fill their worldly needs as well.

Many of these displaced Southerners started their own churches, in storefronts or in homes. Again, there were not always ministers, certainly not paid ministers, for all the churches. Worship was in the hands of the people of the congregation. Again, prayer, music, and testimony—the three provinces of black women—were more frequent than preaching.

It was in this time of change, when decisions and policies were being made every time a new church opened its doors, that the Sanctified Church came into being. (The term "Sanctified Church" is used to refer to all churches in the Holiness and Pentecostal movements.)

But, as we have seen, there was something else of importance going on at the same time. And that was the move toward equality of black women. The club movement. The push for ordination in mainstream denominations. The organization of women's societies within the church.

So far, there were two forces at work to ensure women greater participation in these new churches. There was also a third—it was the spiritual nature of the churches themselves.

The direct inspiration of the individual, in Sanctified services, found expression in shouting, ecstatic dancing, and glossolalia, or speaking in tongues. No one—no minister, no church board, no bishop—could forbid this expression. No authority was recognized but that of the spirit.

Black women were strongly drawn to the Sanctified churches for these reasons and for others. Along with the emphasis on the spiritual, there was usually a very strict morality. Drinking, smoking, dancing, theater-going, gambling, and sex outside marriage were all sternly condemned. This fit well with the belief of many black women that they and their people could gain respect from the white community only by being intensely "respectable."

It has been estimated that 90 percent of Sanctified Church members are women. Many of the Sanctified denominations ordained women as ministers. The Fire Baptized Holiness Church of God of the Americas was founded as an entirely egalitarian denomination. The same was true of

The role of women in churches has often been most prominent in the area of music. Pictured here is the Excelsior Temple Band, Brooklyn, New York, 1929. (MOORLAND-SPINGARN)

the Mount Calvary Holy Church of America. Some were founded by women. The Mt. Sinai Holy Church of America was founded by Ida Robinson, and the All Nations Pentecostal Church was founded by Lucy Smith. In others, such as the **Church of God in Christ** (COGIC), women were not ordained but were given significantly greater roles than in the mainstream black churches.

Cheryl Townsend Gilkes writes, "The Sanctified Church took account of at least four specific aspects of [black women's] history when developing churchwomen's roles: the devaluation of black women by dominant culture, the education of black women and their recruitment as educators of 'the Race' during the late nineteenth and early twentieth centuries, the 'relative' economic independence of black women through sustained participation in the labor force, and the autonomous political organizations of black women between 1892 and 1940." The COGIC and other churches in the movement handled the four aspects of black women's history in a variety of ways.

The first point, the devaluation of black women by the dominant culture, was addressed by treating women with meticulous respect in all areas and protecting them against the disrespect of whites. A strict dress code, for both men and women, allowed no opportunity for accusations of low morals or lack of decency. The churches also took care that first names were never used in public settings. In church publications and notice boards, for example, both men and women were referred to by their initials. This, according to Gilkes, was done so that no white person could discover and use their first names.

Women were also given religious titles fitting their responsibilities. This, too, was a way of protecting them from white disrespect. White Southerners who refused to use Mr., Mrs., and Miss when talking to African Americans, were often reluctant to withhold a religious title such as reverend or deacon.

In the case of education, the Sanctified Church embraced the fact that women were educated and educators. In these churches, responsibility for educational programs was not treated as a sop thrown to women who did not have power in the "real" business of the church. It was given great emphasis.

Central to the work of the Women's Department of the COGIC were the Prayer and Bible Study Bands. Like the literary societies of the eighteenth and early nineteenth centuries, these bands were not limited to the functions indicated by their names. They promoted general literacy skills among women. Also, the second president of Saints' Academy in Lexington, Mississippi, a COGIC institution, was a woman, Arenia C. Mallory. For a time, she was the only black woman college president. Women were also teachers of religion in the church. As in the past, this role often was virtually indistinguishable from that of preacher.

Taking into account the third of the aspects Gilkes cites, financial independence, the Sanctified Church encouraged women to raise money for their own projects, separate from the main church budget. These funds were entirely under the control of the women. Women's financial contributions to the church itself were separately and particularly recognized.

Finally, the organization of self-determining women's groups within the church was strongly encouraged. The founder of the COGIC, Bishop Charles Harrison Mason, appointed a women's "overseer" named Mother Lizzie Woods Robertson. She headed the Women's Department and was a well-known revivalist and evangelist. She also founded many COGIC congregations. In time, the Women's Departments of COGIC churches came together to form the Women's Convention.

The strength of women in the Sanctified Church led to an enlargement of their preaching possibilities, even where ordination was still banned. Because of the emphasis on education, teachers of the gospel were highly respected. And many of the "teachers" were strong, effective preachers. They took on the role of evangelist, which differed very little from the role of preacher. Many women from other denominations left to join the Sanctified Church in order to become evangelists. There is reason to believe that the role of women in the Sanctified Church put pressure for change on the mainstream black denominations.

The same ferment that produced the Sanctified Church also gave rise to another form of African-American religion. The Moorish Science Temple was a church founded by Noble Drew Ali in Newark, New Jersey. Its primary importance to black religious history is that it was the forerunner of the Nation of Islam. It was one of seventeen Muslim communities that developed in the United States from the turn of the century to the present.

As in Christian churches, the position of women from one community to another differs, and the leadership of black women who are Muslims is often unofficial and unrecognized. Muslim women have restrictions on dress and behavior similar to those of women in the Sanctified Church and for many of the same reasons. The emphasis on women's groups for education is also strong in Muslim communities.

As the black church changed, the position of women changed with it. There were many more changes ahead for both. The struggle for freedom for black women and men was moving into a new phase.

THE NEW NEGRO AND THE NEW WOMAN

There had always been a political element to the club movement. Life as a black woman in the United States was political by its nature, and neither education nor wealth was a shield. During the last decade of the nineteenth century and the first decade of the twentieth century, the black women's club movement was the largest, strongest organized opponent of racial discrimination.

In 1908, an event occurred that sparked renewed resistance in the community as a whole—a race riot that devastated the black community in Springfield, Illinois. The National Association for the Advancement of Colored People was formed in reaction to the riot. It had both black and white, male and female members. In the beginning, the majority of the officers were white. However, the first field secretary of the NAACP was a black woman named Kathryn Johnson, who was a member of the Independent Order of St. Luke and the African Methodist Episcopal Church. **Mary McLeod Bethune** and Nannie Helen Burroughs were on the board of advisors for more than thirty years.

In the years that followed, the same women who founded black women's clubs and sororities founded local chapters of the NAACP. The same women who raised funds for black churches raised funds for the NAACP. In 1912, Mary Cable, president of

The first field-worker for the NAACP, Kathryn Magnolia Johnson, firmly believed that the leadership of the organization should be all-black. Her outspokenness on this matter may have caused her dismissal from the organization in 1916. (SCHOMBURG CENTER)

the Colored Women's Civic Club in Indianapolis, was responsible for the formation of the Indianapolis branch of the NAACP. She was Indiana's first NAACP president. For the first thirteen months of her term, all officers and members of the board were clubwomen. However, in 1913, they asked the men of the black community "who have more time" to take over.

As the NAACP began its fight for justice, it found unstinting support from the NACW and such black sororities as **Alpha Kappa Alpha** and **Delta Sigma Theta**. Running parallel to and working with the NAACP was Ida B. Wells-Barnett's Anti-Lynching Crusade. Barnett, too, could count on support from the clubwomen.

During this time, the NACW's leaders included **Mary Morris Talbert**, who went from the NACW presidency to the board of the NAACP, and **Hallie Quinn Brown**, who later became a major force in the Republican Party. But the NACW leader who was to make the greatest mark on history was Mary McLeod Bethune. Beginning in the 1920s, the national black women's club movement became the power base for this determined, brilliant, charismatic woman and so fulfilled a destiny no one could have predicted.

Bethune became president of the NACW in 1924. She immediately began to expand its influence. To begin with, she used the primarily white National Council of Women (NCW) of the United States. In this council of thirty-eight national women's organizations, only one, the NACW, was black. In 1925, the conference of the International Council of Women, which met every five years, took place in Washington, D.C. Thirty-five countries were represented. Bethune went into the conference with a plan.

First, she enlisted black women of the NACW from around the country as delegates to the conference. Then, she insisted on a policy of desegregated seating at all conference events. And then, when the policy was violated, she and all the other black Americans at the conference walked out, straight into the arms of the waiting press. Bethune, in one of her typically brilliant moves, appealed to American patriotism. It was humiliating, she said, for black Americans to be segregated in front of women from countries around the world.

Bethune won. The black delegates were assured that they would be seated properly if they would return to the conference, which they did. It was one of the many times that Bethune's keen political sense would lead her to just the right words and actions at just the right time.

After four successful years in office, Bethune was barred by the NACW's constitution from reelection. But she was a woman with vision and a sense of mission. She believed she could be a great leader of her people. She also fiercely believed that it was time for black women to have participation and power in American society. If the NACW could no longer be the base from which she would realize her vision, she would create another.

In 1935, with the help of **Charlotte Hawkins Brown** and other women from both inside and outside the NACW, Bethune founded the National Council of Negro Women (NCNW). This new organization was different from the NACW in that it admitted only national organizations as members. These organizations, fourteen of which were represented at the founding meeting, were diverse. They included sororities, Christian women's societies of different denominations, and academic organizations. The only requirements were that the groups represent black women and have national memberships.

At the first meeting, Bethune was elected president. With one stroke, she had become the executive officer of a group that represented 500,000 women, the total number of members of all the national organizations on the council.

Bethune accomplished much in the next two decades. She rose to such a position of power and influence in the Roosevelt administration that she and her "black cabinet" were directly or indirectly responsible for the establishment of the Fair Employment Practices Commission, the admission of black women into the Women's Army Corps (WAC), the fair treatment of black youth by the National Youth Administration, and the training of black pilots in the Civilian Pilot Training Program, among many other accomplishments. She continued to be active in government after Roosevelt's death, during the administration of President Harry Truman.

Charlotte Hawkins Brown, the long-time head of the Palmer Memorial Institute in Sedalia, North Carolina, was instrumental in helping Mary McLeod Bethune found the National Council of Negro Women.

Mary McLeod Bethune was the National Association of Colored Women president who used her position to make the organization a force to be reckoned with. Her national prominence continued until her death in 1955. She is shown here with Eleanor Roosevelt, one of her most visible and vocal champions. This photo was taken around 1950.   (BETHUNE MUSEUM AND ARCHIVES)

The ethical orientation of activist church women is epitomized in the famous "Last Will and Testament" of Mary McLeod Bethune, in which she encourages a legacy of faith, hope, and love alongside such practical strategies as education, dignity, harmonious living, and devotion to youth. Her "Last Will" is quoted on the base of the statue of Bethune in Washington, D.C., the model for which is reproduced here. (SCHOMBURG CENTER)

Bethune did not, however, neglect her responsibilities as president of the NCNW. Although she managed to get funding for a paid staff and a national headquarters building, she worked under serious financial constraints at all times. Her answer to this was to work with other organizations having greater financial resources. The NCNW became a source of information for, and a partner to, such groups as the Young Women's Christian Association (YWCA), labor unions, the NAACP, the National Council of Women, the National Urban League, the League of Women Voters, and the National Council of Jewish Women.

Bethune used publicity like a sword. She fostered connections, both personal and political, and maintained an image—a truthful image—of such dignity and integrity that she and her council realized many of the wildest dreams of black clubwomen in centuries past. She also helped to lay the groundwork for a new phase of the ongoing struggle, as the modern civil rights movement broke upon the country.

PREPARED FOR STRUGGLE

On May 18, 1955, Mary McLeod Bethune died. On December 1, 1955, a little more than six months later, **Rosa Parks** sat down on a Montgomery, Alabama, bus and refused to move. In an unbroken line, black women continued in the struggle for a better, fairer, freer life.

In recent years, historians have been reviewing and re-evaluating the civil rights movement, looking at it from different perspectives and with different assumptions. One of the things they have discovered is that women were much more crucial to the movement than the books tell us.

In an article entitled "Men Led, but Women Organized," Charles Payne states that in the years before the summer of 1964 women considerably outnumbered men in the civil rights movement. Although the genders were relatively balanced among young and old, women between the ages of thirty and fifty outnumbered men three or four to one. And their participation was not just a matter of numbers. Payne quotes Lawrence Guyot, a member of the **Student Nonviolent Coordinating Committee**, saying, "It's no secret that young people and women led organizationally." The question is why? Historically, women have always been less active in politics than men. Why were black women the exception?

Was it because there were simply more women in the South at the time? There had, after all, been a migration to the North in the 1940s and 1950s of black men seeking work. Payne eliminates that as a possibility by pointing out that even in families where both husband and wife were present, the wife was far more likely to participate in the movement.

Was it because reprisals were likely to be more serious against men? Probably not a deciding factor, says Payne. In the first place, reprisals were usually taken against whole families, regardless of who actually signed a petition or registered to vote. Then, too, reprisals were serious enough against women that they probably didn't perceive themselves as in less danger. They were clubbed and beaten. Payne says that every adult woman he interviewed lost her job.

The answer, according to Payne, lies in the history of religion and community among black women. The difference between black women in the 1950s and 1960s and other women in other times and places in history is that they knew how to organize, were accustomed to working together, and cared deeply about members of the community beyond their immediate families. They also believed that God would take care of them.

Women who came from a background of church and community service were ideal social activists. It didn't matter that the churches they attended often opposed their activities; they were used to disagreeing with the preacher. Because of the strong, independent women's departments in black churches, black women paid their own way and made up their own minds.

As far back as the traveling preachers of the nineteenth century, black women were accustomed to putting their duty to God before their duty to the church. Those same women who had insisted on preaching, no matter what the pastor or the bishop said, were now walking up to the voter registration desk, no matter who told them to go home and behave themselves.

Women often joined the movement when a daughter or nephew or close friend became involved. They knew the cause was just, and often seemed to believe that if loved ones were risking their lives, they should do the same. It might be dangerous, but God would help them through. Although some of the men might be saying it was of no use, the women knew what you could do if you put your mind to it. They had sent missionaries to Africa by running bake sales. They had founded orphanages and hospitals and schools. They had stood up at conventions, stared white women in the eye, and demanded to be seated. And won.

Black women weren't often in the front at press conferences. They didn't get their pictures in the paper or sit down across the table with the mayor as often as the men did. But they were used to that, too. They knew from experience that you can accomplish a great deal, that you can be a leader, without having your name at the top of the church bulletin or on a ballot.

The Montgomery Bus Boycott was the model for black women's participation in the civil rights movement. Montgomery, Alabama, had had racially segregated buses since the city bus line began operation in the mid-1930s. The segregation was enforced by threats and insults. Black women bore the brunt of the abusive treatment because they used the bus far more than black men.

In the early 1950s, the **Women's Political Council** (WPC) of Montgomery decided to

Rosa Parks was not just another tired seamstress who didn't want to give up her seat on a bus. She had behind her "a life history of being rebellious against being mistreated because of my color." (SCHOMBURG CENTER)

make the bus issue its prime concern. Council members met regularly with city officials to discuss the segregation policy, without success. They also looked for a test case suitable to take to court. When Rosa Parks refused to give up her seat to a white man, they had their case. Although Parks had not planned her calm protest, she recalled that she had "a life history of being rebellious against being mistreated because of my color." The time had come "when I had been pushed as far as I could stand to be pushed. . . . I had decided that I would have to know once and for all what rights I had as a human being and a citizen."

When **Jo Ann Gibson Robinson**, president of the WPC, learned of Parks' arrest, she decided to begin a boycott. For the next year, the women of the WPC passed out flyers, raised funds, and ran a car pool. They also worked with twenty-six-year-old Dr. Martin Luther King, Jr., whose charismatic personality drew interest to the boycott and who became its spokesperson.

While Robinson, Irene West, Euretta Adair, Hazel Gregory, Johnnie Carr, and other middle-class women served on committees, managed the Montgomery Improvement Association (MIA) office, and

Jo Ann Gibson Robinson had been traumatized by her own deeply humiliating experience at the hands of an abusive and racist Montgomery City Lines bus driver several years before she became the mobilizing force behind the boycott of the buses in Montgomery, Alabama.

played vital leadership roles, dozens of less-educated women supported the boycott. Georgia Gilmore, a self-employed cook, organized a club that sold pies and cakes, donating the proceeds at the mass meetings. Inez Ricks formed a rival club, and the meetings were enlivened by a weekly contest over which club raised more money.

The female leadership network was crucial to the boycott's success, but the backbone of the long protest was several thousand working-class women who, in the face of intimidation and threats, rode in the car pools or walked as far as twelve miles a day, even in the rain. "I'm not walking for myself," said an elderly woman refusing a ride. "I'm walking for my children and my grandchildren."

Another woman, Mother Pollard, promised King that she would walk until it was over. "But aren't your feet tired?" he inquired. "My feets is tired," she answered, "but my soul is rested."

The Montgomery Bus Boycott was not an isolated case. Women were leaders in the movement everywhere and at every moment. As individuals, churchwomen and clubwomen often became social activists.

Daisy Lampkin was chief of the executive board of the NACW before she became national field secretary of the NAACP. She used the fund-raising skills she had developed in the NACW and the National Council of Negro Women to raise millions for the NAACP's school desegregation fight, while her own salary never rose above $100 a week. **Juanita Jackson Mitchell** found her political consciousness raised in her sorority, Alpha Kappa Alpha, and went on to become the first national youth director for the NAACP.

Septima Poinsette Clark, a teacher who belonged to the Federated Women's Club of South Carolina, worked with the **Highlander Folk School** and became director of education and teaching for the Southern Christian Leadership Conference (SCLC). **Dorothy Foreman Cotton** followed her pastor at the Gillfield Baptist Church into the NAACP and ended up an officer in the SCLC and an advisor to Martin Luther King, Jr.

Devout churchwoman **Annie Devine** joined the civil rights movement at the age of fifty, organized widely for voter registration, and helped to found the **Mississippi Freedom Democratic Party** (MFDP) with her friend **Fannie Lou Hamer**. Hamer herself came straight out of the church and led off gatherings of SNCC and the MFDP with hymns.

The groups in which these women trained for the fight were not often so radical. And yet, such is the nature of the black struggle, that the goals of the National Council of Negro Women now read very much like those of the most militant civil rights organization.

Today, it is difficult to draw the line between "clubs" and activist groups, between political organizations and professional associations. The **National Coalition of 100 Black Women**, for example, is a networking group for black professional women, which also focuses on building career opportunities, developing leadership talents, and recognizing the contributions of black women. It is hardly a club, but one can't help feeling that **Mary Church Terrell** and Josephine St. Pierre Ruffin would feel right at home in its ranks.

The major black sororities, Alpha Kappa Alpha and Delta Sigma Theta, which have

Daisy Lampkin used her fund-raising skills to raise millions of dollars for the NAACP's school desegregation fight, while her own salary never rose above $100 a week.

been active for decades, are asserting a growing influence in the community of black women. They represent more than a quarter-million educated women who have moved into positions of authority in business, politics, the church, and every other aspect of American life.

Black women are still on the outside of many of the centers of power in the United States. And they are still finding strength in community.

AND VICE VERSA

If churchwomen were among those who gave most freely to the civil rights movement, they were also among those who received much in return. The political atmosphere generated by the movement caused widespread changes in the church.

In 1948, the African Methodist Episcopal Church agreed to ordain women, making official the position of all those traveling evangelists and teachers. The United Methodist Church had approved ordination for women in 1924, but it was limited. In 1956, women attained full status as ministers, as they also did in the United Presbyterian Church. By 1976, every major Protestant denomination in the United States had approved the ordination of women. The Church of God in Christ still has not done so. In the Roman Catholic Church, a few nuns have been assigned as pastors of churches.

Today, while most women, black and white, still exert their primary influence in the church in traditional roles, there are exceptions who have entered powerful positions formerly reserved for men. In 1984, Leontine T. C. Kelly was elected a bishop of the United Methodist Church. She was the first African-American woman to become a bishop in any major denomination in the United States. In 1989, **Barbara Harris** was consecrated a bishop of the Episcopal Church. She was the first woman of any race to fill that position. In 1989, Joan Salmon Campell was elected moderator of the Presbyterian Church, U.S.A. She was the first black woman and the sixth woman to head that church.

Kelly has stated with clarity how the church can expect to benefit from its new leaders. "For me," she has said, "the crux of the gospel message is the way we share power. One of the things women bring to the situation in terms of sharing power is new styles of leadership. I am no less the bishop. I know where the buck stops and who is responsible. But that doesn't mean I have to exert power in such a way that other people feel they are less than who they are because of who I am."

In any religion, in any community, that is a magnificent dowry for women to bring with them.

[This introduction incorporates material from the following articles in *Black Women in America: An Historical Encyclopedia*: "Religion," by Cheryl Townsend Gilkes; "Mutual Benefit Societies," by Walter Weare; "African Methodist Episcopal Preaching Women of the Nineteenth Century," by Jualynne E. Dodson; "African Missionary Movement," by Sylvia M. Jacobs; "Antilynching Movement," by Jacqueline Dowd Hall; and from many of the individual entries included in this volume. Other sources include the article "Together and in Harness: Women's Traditions in the Sanctified Church," by Cheryl Townsend Gilkes, which was originally published in *Signs*, volume 10, number 4, Summer, 1985.]

A

Alpha Kappa Alpha Sorority

Summer 1935 in the heart of the Mississippi Delta was typical—full of famine and disease. Malnutrition and no medical attention continued to lead to a rampant growth of diphtheria, smallpox, and syphilis. Other venereal diseases went unchecked. Child mortality increased. After years of being held hostage, people in the mud-sogged, fever-infested region accepted their plight and learned to subsist in spite of the conditions. They were hostages who did not expect to be released.

Still, by summer's end, the people in Holmes County had been given a reason to hope. Mobile health units staffed by twelve visiting doctors, nurses, and health care providers—unheard of in Mississippi or elsewhere—had traveled 5,324 miles to even the most remote areas to administer more than 2,000 immunizations to the children, give medical attention to 2,267, and distribute 6,800 health pamphlets. The mobile health clinics would continue to bring hope for eight years, expanding both the territory covered and the services rendered, and assisting more than 15,000.

Called the Mississippi Health Project (MHP), the clinics were the first national show of strength for twenty-seven-year-old Alpha Kappa Alpha (AKA) sorority. The impact was noted far and wide—from articles in periodicals such as the *Journal of Public Health* to magazines such as *Reader's Digest* to commendations by the surgeon general of the U.S. Public Health Service, Thomas Parren, who called MHP one of the finest jobs of volunteer public health work he had ever seen.

With the clinic, AKA—founded January 15, 1908, at **Howard University** as the first black Greek-letter organization for black women—was at the vanguard of a movement, and the exigencies of the times determined the response. The same was true in 1908. Then, there were a small number of women enrolled at Howard, limited opportunities for cultural enrichment, and the awareness that membership in this privileged class obligated black women to develop their potential to its fullest. The combination of circumstances led undergraduate **Ethel Hedgeman Lyle** and her eight associates to draft a blueprint that incorporated self-pride, social interaction, ethical standards, cultural stimulation, and scholarly pursuits: issues that had to be addressed to improve the quality of life for themselves and their people.

One of the earliest projects was the presentation of a concert in Rankin Chapel by AKA members during spring 1908. By 1913, the cultural program included national figures such as Nathaniel Guy, an elocutionist in classical repertoire, and Jane Addams of Hull House. AKA women also worked cooperatively with groups that fostered social action, marching for women's rights in suffragette parades, giving countless hours of service to aid black Americans migrating from the Deep South in 1917 and 1918, and taking leadership roles in the **National Association for the Advancement of Colored People** (NAACP), the **Young Women's Christian Association** (YWCA), and other organizations that worked for the betterment of humankind.

In the 1920s, as AKA, having been incorporated in 1913, grew into a national organization, a national agenda began to take shape. Beginning in 1921, AKA chapters used their January founders' day celebrations to feature programs that increased race consciousness. By 1922, national programs to foster "aesthetic development of the public" and increase community involvement had been added.

The 1930s, reeking with the Great Depression and intense antiblack feelings, signaled the need for social action programs. At its 1934 national meeting, AKA developed plans for a summer school for rural teachers, the precursor to the Mississippi Health Project; laid the groundwork to pressure Congress to pass the Costigan-Wagner Anti-Lynching Bill; and joined forces with other fraternal groups and the NAACP in monitoring fair employment and lynching legislation. In 1938, feeling the need to do even more to promote and safeguard the interests of black Americans, AKA established a full-time lobby to secure decent living conditions, permanent jobs, and a voice for determining working conditions.

The lobby continued to be a focal point during the 1940s, adding as targets the elimination of discrimination, disfranchisement, lynching, and inequities in federal housing and hospitalization programs. In 1946, buoyed by the lobby's success and excited about its potential, AKA invited the seven other Greek-letter organizations (sororities Delta Sigma Theta, Zeta Phi Beta, and Sigma Gamma Rho, and fraternities Alpha Phi Alpha, Kappa Alpha Psi, Omega Psi Phi, and Phi Beta Sigma) to become partners, and the American Council of Human Rights (ACHR) was created, with the elimination of racial discrimination and inequality as its primary goals.

The awarding of grants during the 1950s brought another dimension to the program. In 1952, AKA gave its first grant-in-aid—$6,000 over a three-year period—to the Howard University College of Medicine for research in child development. Sickle cell anemia was the focus for additional grants, with $15,000 contributed between 1958 and 1961.

The 1960s dictated further program expansion. As a response to the increase in black poverty, AKA developed a partnership with the federal government to prepare young women for economic independence under the aegis of the Anti-poverty Program. A $4 million grant resulted, and in 1965 AKA began its operation of the Cleveland Job Corps Center, thereby becoming the federal government's first women's Job Corps contractor. Subsequent awards of more than $40 million over a twenty-five-year period and a 1991 award of $15 million attested to the center's effectiveness, providing a second chance for more than 20,000 youths. AKA also developed its interest in the preservation of black culture, instituting a domestic travel tour on historical black figures, events, and places, and a heritage publication series on black women in the judiciary, politics, business, medicine, and dentistry.

The 1970s ushered in an era when AKA could give large awards to others. A $20,000 award was given to underwrite the purchase of Dr. Martin Luther King's birthplace; Central State University received $25,000 to restore a rare book collection destroyed by a tornado in 1974; the NAACP was given $50,000; and AKA presented the final installment on its pledge of $500,000 to the United Negro College Fund. AKA also launched its Educational Advancement Foundation, which by 1991 was making annual awards of $300,000 for scholarly pursuits.

With the realization that the world was becoming smaller, global initiatives became program targets in the 1980s. More than 300 African villages were adopted by AKA chapters in partnership with AfriCare. Additional support also was given to education through the award of $200,000 to historically black colleges.

In the 1990s, education, heritage, black economic development, and benevolent support continued. The Ivy AKAdemy, a community-based comprehensive learning center, opened in January 1991 in communities across the nation. The donation in October of a memorial honoring World War II hero Dorie Miller marked the inauguration of Black Faces in Public Places, a campaign by AKA to increase the number of black images on government property and in public parks. The inauguration of Black Family Month reemphasized the strength of the black family. A Black Dollar Day campaign called attention to the plight of black businesses and promoted a "buy Black philosophy." Other special programs raised thousands of dollars for victims of an economy in distress.

When the leadership changed in 1990, AKA's president outlined the critical issues that require responses if AKA is to move itself and black people into the next century. Although she found herself addressing a membership that had grown from the original nine in a single chapter to more than 120,000 in more than 800 chapters in the United States, West Africa, Germany, the Virgin Islands, and the Bahamas, the approach used by Mary Shy Scott paralleled the one used by Ethel Hedgeman Lyle when she established AKA in 1908: developing a program that would improve the quality of life for AKA and its people was still the order of the day.

EARNESTINE GREEN McNEALEY

B

Baha'i Faith

Weary and heart sore, discouraged with the Churches that close their doors to them, the silent pulpits that should thunder forth in trumpet tones against the iniquities in the pews, it were strange indeed if the Baha'i teachings wakened no response of great hope in the hearts of colored people.

Coralie Franklin Cook,
March 2, 1914

With these words, Coralie Cook declared her commitment to the Baha'i Faith and her expectation that this new religion would unite black and white believers as was promised in its holy scriptures. Coralie and her husband, George William, became Baha'is around 1913, but had learned about the religion as early as 1910. Coralie Cook was educated at Storer College, Emerson College, and Shoemaker School of Oratory. She served as superintendent of the Washington Home for Destitute Colored Women and Children, and was chair of oratory at **Howard University**. An outstanding speaker and educator, Cook was appointed to the District of Columbia Board of Education in 1914 and served until 1926, the longest term of any board member at that time.

Cook and her husband were married in 1898 and had one son, George Will, Jr. George Cook was born into slavery in 1855,

but escaped and later earned degrees from Howard University. He taught at Howard and became dean of the university's School of Commerce and Finance. The couple devoted their energy to making Howard University a first-rate institution of higher learning. In addition, Coralie was deeply involved in community affairs and was a veteran of the Colored Women's League founded in 1892. She maintained a close friendship with Susan B. Anthony and represented the "women of the Race" at the Susan B. Anthony eightieth anniversary mass meeting in Washington, D.C. Coralie Cook was an ardent civil rights and women's rights activist who brought the same zeal for these issues to the Baha'i faith, a religion based on the principle of the oneness of mankind and the equality of women and men. She was a masterful rhetorician who published several essays in the **National Association for the Advancement of Colored People** (NAACP) journal, the *Crisis*.

Coralie and George Cook are just two examples of African Americans who were attracted to the Baha'i faith in its early days in the United States. An independent world religion, the Baha'i faith was founded in Iran in 1844 and spread to the United States in the early 1890s. Baha'u'llah, the prophet-founder of the faith, focused his teachings on a fundamental principle of unity: unity or oneness of God, religion, and mankind.

Baha'i tenets revolve around the principle that mankind must unite in a spirit of peace and harmony. Animosity and strife between the races must be eliminated just as all other prejudices must be condemned and abolished. Other principles include the equality of women and men, compulsory education for all children, eradication of extremes of wealth and poverty, and the belief that the primary purpose of religion is the promotion of concord among the peoples of the world.

There are more than five million Baha'is worldwide, and over 100,000 in the United States. Among the followers of the Baha'i faith are people from all religious backgrounds, nationalities, racial groups, and social classes. More than 2,100 ethnic groups and tribes are represented. Baha'i literature has been translated into more than 700 languages and dialects. The Baha'i faith has no clergy. Its affairs are administered by democratically elected spiritual assemblies on both local and national levels.

Before the Cooks became Baha'is, Robert Turner was the first black American to embrace the religion, in 1898. He was the butler of Phoebe Apperson Hearst, a philanthropist and mother of William Randolph Hearst, the publishing magnate. Turner lived with his wife and mother-in-law in San Francisco. Nearly one year later, Olive Jackson was the first black American woman to become a Baha'i. She was a dressmaker who lived in New York City. Information about these first black American Baha'is is sketchy, but suggests that the black community was aware of this new religion from its infancy in the United States.

Some of the earliest black American believers include several black citizens who enrolled in the faith when Abdu'l-Baha', son of Baha'u'llah, visited the United States in

Dorothy Champ, who gave up her Broadway acting career to promote the Baha'i faith, was one of many black people who believed that this multicultural religion could unite the races. (NATIONAL BAHA'I ARCHIVES)

1912. **Harriet Gibbs Marshall** was one of them. She was born in Victoria, on Vancouver Island, British Columbia, in 1870 and grew up in Oberlin, Ohio. She died on February 25, 1941. Harriet was the daughter of Judge M. W. Gibbs and Marie Alexander. She married Army Captain Napoleon B. Marshall, a Harvard graduate in the class of 1897.

Talented and well-educated, Harriet Gibbs Marshall was the first black American woman to graduate from the **Oberlin Col-**

lege Conservatory of Music, in 1889. She studied piano in Paris, France, with Moskowski and in 1900 was appointed director of music for the public schools of Washington, D.C. In 1903, she founded the Washington Conservatory of Music and School of Expression for the purpose of providing black students with the opportunity to study music through a conservatory approach. In 1937, she established the National Negro Music Center as part of the conservatory. The center was designed to be a resource in the research and preservation of black American music. The conservatory was closed in 1960. Harriet Gibbs Marshall was an active Baha'i and offered the conservatory for Baha'i meetings at a time when few other public facilities would allow integrated gatherings.

A prominent Cleveland couple, Mary B. Martin, a school teacher, and her husband, Alexander, an attorney, became Baha'is in 1913. They were initially invited to Baha'i meetings by Louis Gregory, high-ranking black Baha'i who also was an attorney. Mary was born in North Carolina on May 31, 1877, and died in 1939. She was active in the suffragists' movement and in 1929 was elected to the Cleveland Board of Education. She was the first black American and the second woman to serve on the board. Mary again was elected to the board in 1933 and in 1939 by nonpartisan ballot. She passed away only two weeks after the 1939 election; hundreds of people attended her funeral. In 1965, the Cleveland Board of Education named a new elementary school after her, the Mary B. Martin Elementary School. Of her four children, two boys and two girls, Lydia Martin and Sarah Martin Pereira became well-known Baha'is who introduced the religion to people around the world.

Sadie and Mabry Oglesby enrolled as Baha'is in 1914. Sadie Oglesby and her daughter, Bertha Parvine, became the first black American women to make a pilgrimage to the Baha'i holy places in Haifa, Israel, in 1927. This trip created a dramatic change in Oglesby's life. While on pilgrimage, Shoghi Effendi, grandson of Abdu'l-Baha', urged her to actively help Baha'is understand and bring about racial unity among themselves and the world at large. Sadie Oglesby reported that during most of the pilgrimage Shoghi Effendi focused on issues of racial harmony and constantly encouraged her to play a key role in this "most challenging issue." She agreed to take up this task and immediately upon her return to the United States began giving public speeches on the need for unity among the races. She constantly brought the issue to the floor of Baha'i conventions and exchanged several letters with Shoghi Effendi regarding her plans and progress. Subsequent reports of Baha'i activities indicate that Sadie was indeed successful in generating unity among the races.

Zylpha O. Johnson was born on October 7, 1890, in Boston, Massachusetts, and became a Baha'i in September 1916. She raised her five children as Baha'is. Her husband, Alexander Mapp, was an architect from Barbados, West Indies.

In 1908, Zylpha Mapp became the first black American woman to graduate from Plymouth High School. Her father, William Johnson, had been the first black American to graduate from that same high school in the mid-1880s.

On her own property, Zylpha Mapp established a camp for underprivileged children from the Boston area. The project was cosponsored by the Boston Urban League. While her children were still in school, Zylpha Mapp enrolled in law school, but after two and one-half years she had to quit due to the illness and death of her father, and the Great Depression. In 1960, she became active in the Springfield Federation of Women's Clubs. She became its first black president and served for four consecutive years. During that time she made fifty to sixty dresses a year as a service for the Indian children that the club supported. In her spare time, Zylpha wrote eloquent poetry about various subjects, including her acquaintance with Eleanor Roosevelt.

Elected to the Boston Spiritual Assembly in 1929, Zylpha Mapp served until 1934. She corresponded regularly with Shoghi Effendi and Louis Gregory, with whom she later worked in leading discussion groups at the Green Acre Baha'i summer school. Zylpha Mapp Robinson, her daughter, continued in the tradition of her mother and became an extraordinary Baha'i in her own right.

The end of the decade of this first generation of black Baha'is was highlighted by the enrollment of Dorothy Champ in 1919. That same year, Champ became the first black American to be elected to the New York City Spiritual Assembly. She was a Broadway dancer and actress who gave up her career in order to promote the Baha'i faith in New England. Born in Virginia on February 23, 1893, Champ passed away in Rhode Island on November 28, 1979. She was remembered as a dedicated, steadfast, and unifying force within the Baha'i community: "Her love for God and His Cause was so strong that the fire would flash from her blazing eyes, galvanizing those who heard her speak."

The Baha'i faith continues to be enriched by the contributions of black American women who carry on the legacy of the early believers. Such women include Dr. Wilma Ellis, administrator-general for the Baha'i International Community and member of the Baha'i Continental Board of Counselors for the Americas; the late Dr. Magdalene Carney, member of the Baha'i International Teaching Center; attorney H. Elsie Austin, Baha'i trustee; Dr. Alberta Deas, member of the United States Baha'i National Spiritual Assembly; Dr. Sarah Pereira, member of the Baha'i Continental Board of Counselors; Dr. June Thomas, Michigan State University professor and member of the Baha'i Auxiliary Board; Zylpha Mapp Robinson, international educator and Baha'i pioneer; and Ethel Crawford, staff member at the Baha'i International Center. Black women are represented at various levels within the Baha'i faith. Not all are professional women; they come from a wide range of backgrounds and experiences. They have devoted themselves to active roles in a new religion as exemplified by the words of Annie K. Lewis, who became a Baha'i in 1917: "My only desire is . . . to work interracial till all mankind can live in peace, love, and harmony and go forward with courage in the Cause of God."

GWENDOLYN ETTER-LEWIS

Baptist Church

Black women (and women whose grandmothers were black) are . . . the main pillars of those social settlements which we call churches; and they have with small doubt raised three-fourths of our church property.

W. E. B. DuBois 1918

Although he does not refer to a specific denomination, this statement by W. E. B. DuBois aptly describes women in the black Baptist Church, for today, as well as in 1918, women represent a preponderance of its membership, its financial strength, and its missionary force. These three characteristics form the basis for understanding how black Baptist women, in the face of racial and gender discrimination, contributed to the advancement of the black church and the black community during the nineteenth and early twentieth centuries.

Baptist women constitute the largest group of black Christians in America. It is the very presence of women that explains the magnitude of the black Baptist Church. Census data for the early twentieth century reveal that the black Baptist Church formed a microcosm of the black population in America and included men and women from all social classes and geographic regions. In 1906, black Baptists made up 61.4 percent of all black churchgoers. With a membership of 2,261,607, the black Baptist Church had more than four times the members of the second largest denominational body, the African Methodist Episcopal (AME) Church, with its 494,777 members. By 1916, black Baptists constituted not only the largest black religious group but the third largest of all religious groups, black or white, in America. Trailing only the Roman Catholic and the Methodist Episcopal Churches, black Baptists numbered 2,938,579 that year. In 1936, black Baptists continued to constitute the third largest denomination regardless of race. Equally important, census data consistently have shown that black women make up more than 60 percent of black Baptist membership. From a numerical standpoint, then, the high proportion of female members underscores their vital presence in empowering the Baptist church.

Women's contributions to the church did not begin in the twentieth century but, rather, took root in the efforts of black Baptists to establish congregations independent of white control during the late eighteenth and early nineteenth centuries. Although little is recorded about the black women who participated in this early freedom movement, women certainly were members and financial supporters of those churches founded from the 1750s to 1810 in such places as Mecklenberg, Virginia; Savannah, Georgia; Boston, Massachusetts; and New York City. Mechal Sobel's 1988 study of African-Baptist Christianity during the era of slavery notes instances of women being deaconesses, members of separate women's committees, delegates to associational meetings of both men and women, and active participants in revivals. Yet, the autonomous polity of each Baptist church precluded a consistent participation by women. Ample evidence exists to indicate that there were gender proscriptions: women were categorically denied the right to preach; they were excluded from the business meetings of most black Baptist Churches; and, in many instances, women could not sit beside male members during worship, organize into separate women's societies, or even pray publicly.

The black Baptist Church grew tremendously in the years following the Civil War. With the abolition of slavery, black Baptist women and men expressed their newly won freedom by abandoning the white-controlled churches in which they had been forced to worship. Coming together in black-controlled churches, black

Baptist women found a spiritual haven for individual communion with God and a public space for schooling, recreation, and organizational meetings. Indeed, women, much more than men, attended church not only for Sunday worship but for a variety of activities that took place throughout the week. For many poor black women who worked in domestic service, sharecropping, and other forms of menial employment, the church offered the only form of social and organizational life outside the family. In choirs, deaconess boards, and missionary societies, women with little income found personal dignity, developed leadership and organizational skills, and forged programs for their people's advancement. At the level of the individual church as well as at the level of the regional association of churches, commonly called conventions, the black Baptist Church conflated its private, eschatological witness and its public, political stand, thus becoming a catalyst for the transmission of both spiritual and secular ideas to a broad spectrum of black people.

By means of statewide and other regional conventions, black Baptist churches allied their efforts, embarking upon programs of racial self-help and self-determination. The ministerial-led movement to unite black Baptists into conventions was unique, for, unlike the structured network and hierarchy of other denominations, it emerged only because otherwise independent black Baptist churches voluntarily and freely worked together as race-conscious collectives. Beginning at the local and state levels, the convention movement grew in momentum between the 1860s and 1890s and culminated with the formation of the National Baptist Convention (NBC) in 1895. However, the restricted participation of women in the ministerial-led conventions led Baptist women to form their own, separate local and state organizations in the 1880s and 1890s and, in 1900, a national auxiliary of the NBC, which by 1903 boasted one million members.

State and national women's conventions offered greater opportunity for effective religious proselytism at home and abroad as well as an arena in which women freely discussed and implemented strategies for racial and gender empowerment. The minutes of black Baptist women's state conventions attest to the extensive and sacrificial efforts of overwhelmingly low-income women to meet the spiritual, social, and economic needs of black people, efforts that would have been impossible without their capacity to raise funds. These efforts included visiting homes and reading the Bible, donating clothes and food to the needy, counseling prisoners, caring for the sick, training women in household and parental responsibilities, establishing and supporting orphanages and old folks homes, crusading for temperance, establishing day nurseries and kindergartens, publishing newspapers, instituting vocational training programs, and establishing and/or financing educational institutions.

At a time when Southern states had no public facilities at the high school or college level for black students, late nineteenth- and early twentieth-century women's state conventions worked fervently for the higher education of black men and women. For this reason, black Baptist women's conventions often carried the title "educational" as part and parcel of their missionary identity; for example, the Baptist Women's Educational Convention of Kentucky, the Women's Baptist Educational and Missionary Convention of South Carolina, and the Woman's Baptist Missionary and Educational Association of Virginia. Unquestionably, the black church was the most important institution in the black community, and it was largely through the organized fund-raising of church women that this claim came to be actualized. In the racist climate of segregation, disfranchisement, and lynching, women's missionary and financial efforts were decisive factors in the black Baptist church's ability to rally the impoverished masses for the staggering task of building and sustaining self-help institutions.

Women's conventions, notwithstanding their auxiliary relationship to the ministerial-dominated conventions, generated their own distinct dynamism and assertiveness. Women's conventions controlled their own budgets and determined the allocation of funds, and they explicitly denied male participation in any role other than as honorary members. Black women found enormous satisfaction in accomplishing the goals of their conventions and in developing their own individual skills and abilities. In 1888, the president of the Kentucky Baptist group told a predominantly male Baptist audience that the women had learned to delegate authority, to raise points of order, and to transact business as well as men. In 1904, the president of Arkansas Baptist women credited her state association with building the self-confidence of ordinary women regarding their skills and abilities. She explicitly mentioned women's financial contributions and informed black Baptist ministers: "From a financial standpoint we are prepared to prove that we have given thousands that you would not have, had it not been for the untiring and loyal women in the State." Emboldened by the successes

of their separate conventions, black women also were cognizant of their crucial role in building the denomination as a whole.

The founding and growth of black Baptist women's societies during the 1880s and 1890s did not occur without gender conflict, however. Ironically, the black Baptist convention movement that united men and women in the struggle against racial inequality betrayed a masculine bias in its institutional structures and discourses. Tensions arose when male ministers expected women to be silent helpmates. Yet the rising prominence of black churchwomen and their growing demand for a separate organizational voice during the last two decades of the nineteenth century reflected a heightened gender consciousness on the part of women who were no longer content to operate merely within the boundaries of individual churches or silently within ministerial-led state conventions.

Throughout the 1880s and 1890s, black Baptist women challenged gender proscriptions that thwarted the full use of their talents. The debate over women's rights in Arkansas typified that in other states. Ministers argued that separate organizations under the control of women would elicit a desire to rule the men. Some Arkansas ministers contended that women's financial contributions would cease to be under the men's control, whereas others demanded that male officers preside over women's societies—if they were permitted to form. The women of Arkansas responded by stressing their critical importance as a missionary force, insisting that they could better accomplish the work of religiously training the world by uniting as a separate organization. The women claimed their right to be an independent voice in the church on the assumption that they were equally responsible, in proportion to their abilities, as men.

Outstanding leaders such as Virginia W. Broughton of Tennessee and Mary V. Cook of Kentucky turned to the Bible to defend women's rights in the church and the larger society. Broughton, a schoolteacher and zealous missionary, published *Women's Work, as Gleaned from the Women of the Bible* (1904) in order to disclose biblical precedents for gender equality. Her feminist interpretation of the Bible shaped her understanding of women's roles in her own day, and the book summed up the ideas that had marked her public lectures, correspondence, and house-to-house visitations since the 1880s. Broughton led the women of her state in forming Bible bands for the study and interpretation of the Scriptures, and her gender consciousness united black Baptist women in other states as well, emboldening them to develop their own societies. Traveling throughout the urban and rural areas of Tennessee, Broughton was instrumental in organizing a statewide association of black Baptist women. She advocated training schools for mothers in order to better the home life of black people, and she ardently promoted higher education for women.

Mary Cook of Kentucky also appropriated biblical images to prove that God used women in every capacity. During the late 1880s, Cook, a professor at the black Baptist-owned State University at Louisville (later renamed Simmons University), was the most prominent woman in the ministerial-led convention movement that ultimately led to the founding of the NBC. She urged women to spread their influence in every cause, place, and institution. In

Mary Cook of Kentucky was prominent in the movement that led to the founding of the National Baptist Convention. In newspaper articles and speeches, she urged women to use their influence in every sphere to achieve suffrage as well as full equality in employment, education, social reform, and church work. (MOORLAND-SPINGARN)

newspaper articles and speeches, she emphasized woman's suffrage as well as full equality for women in employment, education, social reform, and church work. In a speech given in 1887, Cook praised female teachers, journalists, linguists, and physicians, and she insisted that women must "come from all the professions, from the humble Christian to the expounder of His word; from the obedient citizen to the ruler of the land." Both Cook and Broughton noted male resistance to the formation of women's societies; for example, they claimed that ministers and laymen had locked the doors of their churches, refusing to accommodate women's societies. In her autobiography, *Twenty Years as a Missionary* (1907), Broughton even recalled potentially fatal confrontations and physical threats made against women.

Although the black Baptist convention movement had served the critical role of uniting women and men in the struggle for racial self-determination, it had simultaneously created a separate, gender-based community that reflected and supported women's equality.

In 1900, at the annual meeting of the NBC held in Richmond, Virginia, **Nannie Bur-**

In her speech at the 1900 meeting of the National Baptist Convention, Nannie Burroughs expressed the discontent and burning zeal of black Baptist women to work unrestricted as a missionary force for the betterment of society. (MOORLAND-SPINGARN)

roughs delivered a speech entitled "How the Sisters Are Hindered from Helping," based on the biblical text, "Ye entered not in yourselves, and them that were entering in ye hindered" (Luke 11:52). Burroughs expressed the discontent and burning zeal of black Baptist women to work unrestricted as a missionary force for the betterment of society. Burroughs' eloquence triumphed. In response to the motion of the influential NBC officer Lewis G. Jordan, and a second from Charles H. Parrish, the male-led convention approved the establishment of the Women's Convention Auxiliary (WC) to the NBC. It is interesting to note that Burroughs worked as Jordan's secretary at the time, and Parrish was married to the aforementioned Mary V. Cook.

By the close of the Richmond meeting, the women had elected the following officers: S. Willie Layten of Philadelphia, president; Sylvia C. J. Bryant of Atlanta, vice president at large; Nannie H. Burroughs of Washington, D.C., corresponding secretary; Virginia Broughton of Nashville, recording secretary; and Susie C. Foster of Montgomery, Alabama, treasurer. The minutes for 1900 listed twenty-six state vice presidents, including one each from Indian Territory, Oklahoma Territory, and Washington, D.C. The women described their mission as coming to the rescue of the world, and they adopted the motto "The World for Christ. Women Arise. He Calleth for Thee." The formation of the WC signaled not only a national identity for black Baptist women but also a black women's congress, so to speak, where women as delegates from local churches, district associations, and state conventions assembled annually as a national body to discuss and debate issues of common concern, disseminate information to broader female constituencies, and implement nationally supported programs.

In her first open letter to the black Baptist women of America, S. Willie Layten urged all existing societies to affiliate with the WC, to work closely with the state vice presidents, and to welcome the formation of new societies where none existed at the state and local level. Layten had a long familiarity with the organized work of black Baptists. Her youth was spent in Memphis, where she acquired her early education and probably her first knowledge of women's missionary activities. After living in California during the late 1880s and early 1890s, Layten moved to Philadelphia in 1894 and became active in religious work and secular social reform. During the first decade of the twentieth century, Layten was a member of the **National Association of Colored Women** (NACW) and was a leader in the National Urban League and the Association for the Protection of Colored Women.

By the second decade of the twentieth century, WC programs reflected the influence of both Progressive-era reform and black urbanization. The changing circumstances of employment, housing, and social problems related to the massive migration of black people from the rural South to the urban North prompted the WC to adopt new methods of mission work. The Baptist women's national organization played an important mediating role in connecting local church and state activities throughout the nation with more sophisticated and changing reform trends. Their organizational networks at the state and national level facilitated a wide dissemination of ideas and expertise for use at the local level.

Officers of the WC alluded to the educational role of their annual meetings when they referred to them as "institutes" and "schools of methods" for local communities. Through the convention, a national network of communication and cooperation identified women with a particular expertise, collected data, and introduced new methods. The annual meetings of the WC featured papers delivered by physicians, social workers, and civic-improvement activists. Convinced that society and not merely the individual soul was at stake, women in the black Baptist Church involved themselves in the practical work of social salvation—establishing settlement houses, holding forums to discuss industrial problems and public health, creating social service commissions, and working to improve the conditions in city slums.

Support for foreign missions constituted another important aspect of the work of the convention. In 1901, the WC contributed money to support Spelman graduate Emma Delaney, who worked as a missionary to Chiradzulu in British Central Africa (now Malawi). In 1902, the women supplied funds to build a brick mission house for her. Through their support of Delaney, the women learned of the harsh consequences of European colonialism on African people. In a visit to America in 1905, Delaney spoke of the need for black Americans to redeem Africa from colonial rule. In her speech before the WC's annual meeting, she poignantly described the suffering of African people "who were compelled to secure rubber for the Belgium Government at any cost, even the loss of their limbs, if the required quantity of rubber was not brought." During the early decades of the twentieth century, the WC shipped boxes of food and clothing to missionaries in foreign fields, underwrote the educational expenses of African students in the United States, contributed to mission stations in various parts of Africa, and built a hospital in Liberia.

The role of black Baptist women as a force for missions also entailed the effort to rid American society of the sins of racial and gender discrimination. In this regard, the WC went on record against segregation, lynching, injustice in the courts, the inequitable division of school funds, and barriers to voting rights and equal employment. It supported the civil rights agenda of the **National Association for the Advancement of Colored People** (NAACP) and invited representatives from that organization to appear at the Baptist women's annual meetings. In 1914, the WC joined forces with the NAACP in a national campaign to end negative stereotyping of black people in literature, film, textbooks, newspapers, and the stage. According to their minutes, they also advocated boycotts and written protests to publishers and others who used racial slurs.

The WC afforded black women an arena in which to transcend narrow social and intellectual confines and become exposed to new places, personalities, and ideas that negated both racist and sexist stereotypes and limitations. At the very time when Booker T. Washington refused to use his influential voice publicly to criticize black disfranchisement in the South, the leadership of the WC loudly called for suffrage for black women and men. In 1909, these Baptist women specified that their political input in state legislatures and the federal government would help improve the living and working conditions of black people in general and black women in particular.

Understanding the historic role of black Baptist women ultimately must evoke recognition of the multivalent character of the black church itself. The church was not the exclusive voice of a male ministry but the inclusive voice of men and women in dialogue. As the majority of church members, the mainstay of financial support, and the missionary impetus for social change, black Baptist women were never silent. In the struggle to come into their own voice, they empowered their church, their community, and, not least of all, themselves.

EVELYN BROOKS HIGGINBOTHAM

Barrett, Janie Porter (1865–1948)

Brought up and educated in a white family and looking Caucasian, Janie Porter was urged by her benefactor to go north for college and prepare to pass into white society. Had she done so, we might now see her name along with Lillian Wald, Jane Addams, and Mary McDowell as founders of the American settlement movement. As it was, she went instead to Hampton Institute, the school for freedpeople, and founded the first social settlement in Virginia, and one of the first in the country for black people.

Janie Porter was born in Athens, Georgia. Nothing is known of her father; possibly he was white. A white woman in Macon, Georgia, for whom Julia Porter, Janie's mother, worked as housekeeper virtually adopted the child. It was she who urged the fifteen-year-old Janie to go north to school. Julia Porter, by contrast, wanted her to maintain her African-American identity, and pushed her to attend Hampton. Although the transition from her sheltered life in Macon was occasionally rough, she graduated from the institute in 1884 and began teaching, first in

Georgia and then back at Hampton, where in 1889 she married Harris Barrett, a member of the staff. Walter Besant's novel *All Sorts and Conditions of Men* is said to have been the inspiration for her decision to devote her life to helping the weakest and most vulnerable members of her race.

She began holding weekly meetings for young girls in her home. The response was so great that in time her husband built another structure to accommodate people of all ages who came for help, training, inspiration, comfort, and advice. This informal institution came to be called the Locust Street Social Settlement. Barrett raised money from Northern philanthropists and recruited Hampton students to teach the practical skills they were learning to the people who came to the settlement.

In 1907, Janie Barrett was one of the founders of the Virginia Federation of Colored Women's Clubs, of which she became the first president in 1908. Clubwomen throughout the United States were by that time a major force in what was called the progressive movement. The needs of their community were so glaring that black clubwomen were tackling serious social problems. Thus it was that the federated black clubwomen of Virginia, under Barrett's leadership, raised enough money to create a rehabilitation center for black girls in trouble. In 1915, the Virginia Industrial School for Colored Girls was built on a farm eighteen miles north of Richmond, and the Virginia legislature agreed to provide some support.

After Harris Barrett died, Janie Porter Barrett, whose four children were reaching an age of independence, took over as resident head of the school. She proceeded to make it one of the model schools of its kind

Rejecting suggestions that she pass for white, Janie Porter Barrett became one of the foremost black organizers in the social settlement movement of the late nineteenth and early twentieth centuries. (HAMPTON UNIVERSITY ARCHIVES)

in the country, based on the accepted principles of contemporary progressive reform. Barrett's own personality contributed to the atmosphere of trust and hope that visitors noted and other states tried to emulate.

In addition to her remarkable accomplishments at the school, Barrett worked with many groups to develop interracial cooperation in Virginia. Her own school had a biracial board, and she seldom failed to praise the white women who had had the courage to join in the undertaking. She understood how women's voluntary associations could multiply individual effectiveness and made the most of the parallel networks: the white clubwomen and the black. In 1940, at the age of seventy-five, she retired and returned to live in Hampton for the eight remaining years of her life, honored in Virginia and among social reformers in the North for her work and her example. After her death the school was renamed the Janie Porter Barrett School for Girls.

ANNE FIROR SCOTT

Bearden, Bessye (1891–1943)

Bessye Bearden was a complete extrovert, an intensely social person whose New York home was the focal point for gatherings of personalities from the varied worlds of politics, journalism, show business, and the arts. Her outgoing personality helped contribute to her formidable achievements as a journalist and community activist.

Bessye Bearden was born in Goldsboro, North Carolina, the daughter of George T. and Carrie G. Banks. Educated in the public

One of the most visible and influential black female leaders in New York City during the 1920s and 1930s, Bessye Bearden was New York news representative of the Chicago Defender, among other responsibilities. (MOORLAND-SPINGARN)

schools of Atlantic City, New Jersey, Bessye Banks attended Hartshorn Memorial College in Richmond, Virginia, and graduated from Virginia Normal and Industrial Institute in Petersburg. She also took special courses in journalism at Columbia University.

She married R. Howard Bearden in 1910, and they had one son, the painter Romare Bearden. After living in Charlotte, North Carolina, for several years, they moved to New York City in 1915. For many years Bearden was in charge of the New York office of the E. C. Brown Real Estate Company of Philadelphia. She became the New York news representative for the *Chicago Defender* in 1927 and stayed with the paper until her death in 1943. Bearden was an active member of the Utopia Neighborhood Club, the New York Urban League, and the **National Association for the Advancement of Colored People** (NAACP). She also served on the executive board of the Harlem Community Council (head of the Widow Pension Bureau) and the executive board of the Citizens Welfare Council of New York. She also was founder and president of the Colored Women's Democratic League and an honorary member of Phi Delta Kappa sorority.

In 1922, Bearden was elected to serve on her local school board, District no. 15 of the Board of Education of the City of New York. She served as secretary for two and a half years. Later, when this board was changed to District No. 12, she was elected chair. Bearden was a member of Saint Martin's Protestant Episcopal Church and the Independent Order of Saint Luke.

Bearden also was a member of the advisory committee to the Special Assistant on Racial Problems of the Emergency Relief

Among the many responsibilities Bessye Bearden assumed was that of secretary of her local school board. She is shown here signing diplomas. (SCHOMBURG CENTER)

Bureau and was secretary of the Harlem Tuberculosis and Health Committee.

In March 1938, **Mary McLeod Bethune** invited Bearden "to discuss the part that Negro women and children are playing in the program of the government as it is being administered," and by June 1940 Bearden had been appointed treasurer of the **National Council of Negro Women**. In September 1940, Bearden was elected chair of the executive board of the Harlem Committee Art Center. In October of that year, she was hostess of the temple of religion at the New York World's Fair.

Bessye Bearden was a multitalented woman who successfully negotiated diverse responsibilities as a woman leader committed to a life of service. She died on September

25, 1943. The *New York Amsterdam News* reported that thousands of people attended her funeral.

JEAN B. HUTSON

Boone, Eva Roberta Coles (1880–1902)

Wives who accompanied their husbands to Africa were designated as assistant missionaries and were engaged in so-called women's work. Such was the case for Eva Boone. Eva Roberta Coles was born on January 8, 1880, in Charlottesville, Virginia. In May 1899, she graduated from Hartshorn Memorial College (Richmond, Virginia; later merged into Virginia Union University), which had

One of Eva Boone's most difficult missionary tasks was teaching sewing to African women; they viewed it as "men's work." (SYLVIA M. JACOBS)

been established to train young black women as teachers and in the domestic arts.

Coles taught in Charlottesville for a short time before marrying Clinton C. Boone on January 16, 1901. Coles probably met Boone in Richmond while he was a student at Richmond Theological Seminary (now Virginia Union University).

The couple traveled to Africa in April 1901, under the auspices of the American Baptist Missionary Union (ABMU; now the American Baptist Churches in the U.S.A.) in cooperation with the Lott Carey Baptist Foreign Mission Convention (after 1902, the Lott Carey Baptist Home and Foreign Mission Convention of the United States). They were stationed at Palabala, Congo (now Zaire), the oldest station in Africa of the ABMU, which they reached on May 24, 1901.

Although Clinton Boone was the officially appointed missionary, his wife was also expected to perform mission duties. Consequently, Eva Boone took charge of the kindergarten class in the mission day school, where thirty to forty children attended daily. She organized a sewing group among forty reluctant African women who saw sewing as men's work. In addition, since women missionaries often dispensed first aid, Boone sometimes administered medical treatment. However, after several weeks of illness, brought on by a poisonous bite, Eva Boone died at Palabala on December 8, 1902, only twenty-two years old.

SYLVIA M. JACOBS

Booze, Mary Montgomery (1877–c. 1948)

Mary Cordelia Montgomery Booze was an African-American clubwoman, civic leader, and Republican National Committee member. Born at Brierfield (Davis Bend, Mississippi), the antebellum home of Confederate President Jefferson Davis, she was one of the twelve children of former slaves Isaiah T. and Martha Robb Montgomery.

From childhood, she experienced material comfort and family connections such as few black Mississippians could imagine. Her paternal grandfather, Benjamin Montgomery, and his sons briefly owned the vast Davis plantation (4,000 acres). He was one of the largest cotton producers in Mississippi and the state's first black public officeholder. Her father won fame as town builder, businessman, state Republican leader, and close political ally of Booker T. Washington. In 1887, following the loss of their Davis Bend properties, her parents moved to Mound Bayou, the all-black Bolivar County agricultural colony founded and dominated by her father.

She attended high school and completed two years of college at Straight University in New Orleans, then found employment as her father's bookkeeper and instructor at Mound Bayou Normal Institute. In 1901, she married Eugene P. Booze, a prosperous Clarksdale businessman. The couple had two children and lived briefly in Colorado Springs, Colorado, before returning to Mound Bayou in 1909. Together they acquired extensive agricultural interests; he became a business partner of her father, and she turned to what she often called "race building."

Mary Montgomery Booze was the town example of black achievement. In 1924, she became the first black woman elected to the Republican National Committee, a position she held for two decades. Victimized by the racial and gender values of her time and place, her political life was often plagued by controversy—including allegations that she violated social taboos by both dancing and dining with Herbert Hoover in 1928. With fellow "Black and Tan" leaders she helped deny a "lily-white" takeover of the state Republican organization. She also numbered among Mississippi clubwomen who quietly agitated for more equitable distribution of public services to black Americans. Although she moved to New York City following the unsolved murder of her husband in 1939, she continued to represent Mississippi on the Republican National Committee until 1948.

NEIL R. McMILLAN

Bowles, Eva del Vakia (1875–1943)

As white and colored women we must understand each other, we must think and work and plan together, for upon all of us rests the responsibility of the girlhood of our nation.

Jane Olcott,
The Growth of Our Colored Work

Eva del Vakia Bowles, longtime Secretary for Colored Work for the **Young Women's Christian Association** (YWCA) National Board, can be credited as the architect of race relations in the largest multiracial movement for women in the twentieth century. During the period of the nation's most stringent segregation policies and practices, while she was in charge of work with black women in the YWCA, Bowles supervised an enormous increase in local and national black staff as well as in services to black women.

She was born in Albany, Athens County, Ohio, on January 24, 1875, the eldest of

three children. Her parents, John Hawkes Bowles and Mary Jane (Porter) Bowles, were native Ohioans. Her grandfather, John R. Bowles, served as chaplain of the all-black Fifty-Fifth Massachusetts Infantry during the Civil War and later became the first black teacher hired by the Ohio Public School Fund. Her father taught school in Marietta, Ohio, but quit when he realized that his employment could be used to rationalize segregated education for black children. The family then moved to Columbus, where he became the first black postal clerk for the Railway Mail Service.

Eva del Vakia Bowles was the first Secretary for Colored Work of the Young Women's Christian Association. She is shown here in a 1915 photograph (bottom, center) with the Brooklyn Colored Conference and the YWCA. (YWCA OF THE USA, NATIONAL BOARD ARCHIVES)

After completing high school in Columbus, Bowles attended a local business college and took summer courses at Ohio State University. Later, she attended the Columbia University School of Philanthropy. She began her working career as the first black faculty member at Chandler Normal School in Lexington, Kentucky, and, later, on the faculties of St. Augustine's School in Raleigh, North Carolina, and St. Paul's Normal and Industrial Institute in Lawrenceville, Virginia. In 1905, she was called to New York to work as secretary of the Colored Young Women's Christian Association (later the famous 137th Street YWCA in Harlem). With this position, she became the first black YWCA secretary.

In 1913, after a short assignment as a caseworker in her hometown, Bowles was invited to return to New York as secretary of the newly formed YWCA National Board Subcommittee for Colored Work. Under her careful and cautious leadership, the subcommittee, which was responsible for work among black women in cities, evolved to departmental status with a full staff. However, she maintained what she called "a vision of a truly interracial movement" and fought vigorously any notion of a permanent "colored department." In her view, while black women should be responsible for decision-making for their own constituency, it was equally important that they should be in "constant conference with the white women of the Central Association." Thus, she supported the idea that there should be only one association in a city, with branches to serve black women.

As a secretary under the YWCA's War Work Council during World War I, Bowles supervised the expansion of service to black women and girls from sixteen branches and centers at the beginning of the war to the establishment of recreation and industrial centers in over forty-five cities. To accomplish this, she involved many prominent local and national black clubwomen. Asserting that "the War [gave] opportunity for the colored woman to prove her ability for leadership," Bowles used the influence of these women to press for more equitable representation on local boards and committees. President Theodore Roosevelt was so impressed with the magnitude and quality of Bowles' work during the war that he designated $4,000 of his Nobel Peace Prize award to be disbursed as she designated.

After the war, Bowles concentrated on moving the national association to more active work on race relations. Immediately after the war, when black Southern leaders threatened to leave the association because of their displeasure with what they felt was a governance structure that "could go no faster than the white women . . . would permit," she was able to mediate the situation by having the national board appoint black women to the regional field committees as well as to field staffs. She also led an effort to have the national board sponsor meetings and conventions only in facilities where all participants could be accommodated. In her international work, she was an advocate for increased work with black women in Africa and in the Caribbean. She also served as an important liaison between the association and such organizations as the National Urban League, the National Interracial Conference, the American Interracial Peace Committee, the **National Association for the Advancement of Colored People** (NAACP), the National League of Women Voters, the Commission of Church and Race Relations of the Federal

Council of Churches, and her own denominational Episcopalian women's interracial organization.

When the national board reorganized its staff in 1931, the "colored department" was phased out and black staff were assigned to the organization's three main divisions. While this move was greeted by Bowles as a real achievement in an interracial setup, she resigned from her position in 1932. According to biographer Clarice Winn Davis, Bowles' objective "to have Negro women share fully and equally in all activities" was not fulfilled as she had hoped. Rather, Bowles protested that, in effect, the reorganization "diminish[ed] participation of Negroes in the policy making of the Association."

Following Bowles' retirement from the YWCA National Board staff, she briefly filled an executive position with the National Colored Merchants Association, sponsored by the National Business League. She returned to Ohio and served as acting secretary for the West End Branch of the YWCA in Cincinnati from January 1934 until June 1935. During the 1940 presidential campaign, she was a Harlem organizer for the Wendell Willkie Republicans. She died of complications from cancer while visiting a niece in Richmond, Virginia, on June 14, 1943. She is buried in the Bowles family plot in Columbus, Ohio, where she resided in her final years.

ADRIENNE LASH JONES

Bowman, Sister Thea (1937–1990)

Sister Thea Bowman, singer, dancer, liturgist, educator, evangelist, prophet—all these roles were embodied in one exuberant woman who was able to find the common thread that interweaves people of all races,

Franciscan nun Sister Thea Bowman was a strong black voice in the Catholic Church of the 1980s, speaking widely for intercultural awareness and directing the Hallelujah Singers. (FRANCISCAN SISTERS OF PERPETUAL ADORATION)

colors, and creeds. She spent her life preaching the Good News as a woman, a black American, and a Franciscan Sister. Sister Thea saw herself as a "pilgrim in the journey looking for home," often lamenting, "sometimes I feel like a motherless child." Yet she never doubted she was "God's child—somebody special," adding, "we are all beautiful children of God." Called to share her gift—her song and story, her life—in the end, she envisioned herself not as dying but as "going home like a shooting star."

Sister Thea (Bertha) Bowman was born December 29, 1937, in Yazoo City, Mississippi, the daughter of Dr. Theon Edward and Mary Esther (Coleman) Bowman. She grew up in Canton, Mississippi, where her father had located his medical practice. At the age of nine she became a member of the Catholic Church. Because her parents were not satisfied with the quality of education given their only child in the local public school, the Bowmans enrolled her in Holy Child Jesus School in Canton, staffed by the Franciscan Sisters of Perpetual Adoration from La Crosse, Wisconsin.

When she was fifteen, Bertha decided to enter the community of Sisters who had taught her. At her reception into the novitiate in 1956, she received the name Sister Thea. She was the first and only black member of that religious community—a challenge to both Sister Thea and to the community to look at and accept racial differences.

Sister Thea earned her undergraduate degree in English from Viterbo College, La Crosse, as well as a master's degree and a doctorate in English literature and linguistics from the Catholic University of America in Washington, D.C. As a graduate student, she taught the first class in black literature at the university.

Sister Thea's teaching career included students at all levels—elementary, secondary, and college. She taught at Holy Child Jesus High School in her hometown of Canton during the 1960s. From 1971 to 1978, Sister Thea taught English at Viterbo College and became head of the English department. During these years she had a profound influence on her students, not only as a teacher of English but also as one who prized her own black culture and its values. To enhance

these values she founded and directed the Hallelujah Singers, a choir with a repertoire of spirituals in the tradition of the black South. This group performed throughout the United States.

During her years at Viterbo College, Sister Thea also reached out to the city of La Crosse and the surrounding area by conducting intercultural workshops for elementary schoolchildren, introducing them not only to the customs and values of different races and cultures but also to persons for whom these values and cultures had special meaning.

In 1978, she accepted the invitation of Bishop Joseph Brunini of Jackson, Mississippi, to become the consultant for intercultural awareness for the diocese. She lived in Canton to help her parents, whose health was failing. She also joined the faculty of the Black Catholic Studies Institute at Xavier University, New Orleans, Louisiana. Sister Thea's efforts were not limited to building community between black and white people; her sensitivity extended to Native Americans, Hispanics, and Asian Americans.

Her work in promoting intercultural awareness brought her to the attention of the nation and, in May 1987, CBS television aired a *60 Minutes* segment about her. Since 1984, however, Sister Thea had battled cancer. Confined to a wheelchair by 1988, she continued a rigorous schedule of travel and appearances. To share her message beyond those she could contact personally, she wrote and edited a number of books. She was also the lead singer on an album of spirituals recorded with a group of friends, *Sister Thea: Songs of My People* (1989). Other tapes by and about Sister Thea, both audio and video, plus a book by Sister Christian Koontz, RSM, a good friend from graduate school, have also been published.

In the course of a distinguished career as an evangelist and teacher, Sister Thea Bowman received many honors recognizing her contributions to humanity. In 1982, she received the first La Crosse Diocese Justice and Peace Award. On March 26, 1989, in a surprise presentation, she received four awards: one from former President Ronald Reagan, one from Secretary of Education William Bennett, another from Wisconsin Congressman Steve Gunderson, and one from Wisconsin Governor Tommy G. Thompson. They said in part: "You are, in a single word, an inspiration. You draw potential from our inner beings . . . make us aware of gifts we never knew we possessed . . . and, most importantly, through your ministry of joy, enable us to improve the quality of our lives and those we touch every day." In January 1989, she was the first recipient of the Sister Thea Bowman Justice Award from Bishop Topel Ministries in Spokane, Washington. Sister Thea also received numerous honorary doctorates from colleges and universities in the United States, including the prestigious Laetare Award from Notre Dame University.

Two years before her death, she received the American Cancer Society's Courage Award in a ceremony in the Rose Garden of the White House. Two weeks before her death, Sister Thea granted an interview to Patrice J. Touhy for *U.S. Catholic* in which she stated: "I've always prayed for the grace to live until I die." She died on March 30, 1990. Her prayer was answered.

SISTER MARY GSCHWIND

Brown, Hallie Quinn (1845?–1949)

"Full citizenship must be given the colored woman because she needs the ballot for her protection and that of her children." So said Hallie Quinn Brown, a charismatic public speaker, teacher, and civil and women's rights advocate. Brown was born on March 10, 1845(?) in Pittsburgh, the fifth of six children of Thomas Arthur Brown and Frances June (Scroggins) Brown. A former slave from Frederick County, Maryland, Thomas had purchased his freedom in 1834. Frances, a native of Winchester County, Virginia, was freed by her white grandfather, who was her owner and a former officer in the American Revolution. At the time of Hallie's birth, her father was a steward and express agent on riverboats traveling from Pittsburgh to New Orleans. He owned a considerable amount of real estate prior to the Civil War, and worked actively with the Underground Railroad in assisting fugitive slaves to freedom.

The Hallie Q. Brown Library at Wilberforce University contains records of the life of a most remarkable woman. The "lady principal" of Tuskegee Institute traveled the world in support of civil rights, feminism, and temperance. Brown is seen here (at left center) at the library's dedication. (MOORLAND-SPINGARN)

Thomas Brown moved with his family to Chatham, Ontario, in 1864 because of his wife's poor health and began farming. Hallie's education began in Canada from 1864 to 1870. Later, the Brown family moved to Wilberforce, Ohio, where they built a house, Homewood Cottage, so that Hallie and her brother could attend Wilberforce University, an African Methodist Episcopal (AME) Church institution. Brown received a bachelor's degree in 1873. She later studied at the Chautauqua Lecture School and graduated in 1886 as salutatorian of her class. In 1890, she was awarded an honorary M.S. She received an honorary doctorate in law from Wilberforce University in 1936.

Brown's first position as a teacher was in South Carolina, where she taught children and adults from various plantations to read. She later took charge of a school on the Sonora plantation in Mississippi and held teaching positions in the city public schools of Yazoo, Mississippi, and Columbia, South Carolina. In 1875, she returned to Ohio, where she taught in the Dayton public school system for four years. From 1885 to 1887, Brown was dean of Allen University in Columbia and administered a night school for adults. From 1892 to 1893, she served as dean of women at Tuskegee Institute, under the leadership of Booker T. Washington, to whom she had been introduced a decade before. Then, in 1893, she accepted an appointment as professor of elocution at Wilberforce University. While teaching at Wilberforce, Brown performed and traveled with the Wilberforce Concert Company (later known as the Stewart Company).

In 1894, she began a five-year sojourn in Europe. She lectured for the British Women's Temperance Association and was made a member of the Royal Geographical Society in Edinburgh. In London, Brown was a speaker at the Third Biennial Convention of the World's Woman's Christian Temperance Union in 1895 and a representative to the International Congress of Women in 1897. She also gave a command performance for King George and Queen Mary and was a dinner guest of the Princess of Wales. After she returned to the United States, she again began teaching elocution at Wilberforce in 1906. In 1910, she returned to Europe as a representative to the Woman's Missionary Society of the African Methodist Conference held in Edinburgh. For the next seven months, she raised funds for Wilberforce in England. After returning from her European travels, she was a longtime instructor in the English department and a member of the board of trustees at Wilberforce.

Brown was one of the first to become interested in the formation of black women's clubs. In her club work, she supported the cause of woman suffrage, which she first espoused while a student at Wilberforce when she heard Susan B. Anthony speak. She was an organizer and crusader in the Women's Christian Temperance Union movement. In 1893, her attempt to stimulate a national organization of black women brought into being the Colored Woman's League of Washington, D.C., a forerunner of the **National Association of Colored Women** (NACW). She founded the Neighborhood Club in Wilberforce and was president of the Ohio Federation of Colored Women's Clubs from 1905 to 1912.

Brown served as president of the NACW from 1920 to 1924. During her presidency, two major programs were initiated: the preservation of the Frederick Douglass Home in Washington, D.C., and the establishment of a scholarship fund for the higher education of women. Brown was chair of the scholarship committee for many years, and eventually the fund was named the Hallie Q. Brown Scholarship Loan Fund in her honor.

Brown was a speaker for state, local, and national campaigns in Ohio, Pennsylvania, Illinois, and Missouri. During the 1920s she was vice president of the Ohio Council of Republican Women. In 1924, she spoke at the Republican National Convention in Cleveland and afterward was director of Colored Women's Activities at the Republican national campaign headquarters in Chicago. Brown was instrumental in securing the support of the NACW for the presidency of Warren G. Harding. Skilled at uniting women on all fronts, she also organized women to "render aid in the battle waged against lynch law and mobocracy and plead for Federal interference in eradicating evils."

In May 1925, she delivered a scathing speech against discrimination in the seating of black Americans at the All-American Music Festival of the International Council of Women, which was held in Washington, D.C. Brown declared in her protest that unless the policy of segregation was changed, all black performers in the program would withdraw. She maintained that it was a gathering of women of the world, wherein color was irrelevant. The policy was not changed, but her speech was so powerful that all black performers as well as audience members boycotted the proceedings.

Brown's published writings include *Bits and Odds: A Choice Selection of Recitations* (1880), *First Lessons in Public Speaking* (1920), *The Beautiful: A Story of Slavery* (1924), *Tales My Father Told* (1925), *Our Women: Past, Present, and Future* (1925), *Homespun Heroines and Other Women of Distinction* (1926), and *Ten Pictures of Pioneers of Wilberforce* (1937).

Hallie Quinn Brown died of coronary thrombosis on September 16, 1949, in Wilberforce. She was buried in the family plot in nearby Massie's Creek Cemetery. Two buildings serve as a memorial to this outstanding woman: the Hallie Quinn Brown Community House (St. Paul, Minnesota) and the Hallie Q. Brown Memorial Library (Wilberforce).

VIVIAN NJERI FISHER

Brown, Sarah Winifred (b. 1870–?)

Sara Winifred Brown, a founder of the College Alumnae Club and assistant principal of the District of Columbia Normal School, was a member of Washington's elite professional community. In 1894, while a teacher of English in the District of Columbia Normal School, Brown took a leave of absence to earn a B.S. from Cornell University. Upon her return to Washington in 1897, she taught science at the prestigious M Street School and enrolled in the **Howard University** medical department, from which she later graduated. While progressing in her career as an educator, Brown took advanced courses in pathology and physiology at Howard and maintained a part-time medical practice for twenty-five years.

In 1910, with a group of friends, including **Mary Church Terrell**, a graduate of **Oberlin College** and the first woman trustee of the District of Columbia Board of Education, Brown founded the College Alumnae Club. Although technically eligible for membership in the predominantly white Association of Collegiate Alumnae (ACA) because she was an alumna of Cornell, Brown contributed her efforts to the segregated society to enable graduates of Howard and other "colored colleges" who were denied membership in the ACA to enjoy the benefits of professional affiliation.

GLORIA MOLDOW

Burrell, Mary (1863–c. 1920)

We have not been working long, but I believe we have wrought well, and I hope we will merit at the end of our day the Master's well done thou good and faithful servant enter thou into the joys of thy Lord.

Women's Baptist Missionary and Educational Association of Virginia, 1910

Mary E. Cary Burrell, along with many African-American women, labored faithfully to improve the lot of black women in the late nineteenth- and early twentieth-century United States. The work done by Burrell and others indicates the important role black women played in the attempts to advance African Americans everywhere. Mary E. Burrell was a tireless and willing activist who worked to improve the material, educational, medical, and social well-being of black people in both Virginia and New Jersey.

Mary E. Cary was born in 1863, the daughter of slave parents, in Richmond, Virginia. Educated in the public schools of Richmond, Cary graduated from the Richmond High and Normal School in 1883. She taught in the local schools for the next two years, after which she married William P. Burrell, an active participant in numerous benevolent associations including the Grand Fountain, United Order of True Reformers. The Burrells had two sons.

Mary Burrell joined the True Reformers in 1885 and became intricately involved in its work. She became the first female canvasser for the organization, its first bank clerk, president of the Rosebud Board of Managers, and treasurer of the Rosebud Nursery Convention of the Southern Grand Division, organizing several Fountain and Rosebud chapters during her tenure.

As an active participant in church activities, Mary Burrell was a leading force in the Women's Baptist Missionary and Educational Association of Virginia as chairman of the executive board. This organization aimed to "spread the light of Christian intelligence among the masses." To accomplish this goal, the association established educational institutions throughout Virginia staffed by "a mighty army of intelligent and consecrated teachers" who were to "develop the noblest ideas and highest character" in black youth.

In 1907, various black women's clubs in Virginia organized a State Federation of Colored Women's Clubs headed by **Janie Porter Barrett** of Hampton. This organization was an outgrowth of the Hampton Negro Conference and the general movement among black women to organize. The avowed purpose of the Virginia federation was to encourage cooperation among black women in order to elevate the home, moral, and civil life of black people in Virginia. Specifically, the Virginia Federation attempted to secure funding for an Industrial Home School for wayward girls. Mary E. Burrell became the Virginia federation's secretary.

Mary Burrell's activities encompassed more than moral and spiritual uplift. She was a prominent force in the activities of the Richmond Hospital. As was the case in so many black communities throughout the Jim Crow South, Richmond's African-American community developed institutions to provide vital services inaccessible to blacks in the wider community. The women's auxiliary to the hospital was organized on November 5, 1902, in order to help maintain the charity ward. Burrell was secretary of the auxiliary's Executive Board.

In 1913, Burrell joined the increasing numbers of black Americans who trekked northward. Migrating to Newark, New Jersey, she did not abandon her efforts on behalf of others. For example, Burrell operated a soldier's canteen during World War I. This operation was part of the Women's Volunteer Service League's efforts to have a building that provided both the canteen and a rest house for black soldiers and sailors. In addition, this house became a training ground for black women in various trades. For her efforts, the government conferred on Burrell the distinguished service badge.

When the war ended, Burrell continued her life of service as a member of the executive board of the Newark branch of the **National Association for the Advancement of Colored People** (NAACP), and she headed the home economics department of the **National Association of Colored Women** (NACW). She also worked for her local federation as chairman of the legislative department of the Federation of Colored Women's Clubs of New Jersey. Truly, Mary E. Burrell "wrought well . . . thou good and faithful servant."

MICHAEL HUCLES

Burroughs, Nannie Helen (1879–1961)

Nannie Helen Burroughs was only twenty-one years old when she became a national

Among numerous other accomplishments, Nannie Helen Burroughs (right) created the National Training School for Women and Girls in Washington, D.C. Not without a sense of humor, she is pictured here with two unidentified women in an obviously posed photograph. (LIBRARY OF CONGRESS)

leader, catapulted to fame after presenting the speech "How the Sisters Are Hindered from Helping" at the annual conference of the National Baptist Convention (NBC) in Richmond, Virginia, in 1900. Her outspoken eloquence articulated the righteous discontent of women in the black Baptist church and served as a catalyst for the formation of the largest black women's organization in America—the Woman's Convention Auxiliary (WC) to the NBC. Some called her an upstart because she led the organization in the struggle for women's rights, antilynching laws, desegregation, and industrial education for black women and girls. Most, however, considered her an organizational genius—a religious leader, educator, clubwoman, political organizer, and civil rights activist all in one. At the helm of the WC for more than six decades, Burroughs remained a tireless and intrepid champion of black pride and women's rights.

Burroughs was born on May 2, 1879, in Orange, Virginia, to John and Jennie (Poindexter) Burroughs. Her paternal grandfather, who was known during the slave era as Lija the slave carpenter, had been able to buy his own freedom. Her father, John Burroughs, attended the Richmond Institute (renamed Virginia Union University) and afterward became an itinerant preacher. Her mother was born a slave in Orange County. Burroughs described her mother as an independent type who, without her husband, took her two daughters (Burroughs' sister died in childhood) to Washington, D.C., in order to find employment for herself and schools for her children. Burroughs and her mother lived in the home of her mother's older sister, Cordelia Mercer.

Nannie Burroughs attended public schools in Washington, D.C., and considered her education at the Colored High School (later called M Street High and still later renamed Dunbar High) to have been a glorious experience. She identified black women teachers such as **Mary Church Terrell** and **Anna J. Cooper** as important role models during her formative years. Her oratorical talents were nurtured in the literary society of her high school and especially in the black Baptist Church. A member of the Nineteenth Street Baptist Church in Washington, D.C., Burroughs noted the interest of her pastor, Rev. Walter H. Brooks (1851–1945), in the young people of the church. Race conscious and active in the formation of the NBC during the 1880s and 1890s, Brooks encouraged Burroughs in church programs when she was a girl, and he remained her mentor and friend throughout his life.

Yet Burroughs' future greatness also was influenced by a disappointment she experienced soon after graduation from high school. Her domestic science teacher failed to keep her promise to ask that Burroughs become her assistant, a position Burroughs sorely wanted. (Some published accounts assert that Burroughs sought the position of domestic science teacher, but her own handwritten notes state otherwise.) It was suggested to Burroughs that her dark skin color and her lack of social pull had thwarted her being chosen for the appointment, but whether or not this was true, Burroughs later confessed that "the die was cast [to] beat and ignore both until death." This early disappointment inspired a zeal to provide opportunities for black women of low income and social status. Her goal of empowering women in the black Baptist church and her dream of establishing a training school for women and girls grew directly out of her determination to fight injustice.

Undaunted, Burroughs sought work outside of the Washington, D.C., area. In 1896, she wrote to Booker T. Washington with the hope of acquiring a job as a typist and stenographer at Tuskegee Institute. Unable to get work at Tuskegee, she finally found clerical work in Philadelphia at the office of the *Christian Banner*. During her stay in Philadelphia, she met Rev. Lewis G. Jordan, pastor of the city's Union Baptist Church and an officer of the Foreign Mission Board of the NBC. Burroughs worked on a part-time basis for Jordan in order to supplement her income from the *Banner*, but she later moved to Louisville, Kentucky, when Jordan relocated there. While in Louisville, Burroughs won acclaim in the local press for organizing a women's industrial club. A harbinger of her future educational work, the Louisville club offered evening classes in bookkeeping, sewing, cooking, typing, and other vocational skills.

During her years in Louisville, Burroughs traveled to the Richmond Convention and delivered her historic speech, "How the Sisters Are Hindered from Helping." Her dynamic presence at the NBC annual meeting in 1900, coupled with the long-standing efforts of black Baptist women to form a national organization, culminated not only in the birth of the WC but also in the election of Burroughs as its corresponding secretary. Her youthful energy, resourcefulness, and speaking abilities assured the growth of the newly formed convention. During her first year in office, Burroughs reported having worked 365 days, traveled 22,125 miles, delivered 215 speeches, organized 12 societies, written 9,235 letters, and received 4,820 letters. In 1903, Burroughs reported that the WC represented nearly one million black Baptist women; by 1907, she boasted 1.5 million. Burroughs tried to systematize the work of women's state and local societies by publishing the handbook *What to Do and How to Do It*, and by distributing uniform record books and bookkeeping advice. In 1908, she conceived of National Woman's Day and inaugurated its annual celebration in local churches as an expression of sisterhood and as a means of garnering financial support for the WC. That same year she wrote *The Slabtown District Convention*, a humorous play that continues to be reprinted and performed.

Never married, Burroughs devoted her energies to a variety of causes, but her life's work clearly was rooted in the religious and educational work of the WC. Despite her at times stormy relationship with the ministerial-led NBC, Burroughs maintained the love and loyalty of the women. They elected her corresponding secretary year after year between 1900 and 1948. In 1948, she was voted president of the WC, a position she held until her death on May 20, 1961. Under Burroughs' long and illustrious leadership, the WC provided a deliberate arena for black women to address freely their religious, political, and social concerns.

On the lecture circuit, in the press, and in her speeches to the WC, Burroughs boldly denounced lynching, segregation, employment discrimination, and African colonialism. Her verbal attacks were coupled with calls to action. During World War I, her militant demands for racial equality and her strong criticism of President Woodrow Wilson's silence on lynching led to her being placed under government surveillance. Her uncompromising stand on racial equality included a woman's right to vote and equal economic opportunity.

Challenging black churches to educate their female members about their political rights and responsibilities, Burroughs stressed the importance of woman's suffrage for both racial and gender advancement. Black women voters, she argued, would oppose candidates who supported segregation, job discrimination, and Southern disfranchisement. In articles in the secular and religious press, Burroughs also disclosed her strong feminist convictions when she referred to woman's suffrage as a safeguard against male dominance and sexual abuse. In August 1915, in the *Crisis*, magazine of the **National Association for the Advancement of Colored People** (NAACP), Burroughs emphasized that the vote would help black women "reckon with men who place no value on her virtue." Nor did she hesitate to condemn those black men who quietly accepted the South's policy of black disfranchisement. She called for a united leadership that would "neither compromise nor sell out." In her report to the WC in 1912, she threatened: "If women cannot vote, they should make it very uncomfortable for the men who have the ballot but do not know its value."

As a clubwoman, Burroughs joined with other women in the **National Association of Colored Women** (NACW) to promote the political mobilization of black women after the ratification of the Nineteenth Amendment. Also during the 1920s, Burroughs became actively involved in partisan party politics. At that time, the great majority of black voters were loyal to the Republican party, identifying it with the party of Abraham Lincoln and the abolition of slavery. Most black voters identified the Democratic party, on the other hand, with segregation and disfranchisement. At the same time, ever growing numbers of black Southerners were migrating to Northern cities where racist voting restrictions no longer dominated the political landscape. Realizing the potential of black women voters to augment the black electorate, Burroughs and other clubwomen founded the National League of Republican Colored Women in 1924. Burroughs was elected the league's president; other officers included such notables as **Daisy Lampkin** of Pennsylvania, treasurer and chairman of the executive committee; Mary Church Terrell of the District of Columbia, treasurer; and **Elizabeth Ross Haynes**, parliamentarian.

Like Burroughs, the other officers were well known for their visibility in numerous organizations such as the NACW, the NAACP, and the Urban League.

Burroughs' oratorical abilities made her particularly attractive to the Republican high command. She was placed on the party's national speakers' bureau and was highly sought after during the presidential races of the 1920s. On January 12–14, 1927, Burroughs represented the league at a conference sponsored by the women's division of the Republican National Committee. She was one of three black women along with eighty-two white women from thirty-three states invited to the conference for a discussion of such topics as women's political roles, problems of organizing and fund-raising, and overcoming differences among Republican women. With the inauguration of Herbert Hoover as president in 1928, Burroughs was appointed to chair a fact-finding commission on housing. The commission was composed of outstanding black scholars and community leaders such as the sociologist Charles S. Johnson of Fisk University, the architect Moses McKissick of Nashville, and clubwoman and political activist Daisy Lampkin of Pittsburgh. Research conducted by this group was published in the book-length study *Negro Housing: Report of the Committee on Negro Housing* (1932).

Burroughs so linked her religious and political ideals that she saw the black church as a critical vehicle for the political education and mobilization of the masses of working-class black women. At election time, Burroughs frequently addressed church congregations, soliciting support for candidates. Her political visibility was eclipsed in the 1930s, however, by the ascendancy of Franklin Roosevelt and the New Deal. Burroughs continued to support the Republican Party despite her periodic frustration with its racial policies and the shifting allegiance of the majority of black voters to the Democrats. Although her direct influence in electoral politics waned considerably from its highpoint in the 1920s and early 1930s because of, Burroughs maintained a wide following in the black community. Her popularity continued beyond the 1930s because of her public statements on black pride and racial self-help and because of her participation in a diverse array of religious and secular organizations, some of which included Baptist and other ecumenical groups, the NAACP, the Association for the Study of Negro Life and History, and the Commission on Interracial Cooperation.

Perhaps Burroughs' most challenging achievement was the **National Training School for Women and Girls,** which, founded in 1909, continues to operate. (It was renamed the Nannie Helen Burroughs School in 1964 and today serves elementary school children.) As early as 1901, Burroughs introduced the idea of founding a school to the fledgling WC, and on October 19, 1909, the National Training School, with Burroughs as president, opened its doors to thirty-five students. In the school's first twenty-five years, more than 2,000 women from across the United States and from Africa and the Caribbean matriculated at the high school and junior college levels. Burroughs dubbed her institution the "school of the three B's" because of the importance she placed on the Bible, bath, and broom as tools for race advancement. The school's first motto, "Work, Support Thyself, to Thine Own Powers Appeal," captured Burroughs' valorization of work as

a central tenet of racial pride and self-help. In a similar vein, the later motto, "We Specialize in the Wholly Impossible," stressed Burroughs' belief in the need of black women to be self-sufficient wage earners.

The school offered missionary training as well as an industrial curriculum that prepared women for jobs as cooks, laundresses, chambermaids, ladies' maids, nurses, housekeepers, dressmakers, stenographers, bookkeepers, and clerks. Although the school emphasized domestic service, its industrial training curriculum also prepared black women to seek work outside the realm of traditional female employment by offering courses in printing, barbering, and shoe repair. Like Booker T. Washington in her pragmatic approach to the reality of job discrimination, and in her belief in the primacy of industrial rather than liberal arts education for the masses, Burroughs extolled all forms of honest labor, no matter how menial. "Don't scorn labor nor look with contempt upon the laborer," she once said. "Those who encourage Negro women to loaf, rather than work at service for a living are enemies to the race." Indeed, Burroughs sought to professionalize domestic service and to redefine the work identities of black women as skilled workers rather than incompetent menials.

In 1920, Burroughs launched the short-lived National Association of Wage Earners in order to improve the living and working conditions of domestic servants. Burroughs spoke ardently in defense of domestics, and repudiated policies that treated them differently from other unskilled workers. That same year, for instance, the federal government recommended a minimum wage for laundresses that was two dollars less than that for other unskilled laborers. Sensitive to the fact that most laundresses were black women, Burroughs wrote to Archibald Grimké, then president of the Washington, D.C., branch of the NAACP, in hopes of organizing a broad-based demand for a decent living wage.

Through her speeches and press releases, Burroughs became a familiar voice among black Americans of all classes and regions. Her eloquent and dynamic voice commanded many followers, ranging from uneducated domestic servants to Harvard-trained educators such as Carter G. Woodson. Rev. Earl L. Harrison, in his 1956 biography of Burroughs, recalled her impact on him when he heard her speak in a rural and remote part of Texas. Seeing her for the first time, and admiring her spellbinding style, Harrison recalled, "I shall not forget that day, when the young woman from Washington, D.C., charmed the old and the young with her logic, wit and wisdom. She made us country folk proud. We had not seen or heard such gift displayed in a Negro woman."

In the final analysis, Burroughs' appeal rested in her commitment to overcome what seemed to be wholly impossible. She fervently believed that self-esteem and self-determination developed independent of race, gender, and income. Although she acknowledged the damaging effects of institutional racism, she believed that achievement ultimately was a question of individual will and effort. Burroughs decried the abridgement of her people's civil and political rights but exalted the resultant rise of black-owned businesses and other expressions of racial self-help. Submission to the Jim Crow laws, she asserted in 1905, denied black Americans civil equality but never human dignity: "Men and women are not made on trains and on streetcars. If in our homes there is implanted in the hearts of our children, of our young men and of our young women the thought they are what they are, not by environment, but of themselves, this effort to teach a lesson of inferiority will be futile."

At the same time, she demanded that black people fight in season and out of season for equal justice. In 1933, she told an overflowing audience of young people at the Bethel African Methodist Episcopal (AME) Church that black people must give notice to the world that they were willing to die for their rights. In the apocalyptic language of the Old Testament, she admonished her listeners not to wait for a deliverer: "We must arise and go over Jordan. We can take the promised land." For decades, she supported the NAACP's crusade against racial discrimination and violence by advocating boycotts, petitions, prayer vigils, and other forms of protest. In 1934, she insisted that black Americans fight for their rights with "ballots and dollars" rather than "begging the white race for mercy." She proclaimed in the black press that "It is no evidence of Christianity to have people mock you and spit on you and defeat the future of your children. It is a mark of cowardice." She was equally militant in her attacks against sexism: "We must have a glorified womanhood that can look any man in the face—white, red, yellow, brown, or black—and tell of the nobility of character within black womanhood.

When Nannie Helen Burroughs died on May 20, 1961, at the age of eighty-two, Mary O. Ross, who would soon take Burroughs' place as president of the WC, exclaimed that "womankind has lost a conquering heroine." The *Afro-American* reported that 5,500 people came to the Nineteenth Street Baptist Church to pay their last respects. Nannie Helen Burroughs, by her life's example and teachings, laid a strong foundation upon which to build a more just and equitable America.

EVELYN BROOKS HIGGINBOTHAM

Butler, Selena Sloan (1872?–1964)

Whenever life around Selena Sloan Butler was uncertain, she simply took affairs into her own hands. When there was no kindergarten for her son to attend, she created one. When there was no support organization for his public school, she founded one. When there were no community organizations for black women to work through, she banded with others and established them. And later, when her husband died, she simply packed up and moved on. Her efforts, particularly on behalf of schoolchildren, have been recognized in her designation as one of the founders of modern-day parent-teachers associations.

Selena Butler never revealed much information about her early life; only a few facts are known. She was born Selena Sloan in Thomasville, Georgia, on January 4, 1872(?), to Winnie Williams, a woman of African and Indian descent, and William Sloan, a white man. Her father took care of her, her elder sister, and her mother, but he did not reside with them. Selena's mother died while Selena was still young; she may have lived a short time with her married sister.

Selena received elementary school training from missionaries in Thomas County and was sponsored for admission to Spelman Seminary (later **Spelman College**) in Atlanta, Georgia, by her mother's minister.

After six years of schooling, at age sixteen, she graduated. After matriculating, she began a career teaching English and elocution, first in Atlanta and then in Florida. While teaching in Atlanta, she met and later married Henry Rutherford Butler, destined to be one of Atlanta's finest and foremost doctors. They traveled together to Boston, where Henry went to medical school at Harvard and she studied oratory at Emerson School. In 1895, the couple returned to Atlanta.

When Butler's son, Henry Rutherford, Jr., was born, she began her lifelong involvement in parent-teacher associations. There was no preschool teacher in her neighborhood, so she set up a kindergarten in her own living room. When Henry went to public school, she followed a supportive course by establishing the first black parent-teacher association in the country at Yonge Street School. From this small beginning, Butler went on to establish an association at the state level (1920), and then, six years later, at the national level (1926). The National Congress of Colored Parents and Teachers maintained a good relationship with the white national Parent-Teacher Association organization because Butler made every effort to see that the policies and programs of both organizations were coordinated. The black association serviced primarily the Southern states, where there were the largest concentrations of racially segregated schools. When the two organizations were joined nationally, after Butler's death, Butler was elevated to national founder status along with two white women, Alice McLellan Birney (also from Georgia) and Phoebe Hearst.

Selena Butler was an active clubwoman in arenas other than education. She served as a delegate to the founding convention of the

National Association of Colored Women, the first president of the Georgia Federation of Colored Women's Clubs, and a member of the Georgia Commission on Interracial Cooperation. In addition, the Chautauqua Circle, the premier black women's social organization in Atlanta, claimed her as a member, as did the Ruth Chapter of the Order of the Eastern Star. She maintained her interest and activity in the Eastern Star long after she left Atlanta.

In 1931, when her husband died, she moved with her son to England. Her son also pursued a career in medicine and had studied, as his father had, at Harvard. Unlike his father, however, Henry Rutherford, Jr., felt no particular loyalty to the South. Light-skinned, educated, articulate, sophisticated, and polished in manner, Butler's son voiced a deep-seated denunciation of the South's racial constrictions with his own permanent exile from home. World War II forced Dr. Butler to leave England. He and his mother moved to Fort Huachaca in Arizona, where he served in the army hospital. At the same hospital, Butler organized the first Gray Lady Corps for black women.

When Dr. Butler married and moved to California, Butler returned to Atlanta, where she kept up an active community service career until 1953. Some late-life health problems required her retirement from strenuous activity, and she moved in 1953 to Los Angeles to live with her son and daughter-in-law. She died in 1964 in Los Angeles, but she is buried in Atlanta next to her husband in Oakland Cemetery.

During her lifetime Butler was recognized for her philanthropic and charitable service, especially in the field of child welfare. The Lord Mayor of London, the American Red Cross, Spelman College, and President Herbert Hoover, all honored her. Her portrait hangs in the State Capitol of Georgia and Atlanta named a park after her, which sits next door to the Henry Rutherford Butler Elementary School, formerly the Yonge Street School, where her first PTA was founded.

DARLENE ROTH

C

Cass, Melnea (1896–1978)

She had a high school education and never held a paying job more prestigious than domestic. Yet she was wise, determined, and a powerful force in her community. Melnea Cass was known as "The First Lady of Roxbury," and she counted among her friends and admirers mayors, governors, and senators.

Born in Richmond, Virginia, on June 16, 1896, Melnea Agnes Jones Cass was the oldest daughter of Mary Drew Jones and Albert Jones. Her mother was a domestic worker, and her father a janitor. Neither had beyond a grade-school education, but they were described as intelligent, literate, and "wide-awake." With the encouragement of Ella Drew, Cass' aunt, the family moved to Boston when she was five.

The urban North held more promise, though Cass' parents continued to work at similar jobs. Cass' mother died when she was eight. Drew stepped in as a second mother, although her own job as a live-in domestic made it difficult to spend as much time with the family as she wished. In time, Drew arranged for the children to be sent to Newburyport, near Boston, where Drew's employers spent their summers. There Drew found a household to care for the children. After early schooling in Boston, Cass graduated from grammar school in Newburyport.

Cass attended Girls' High School in Boston for a year, then was sent to boarding school at St. Francis de Sales in Rock Creek, Virginia. This was a Catholic school founded for black children and Native Americans, a short way up the river from her father's relations in Richmond. The Richmond branch of the family had prospered and sent several children to college. This household became Cass' home base during her vacations from St. Francis. In 1914, Cass graduated from St. Francis, valedictorian of her class.

In keeping with the times, the school trained girls in practical skills, including domestic science. When Cass returned to Boston, she applied for work as a salesgirl, but African Americans were seldom hired in such jobs. Instead, she became a domestic, continuing to do that kind of work until she married Marshall Cass in 1917.

Marshall Cass had enlisted to fight in World War I. Before he sailed, Cass married him and went to live with his mother, Rosa Brown. Brown was a prominent woman in the Boston community, interested in a wide variety of civic affairs. She was a suffragette, lobbying for women's right to vote. Cass was exposed to many of her mother-in-law's beliefs. After women won the right to vote in 1920, Cass helped organize black women to get out and exercise their right.

Along with women's rights, civil rights were a burning issue of the day, with many great speakers appearing in local lectures.

Among them were W. E. B. DuBois and William Monroe Trotter, whom Cass especially admired. She became a member of the **National Association for the Advancement of Colored People** (NAACP) soon after her marriage and worked with Trotter on civil rights campaigns for many years.

Cass was active in the black women's club movement and the Massachusetts State Union of Women's Clubs. She belonged to the Northeastern Region of the National Association of Colored Women's Clubs, acting as secretary, chairman of the board, vice president, and finally president. She was vice president of the national organization during the 1960s.

For seventeen years, Cass was president of the Women's Service Club, which set up a dormitory to aid young black women who had just immigrated from the South. In the 1920s, she helped organize the Boston chapter of the Brotherhood of Sleeping Car Porters, one of the early black unions. During the 1930s, she worked with Trotter to organize demonstrations to get African Americans hired as department store clerks, the job she was denied herself. This campaign was followed by another to get Boston Hospital to hire black doctors. After Trotter's death, she continued his work to maintain the memory of Crispus Attucks, the first person to fall in the Boston Massacre. She also lobbied to get Frederick Douglass' birthday commemorated in Boston.

Cass was one of the organizers of Women in Community Service, which was set up to meet the needs of the community during World War II. This group later became the Boston sponsor of the Job Corps.

Cass' formal political influence began in the 1950s. By this time, white government officials had begun to recognize the treasure trove of talent to be found in black community leaders. It was both politically and practically wise for elected leaders to ask the non-elected leaders for advice. During the 1950s, the mayor of Boston appointed Cass the first female and community member of Action for Boston Community Development (ABCD). This group was established to help relocate people displaced during urban renewal projects. ABCD later became a permanent organization with several ongoing community projects. Cass was a member of the Board of Overseers of Public Welfare for ten years, advising the mayor and the Welfare Department.

Cass was president of the Boston branch of the NAACP from 1962 to 1964, during the Kennedy years in the White House. This was a time of struggle to desegregate the Boston school system. From 1975 to 1976, she was appointed by the governor as a member of the state Advisory Committee for the Elderly. In 1975, she served on a similar mayoral committee. In 1973, she was appointed by the Secretary of Health, Education, and Welfare to represent consumers' interests in Medicare on the National Health Insurance Benefits Advisory Council.

While prominent in the **Young Women's Christian Association** (YWCA) for many years, Cass left the organization in 1951 because of racial discrimination. She rejoined the organization in 1976, when she was honored in their Women of '76 program. At that time, the main branch of the Boston YWCA was renamed the Melnea A. Cass Clarendon Street Branch.

Cass was awarded numerous honors after her long years of service. On May 22, 1966, the mayor of Boston declared Melnea Cass

Day in a ceremony attended by more than two thousand people. Two years later, the city of Newton repeated the honor. In 1977, she was named one of the seven "Grand Bostonians." She was awarded honorary degrees from Boston College, Northeastern University, and Simmons College. After her death in 1978, Boston dedicated Melnea A. Cass Boulevard to preserve the memory of this great lady.

ANDRA MEDEA

Catholic Church

> O, write my name. / O, write my name. / O, write my name. . . . / Write my name when-a you get home / Yes, write my name in the book of life. . . . / The angels in the heav'n going to write my name.

> Spiritual—Underground Railroad

Within the history of women in America, black Catholic women occupy a unique place, but one that has been ignored or portrayed in distorted ways. Their triple burden and challenge—that of being woman, black, and Catholic—has required them to cope with realities affecting their essential humanity. The history of their perseverance and faith extends hundreds of years in both Africa and America.

PRE-CIVIL WAR

Black Catholic women have been an active and persistent presence in the long struggle for freedom and justice in America and within the American Catholic Church; however, they have been portrayed from a male (both black and white) perspective. Nonetheless, selected public records and church documents reveal fascinating glimpses of their lives.

The most substantial Catholic settlement was in Maryland, a proprietary colony founded in 1632 and settled by English Jesuits. Along with Catholic laymen, these Jesuits bought, kept, and sold black slaves. Since Jesuit policy was to catechize and baptize all slaves, a substantial number of slaves became Catholic. Perhaps as early as 1634 or 1635, Rev. Andrew White brought two mulattos into the province, Matthias de Sousa and Francisco, who had been taken aboard the *Ark* and the *Dove* in the port at Barbados Island.

Early mention of a black woman in a Catholic setting appears in a 1656 description of St. John's Manor, Maryland, which housed the seat of government in St. Mary's County. A notice for a court case, *Attorney General* v. *Overzee*, states that "a pear tree stood near the dwelling house. A Negro woman was not a witness since she stayed in the quartering house [servant's quarters]."

Black Catholics lived in the Louisiana Territory probably as early as 1724. This formal portrait of a group of New Orleans nuns was taken in the twentieth century. (LIBRARY OF CONGRESS)

The development of a single-crop tobacco economy in Maryland relied on slavery. As the slave population increased, laws were promulgated to regulate the slave community. The law of 1664 made black people slaves for life, enslaved white women who married slaves, and made their children slaves for life. Though the law was repealed in 1681, a number of mulatto children had already been enslaved. Even many years later, descendants of mixed unions, including black Catholic women, had to sue for their freedom. In 1771, Mary and William Butler, grandchildren of a Negro slave and a free white Irish Catholic woman named Eleanor, commonly called "Irish Nell," sued for their freedom in a Maryland court. They secured their liberty in a lower court, only to have the case reversed by the Court of Appeals. Sixteen years later, their daughter, also named Mary, initiated another suit and won.

By the late 1790s, the population of black Catholic women increased with the emigration of Catholics from Haiti. Among those who settled in Baltimore were free mulatto women, including the highly educated **Elizabeth Lange**. With several companions, she opened a school in her home for black children. In 1829, these women, with the support of the Sulpician priests, established the first religious community of black women in America. They became known as the **Oblate Sisters of Providence.**

One of the women who joined this community was Anne Marie Becroft, a free black woman from Washington, D.C. In 1820, at the age of fifteen, she had opened a school in Georgetown for black girls. Deciding to join the Oblate Sisters in 1831, she placed the school in the care of a former pupil, Ellen Symonds.

The Sulpician Archives in Baltimore contain a most remarkable document: *Journal of the Commencement of the Proceedings of the Society of Coloured People: With the Approbation of the* Most Rev. Archb. Samuel and the Rector of the Cathedral, Rev. H. B. Coskery. This journal of black Catholics living in Baltimore, Maryland, provides a vivid portrait of the spiritual life of over 250 men and women. An alphabetical listing of the members shows approximately 170 female names. Officers included Mary Holland, first counselor; Elizabeth Berry, third counselor; and Mary Howard, fourth counselor. Land records show that some of the female members owned their own homes. Their listed occupations were domestic, such as washers and ironers.

The entries of the weekly sessions and monthly council meetings indicate that the group met from 1843 until 1845 in Calvert Hall in the basement of the Baltimore Cathedral. Monthly dues for each member were 6 cents. A detailed report of their prayer life includes descriptions of singing, the lending library, their financial status, and provisions for the needy. The group held masses for members who died. In March 1844, Harriet Queen died, followed in August by Lucy Butler, who left $21 to the Society and $21 to the Cathedral. The journal records document the activities of a group of black Catholics in the antebellum period who nurtured a distinctive community within the Catholic Church.

The oldest black Catholic community was established in 1784 in St. Augustine, Florida. In return for military service and conversion to the Catholic faith, slaves who had fled plantations in the Carolinas and Georgia were promised their freedom. They built the fortified town of Gracia Real de Santa Teresa de Mose. Excavations have yielded artifacts including gun flints, buckles, thimbles, buttons, clay pipes, bowls, and even a handmade St. Christopher medal.

Black Catholics lived in the Louisiana Territory probably as early as 1724, when the French Code Noir established the laws governing slavery there. Early Catholic missionaries in the territory owned slaves and profited from their labor. Some black Catholics were able to establish their own communities. Isle Breville, an area on the Cane River in what is now northern Louisiana, became home to one such community.

Coincoin, a slave woman with the French name of Marie Thérèse, was born in Natchitoches in 1742. In 1767, she became the concubine of a French merchant, Claude Metoyer. She bore him seven children who were baptized. After purchasing Coincoin and their children in 1778, Metoyer emancipated Coincoin and the last son. He gave her and the children sixty-eight acres. By diligent work, the family had a thriving business of tobacco, indigo, and bear grease by 1793, and Coincoin purchased the freedom of the rest of her children. She died in 1816. Her son, Augustin, became head of the black Catholic community. He constructed one of the world's oldest black Catholic churches, St. Augustine, in 1829.

By the beginning of the nineteenth century, the practice of concubinage between well-to-do men and free women of color was well established, especially in New Orleans. From this milieu of "genteel immorality" emerged Henriette Delille, founder of the second black religious congregation in America in 1842.

In California, eleven families founded the community of Nuestra Senora de Los Angeles in 1781. Half the adults were black, two were Spanish, and the rest were Native Americans. All were Catholic.

By the mid-nineteenth century, other black Catholic communities had grown up in Alabama, Maryland, and South Carolina. Small settlements could be found in Kentucky; Mobile, Alabama; Savannah, Georgia; St. Louis, Missouri; Philadelphia, Pennsylvania; Baltimore, Maryland; Chicago, Illinois; and New York. Black women lived in all these communities, but church registers acknowledged them in different ways. Many slaves or indentured servants remained unnamed, some were listed with only a first name under "property of . . . ," while "free people of color" were listed with both a first and last name.

POST–CIVIL WAR TO THE 1990S

After the Civil War, black Catholics formed separate parishes, began societies to assist the needy in their communities, and held national lay congresses. Women played supporting roles in these endeavors. By the early 1900s, an urgent need for educational resources became apparent. Through the Federation of Colored Catholics led by Dr. Thomas W. Turner, a biology professor at Hampton Institute in Virginia, appeals were made to every level of the hierarchy for Catholic education.

In many areas, the Catholic schools were the only means of providing an education for blacks. Black Catholic women, serving as religious sisters and laity, staffed most of these schools. In 1910, in Lafayette, Louisiana, Eleanora Figaro, a graduate of St. Paul's School in Lafayette, gathered eighteen children in a shed and began the first Catholic school for black children in that part of the state. She taught at Sacred Heart School for forty-two years. In 1949, Figaro became the first black woman to receive the papal honor "Pro Ecclesia et Pontifice."

In 1924, after much delay, the Cardinal Gibbons Institute opened in Ridge, Maryland, with Victor Daniel as principal and Constance Daniel, his wife, as assistant principal. Both were black Catholics and graduates of Tuskegee Institute. Their school provided academic, vocational, and religious instruction to black students, male and female, from across the United States. Extension courses in agriculture, home economics, and health were also available to black Catholic families. Because of financial difficulties, the institute closed in 1933, but it reopened in 1936 and operated until 1967.

By the 1940s and 1950s, Catholic individuals and groups had begun to organize interracial efforts to combat the serious social and economic problems of that time. Many black women volunteered in the houses of hospitality in the Catholic Worker Movement, begun by Dorothy Day in 1933. Helen Caldwell Day, a young black Catholic, helped at the New York House. In 1950, she returned to her home in Memphis, Tennessee, and began an interracial house of hospitality. Her autobiography, *Color Ebony*, describes her spiritual journey as a black woman in a racist and sexist society.

Black women were highly visible and extremely vocal as staff workers and volunteers in the Friendship House Apostolate, an interracial organization founded by Catherine de Hueck in Harlem in 1938. The group used lectures and articles in the house newsletter to confront and change the institutional racism within the church. One of the staff workers in this New York "settlement type" house was a young black writer, Ellen Tarry. She and a white associate went to Chicago in 1942 to start a Friendship House following race riots there. As in houses in Washington, D.C., Portland, Oregon, and Shreveport, Louisiana, many black women were on the staff or served as volunteers. Ellen Tarry is the author of *The Third Door: The Autobiography of an American Negro Woman* (1955) and *The Other Toussaint: A Post-Revolutionary Black* (1981).

A small group of Catholic women began the interracial *Caritas* in New Orleans in 1950. Six years later, Eunice Royal, a young black woman from Napoleonville, Louisiana, joined. With only three permanent members, including Eunice Royal, and many supporters, *Caritas* continues to serve the parish and community in Louisiana, Guatemala, and Africa.

Since their inception in the 1930s, Catholic Interracial Councils have included black women. One particularly active member in both the Jersey City, New Jersey, and Washington, D.C., chapters was Dr. **Lena Edwards**, a devout Catholic who strongly and effectively protested racism and sexism wherever she encountered them. A wife, mother of six, medical doctor, educator, and missionary to migrant workers in Texas, she received many honors, including the Medal of Freedom.

As a result of the civil rights movement and Vatican II, momentous changes occurred in the United States and in the Catholic Church. Black Catholic women actively participated, and many assumed leadership roles.

With the advent of the Black Power movement, black Catholic men and women formed national organizations of clergy, sisters, and lay persons. In November 1969, the National Conference of Catholic Bishops approved the establishment of the National Office for Black Catholics. Another national organization, the National Association of Black Catholic Administrators, was founded in 1976. Delores Morgan, an early organizer of the Office of Black Catholics in Syracuse, New York, served as the first woman president of the association.

Numerous women have played prominent roles in diocesan offices for black Catholics. A secretariat for black Catholics was established in 1973 in Washington, D.C., where the black Catholic population neared 80,000. Its first director was Cynthia Roberson. Of the five offices for black Catholics existing in the early 1970s, the Washington, D.C., office was the first headed by a black woman.

In 1987, the National Black Catholic Congress met in Washington, D.C., at the Catholic University of America. Theresa Wilson Favors of Baltimore, Maryland, served as the first director of the Black Catholic Congress. Many delegates were women and seven of the twelve major speakers were women, including keynote speaker Sister Francesca Thompson. **Sister Thea Bowman**, whose extraordinary ministry was documented on television's *60 Minutes*, addressed the topic of "History and Culture." She greatly enhanced the times of prayer with her remarkable songs.

Women have also played major roles in enhancing the Catholic Church with liturgy reflecting the African roots of black Catholics. The first Rejoice! Conference on Black Catholic Liturgy was held in 1984, following a series of meetings convened in 1983 by Jacqueline Wilson, executive director of the Office of Black Catholics in Washington,

The extraordinary ministry of Sister Thea Bowman was documented on television's 60 Minutes. (FRANCISCAN SISTERS OF PERPETUAL ADORATION)

D.C. Wilson also served as a regional coordinator for the National Black Catholic Congress. At a special Rejoice! Conference in Rome in 1989, Dr. Diana Hayes spoke on "Tracings of an American Theology: A Black Catholic Perspective." Currently at Georgetown University, Hayes earned her Ph.D. and S.T.D. degrees at the Catholic University of Louvain in Belgium. She is the first black Catholic lay woman to receive these highest degrees in Catholic theology. Sister Eva M. Lumas, also a presenter at the Rejoice! Conference in Rome, is a distinguished lecturer, educator, and leader in Catholic religious education. Other leading black Catholic theologians in the United States who are women include Sisters Jamie Phelps, Toinette Eugene, and Sean Copeland.

Black women have begun to assume increasingly significant positions within the Catholic Church. The nation's first black nun to head a parish, Sister Cora Billings, was installed as a pastor in Richmond, Virginia, on September 23, 1990. In the Archdiocese of New York, Delores Grier was appointed vice chancellor for community relations in 1985. On the national level, Beverly Carroll became the executive director for black Catholics in the National Conference of Catholic Bishops in 1989.

On the threshold of the twenty-first century, black Catholic women enhance the rich legacy of commitment to their freedom and their faith. They will continue to do so.

LORETTA M. BUTLER

Church of God in Christ

The Church of God in Christ (COGIC) is the Pentecostal denomination with the largest and most elaborately organized Women's Convention. Possibly the largest Pentecostal denomination in the United States and the seventh largest African-American Christian church, the COGIC was originally founded in 1895 as a Holiness church. It is currently the largest among those called the Sanctified church. Like other Holiness and Pentecostal denominations, the church emphasizes sanctification as a believer's experience subsequent to or separate from salvation or justification. Bishop Charles Harrison Mason, a Baptist minister in the Mount Helm Baptist Association of Lexington, Missis-

sippi, founded the church along with C. P. Jones, after a conflict with other association members. Upon hearing of the Azuza Street revival of 1906, sparking the emergence of Pentecostalism as a significant force in American religion, Mason and Jones sent several elders to observe and evaluate the revival and its doctrine. Adoption of Pentecostal doctrine led to conflict between Mason and Jones that resulted in Mason's retaining the church's charter and Jones' founding the Church of God in Christ (Holiness).

Women's work and the Women's Convention are central to the history of the Church of God in Christ. Since Bishop Mason believed women should govern other women, he appointed a women's "overseer" (or national supervisor or National Mother), Mother Lizzie Woods Roberson. In addition to her organizing, she was a noted revivalist, evangelist, and founder of congregations. Mother Lillian Brooks Coffey was the second head of what was called the Women's Department. She pioneered a more elaborate women's organizational structure, founding several new organizations within the convention and connecting the Women's Convention with the mainstream of African-American women's organizations, such as the **National Association of Colored Women** (NACW) and the **National Council of Negro Women** (NCNW), through her friendship with **Mary McLeod Bethune**. Another noted leader of the church, Dr. Arenia C. Mallory, was responsible for the church's academy becoming an accredited junior college. Although official church doctrine does not permit the ordination of women to the offices of elder, pastor, or bishop, women may "teach the gospel to others" and may "have charge of a church in the absence of the pastor." In spite of these restrictions, the autonomy of the Women's Convention has enabled it to encourage the development of national evangelists, women who teach the gospel who have conducted revivals successfully in at least seven states, and whose public speaking is indistinguishable from the most exemplary "preaching." Bishops within the church also have ordained women to charges outside of the denomination, such as military chaplaincies. The Women's Convention meets annually in May.

CHERYL TOWNSEND GILKES

Colemon, Johnnie (19??–)

"Holy Materialism, positive thinking, and Practical Christianity," is what Rev. Johnnie Colemon preaches, and those are the tenets of her church, the Christ Universal Temple in Chicago. An ordained Unity minister, she is a practitioner of the New Thought philosophy, which is grounded in the immediate and the material of this world, as opposed to salvation in the next. It focuses on the individual's ability to better the quality of his or her life on Earth, believing that Christ is a part of each person's spirit. In the New Thought philosophy, heaven and hell exist, not after death, but in a person's lifetime. It is up to the individual to determine in which state they will live.

Johnnie Colemon was born in Centerville, Alabama, to John and Lula Haley. Her father (after whom she was named) would have preferred a son, and much of her life was spent trying to overcome that fact. "I spent my entire childhood trying to excel in everything, hoping to win his appreciation

and affection," she told *Ebony* magazine in 1978.

In addition to her fight to win her father's acceptance, Colemon also had to face two kinds of prejudice, that which existed among whites against blacks, and also that among blacks against very dark-skinned blacks (especially women). But though she may have struggled, she found she could overcome, with or without the approval of her father, the white establishment and her lighter-skinned sisters and brothers. She graduated from high school and obtained her bachelor's degree from Wiley College in 1943.

After graduation, Colemon moved first to Canton, Mississippi, and then to Chicago, where she was a teacher in the public school system. Another challenge sent her in the direction that was to become her life's calling.

In the early 1950s, Johnnie Colemon was diagnosed with an incurable illness. Not one to accept this death sentence or to leave her healing in the hands of the doctors alone, she pursued her own cure. Its philosophies of "positive thinking" and personal empowerment led her to the Unity Church. She began to attend the Unity School in Lee's Summit, Missouri.

At the Unity School, she fought against a racism that allowed her to attend classes but wouldn't allow her to live in Unity Village or eat in the restaurant there. Even at services in Kansas City, black worshipers were made to sit in a roped-off section of the balcony. Colemon was successful enough in her fight against this institutional discrimination to become the first African American to be allowed to live on the campus. However, her home was some distance from the white students' cottages.

Still, she persevered and, in 1956, became an ordained minister of the Unity Church. She immediately began her own ministry, opening the Christ Unity Center in a **Young Women's Christian Association** (YWCA) in Chicago. In 1968, she became the first black president of the Association of Unity Churches and, in 1970, organized the association's first successful convention in fifty-two years.

In 1974, a change in the Unity Church's bylaws led Colemon to leave the association and to rename her church the Christ Universal Temple. She then created the Universal Foundation for Better Living (UFBL) and became its president. Johnnie Colemon, Christ Universal Temple, and the UFBL have had great success.

The UFBL has twenty-two study groups and churches from all over the world as members and has grown to include the Johnnie Colemon Institute. The institute trains participants on both the spiritual and worldly aspects of the church. Its first ministers were ordained in 1978. In 1985, in order to house the institute and the temple (which by 1994 had a congregation of more than four thousand), the church and foundation bought Fun Town, a thirty-two acre amusement park on the far South Side of Chicago. The complex contains a bookstore and a prayer ministry in addition to the temple and the institute. A prayer tower, a dormitory, the Johnnie Colemon Elementary School, a performing arts center, and a fitness center are in the development stages.

Colemon has been the recipient of many awards, including the Women's Day Annual Black Excel Award from Operation PUSH (People United to Serve Humanity); the Year of the Woman Award and the Excellence in Religion Award from the PUSH Foundation; the Recognition Award for Service to Humanity from the **Alpha Kappa Alpha Sorority**; and the Golden Anniversary Award from the Association of Unity Churches. She has been asked to speak at the Festival of Mind and Body in London, the 1986 Boule of the Alpha Kappa Alpha Sorority, and the Prayer Breakfast in Atlanta.

In 1981, Colemon began hosting her own television program, *Better Living with Johnnie Colemon*, which ran for several years. She is still a frequent speaker on various radio and television programs.

Johnnie Colemon has been married and widowed twice, first to Richard Colemon, a delicatessen manager, and then to Don Nedd, a minister of her church. There are no children from either marriage. She explained her beliefs in an interview for *Notable Black American Women, Book II* with these thoughts: "If my mind conceives this statement: 'You can have anything you want, if you desire it badly enough.' I can be anything I desire to be. You can accomplish anything you set out to accomplish if you hold to that singleness of purpose. Health, Joy, Love and Prosperity will be yours." If her life is any proof, then the Reverend Johnnie Colemon certainly practices what she preaches.

HILARY MAC AUSTIN

Cummings, Ida Rebecca   (1867–1958)

Ida Rebecca Cummings, educator, organization leader, and clubwoman, was born on March 17, 1867, in Baltimore, Maryland. Her father, Henry Cummings, was a hotel chef who also owned a catering business. Her mother, Eliza Davage Cummings, who descended from free African Americans, operated a boardinghouse at the family residence.

Cummings was reared in an atmosphere that promoted education, black unity, and community service. The family's church, Metropolitan Methodist, which was formerly a station on the Underground Railroad, offered literacy classes prior to the establishment, in 1867, of black public schools in Baltimore. While most African Americans were uneducated laborers, many of Cummings' family members were clergymen, civil servants, and educators. Cummings' brother, one of the first black graduates of the University of Maryland Law School, was, in 1890, the first African American elected to the Baltimore City Council. Her aunt, Charlotte Davage, was for many years president of the Colored **Young Women's Christian Association** (YWCA). A dormitory at Morgan State University is named for her mother, Eliza Cummings, in recognition of her fundraising efforts for the school.

The **Oblate Sisters of Providence**, an order of black nuns, were Cummings' first teachers. She later enrolled in Baltimore's only public school for African Americans. Cummings attended Hampton Institute in Virginia; Morgan State College in Maryland, where she earned a bachelor of arts degree in 1922; and Columbia University.

By 1900, Cummings was teaching primary school. She then completed specialized courses in Baltimore and Chicago and became Baltimore's first kindergarten teacher. Affectionately called "Miss Ida" by her students, Cummings taught for thirty-seven years.

Cummings participated in organizations that worked to improve housing, health care, and education for poor children. She founded the **Frances E. W. Harper** Temple of Elks and served for twenty-nine years as Daughter Ruler. She was the Elks' state director of the Department of Education and the national chairman of the Child Welfare Department. A board member of Maryland's Cheltenham School for Boys, she also served as a trustee of Bennett College, as the first woman trustee of Morgan State College, and as president of the Republican Women's League.

In 1904, Cummings, her mother, and other members of the Colored YWCA estab-

Among the many philanthropies of Ida Rebecca Cummings was the Colored Empty Stockings and Fresh Air Circle. For four decades, the Circle provided Christmas gifts and summers in the country for black children from poor families.

lished the Colored Empty Stocking and Fresh Air Circle. The women provided Christmas stockings to children who would otherwise have had no gifts. Also, in order to expose city children to a healthier environment during the summer, the group paid for their board in the homes of rural families. Cummings was president of the Circle for most of its approximately forty years of existence. The group regularly solicited funds from black organizations, and white merchants made occasional contributions. Under Cummings' leadership, the Circle purchased a farm and built a camp staffed by volunteers. Between 1904 and 1907, more than 5,000 children benefited from Circle efforts.

From 1912 to 1914, Cummings was corresponding secretary of the **National Association of Colored Women** (NACW) and chairperson of the planning committee for its annual convention, held in Baltimore in 1916. During this convention, which featured symposia on antilynching and women's suffrage, Cummings was elected vice president.

Cummings died in Baltimore on November 8, 1958. Her will included bequests to the schools and organizations she had supported during her lifetime.

DONNA TYLER HOLLIE

D

Davis, Elizabeth Lindsay (b. 1855–?)

Much of what we currently know about the early club work of African-American women is due to the commitment of Elizabeth Lindsay Davis to building the women's clubs and to documenting their history. Elizabeth Lindsay, the eldest daughter of Thomas and Sophia Lindsay, was born in Peoria County, Illinois, in 1855. At the age of ten, she enrolled in the Bureau County High School in Princeton, Illinois. She was one of three black students to graduate from the institution. She used her teaching skills in several schools throughout the Midwest—Keokuk, Iowa; Quincy, Illinois; New Albany, Indiana—and in Louisville, Kentucky. When she married William H. Davis of Frederick, Maryland, in 1885, she discontinued teaching to do club work.

Davis ardently believed in reform and social uplift. She believed that elite black women should be at the forefront of the reform movement. Thus, she organized the Chicago **Phyllis Wheatley Women's Club** in 1896 and served as president for twenty-eight years. This club, in 1908, opened the **Phyllis Wheatley Home** for young black females who needed a safe place to live. The home provided living accommodations, recreation, and an employment bureau. It also operated a club program and classes in domestic arts. The home and its activities were solely managed and supported by the black community.

Committed reformer Elizabeth Lindsay Davis founded and served for twenty-eight years as president of Chicago's Phyllis Wheatley Women's Club. (SCHOMBURG CENTER)

Davis was also a member of the **Ida B. Wells** Club, the Woman's City Club, the Chicago Forum League of Women Voters, the Woman's Aid, the Giles Charity Club, the E.L.D. Study Club, and the Service Club. In 1918, the Elizabeth Lindsay Charity Club was organized in her honor. The club provided legal counsel, educational facilities, medical aid, food, and clothing to the thousands of Southern black migrants seeking economic opportunity in Chicago.

75

Her long involvement in the **National Association of Colored Women** (NACW)—she was national organizer from 1901 to 1906 and from 1912 to 1916—led to her success as state organizer and president (1910–1912) of the Illinois Federation of Colored Women's Clubs. Under her presidency, the federation endorsed the **National Association for the Advancement of Colored People** (NAACP) and pushed for the ballot for women.

Davis' documentation of the women's club movement in *The Story of The Illinois Federation of Colored Women's Clubs* (1922) is the first record of women's clubs in the state. Her *Lifting as They Climb* (1933) is the first national history of the club movement. A committed reformer and active clubwoman, Davis helped build and document the reform agenda for black Americans throughout the last decade of the nineteenth century and the first decades of the twentieth century.

WANDA HENDRICKS

Delaney, Emma Bertha (1871–1922)

In an address delivered before she left for Africa entitled "Why I Go as a Foreign Missionary," Emma Delaney discussed her interest in mission work: "At the age of thirteen . . . I united with the [Baptist] church, and the spirit of missions increased. After entering Spelman Seminary and spending twelve years there, where our duty to God and humanity, both at home and abroad, is daily set forth, the mere desire for this work was changed to duty and a longing for the work that nothing else would satisfy."

Emma Bertha Delaney (or DeLaney) was born in Fernandina Beach, Florida, on January 3, 1871. She graduated from Spelman Seminary (now **Spelman College**) in Atlanta, Georgia, in 1894. She completed missionary training in 1896, and nurse training in 1900. Afterward she worked for several years as a boarding school supervisor at Florida Institute (Live Oak).

On January 15, 1902, Delaney sailed for Africa and was stationed at Chiradzulu, in Nyasaland (Malawi), where she taught school. Delaney had been sent by the National Baptist Convention (today the

Dedicated missionary Emma Delaney, founder of the Suehn Industrial Mission in Liberia, greatly increased the interest of African-American women in mission work in Africa. (SYLVIA JACOBS)

National Baptist Convention, U.S.A., Inc.) and supported by the Baptist women of Florida. Delaney was influential in establishing a women's society and weekly sewing classes for girls and was responsible for arousing interest among African-American women in African mission work. After four years in Nyasaland, Delaney left the Providence Industrial Mission in 1906.

When the British government denied her permission to reenter Nyasaland, Delaney transferred to Liberia in 1912. She selected a spot near Monrovia, secured a grant of twenty acres of land from the Liberian government, and built the Suehn Industrial Mission. Delaney became the first principal of Suehn Industrial Academy, which was built at Suehn Mission and became a model for industrial centers.

In 1920, Delaney returned to the United States. She died of hematuric fever on October 7, 1922, at her mother's home in Fernandina Beach.

SYLVIA M. JACOBS

Delta Sigma Theta Sorority

On a winter morning in 1913, twenty-two young women of African-American descent were set to march in one of the most important woman's suffrage demonstrations in U.S. history. The date was March 4, the eve of Woodrow Wilson's presidential inauguration in Washington, D.C. The women, students at **Howard University**, a liberal arts college founded after the Civil War to educate former slaves, raised their Delta Sigma Theta banner in anticipation. The contingent was to be led by an honorary member of the student organization, **Mary Church Terrell**, then fifty years old and a revered role model for younger women of the Progressive era.

The suffrage march, organized by the militant Congressional Union (later the Woman's Party), drew some 5,000 participants and marked the suffrage movement's coming of age. As the first public activity of the sorority, the march also marked an important development in the history of the black fraternal movement in general, and Delta Sigma Theta sorority in particular.

Delta had been incorporated as an official sorority on Howard's campus almost two months before, on January 13. It was the fifth such organization in the country, following three black Greek fraternities: Alpha Phi Alpha (1906), Kappa Alpha Psi, and Omega Psi Phi (1911), and one sorority, **Alpha Kappa Alpha** (1908). In addition to fostering scholarship and social bonds among its members, these organizations symbolized the right of black students to pursue a liberal arts education at a time when such studies were deemed to be either beyond the intellectual reach of, or impractical for, the growing number of black students, especially black women, seeking higher education. For Delta specifically, founded at a time when the exigencies of woman's suffrage converged with the new movement toward race reform, as characterized by the creation of the **National Association for the Advancement of Colored People** (NAACP) in 1909 and the National Urban League in 1911, it was inevitable that their mandate would include political concerns.

In subsequent decades, Delta Sigma Theta grew, and its focus evolved as the sorority responded to both external and internal developments. For example, the sorority's tremendous growth during the 1920s was spurred both by the increasing number of black students in both black and white universities and by the racist backlash that accompanied their attendance in predominantly white schools. On many white campuses, the sorority house was not only a social center but also an important refuge for black students who were allowed to matriculate but not permitted to live in university dorms or participate in other interracial activities. This shaped the traditional programs of the sorority, which included bringing well-known activists to speak on campus and raising scholarship funds. By 1930, the sorority included graduate chapters and was established in every region of the country.

The 1930s saw a rise in the academic level of black land grant colleges in the South and their subsequent inclusion in the sorority movement. This, and the crisis of the Great Depression, spurred programs designed to reach out to those with fewer economic resources. In 1937, for example, Delta's National Library Project provided a bookmobile, or traveling library, to several states in the South. In the late 1940s, when gains made by black women during World War II were threatened, Delta's Jobs Analysis and Opportunities Project helped nonprofessional women find training and employment. In 1947, the Detroit chapter purchased the Delta Home for Girls, which provided an alternative to juvenile detention homes.

The 1950s and 1960s were characterized by international outreach and involvement in the civil rights movement. In 1950, Delta established its first non–North American chapter in Haiti; ten years later it would establish its first African chapter in Liberia. In 1961, the sorority raised funds to equip a maternity wing of the Njorge Mungai Hospital in rural Kenya. On the heels of its support for Daisy Bates, leader of the Little Rock, Arkansas, school desegregation struggle of 1957, Delta established the Social Action Commission to provide information and direction on current civil rights issues. In addition to financial support for movement activities, the national office embarked on successful lobbying efforts that culminated in the passage of the Civil Rights Act and the Voting Rights Act of 1964 and 1965, respectively.

In the 1970s, Delta emphasized sorority support for the arts with the establishment of the National Arts and Letters Committee, which produced a full-length feature film, *Countdown at Kusini*, in 1976. Subsequent national initiatives included the establishment of a revolving distinguished endowed professor's chair awarded to black colleges; "summit" calls to action around the issues of inner-city youth, black families, and black single mothers; and educational and informational projects concerning the black diaspora.

From its first chapter comprising twenty-two members in 1913, Delta Sigma Theta has grown to include more than 125,000 women and 750 chapters in the United States, Africa, and the Caribbean.

PAULA GIDDINGS

Duncan, Sara J.   (b. 1869–?)

Through her work on behalf of missions, Sara J. Hatcher Duncan became an important force in the late nineteenth and early twentieth centuries in the African Methodist Episcopal (AME) Church.

Sara J. Hatcher was born in 1869 in Cahaba, Alabama, the youngest of four children. Her father, S. George Hatcher, was an ex-slave who earned his living in the grocery and liquor retail business. Sara's mother, Eliza English, of mulatto heritage, was George's first wife and died one year and one month after Sara's birth.

Sara was raised as one of five foster children and spent her early life helping her grandfather with his postal clerk duties in Cahaba. Jordan Hatcher had received the position of postmaster after the Civil War and encouraged Sara's assistance. She attended public school and continued her education at Presbyterian Knox Academy in Selma, Alabama.

In 1889, Sara married Robert H. Duncan of Rome, Georgia. Her active involvement in church work began early in her youth and continued after she was married. In 1897, she was appointed general superintendent of the Women's Home and Foreign Missionary Society of the AME Church. This was the second and specifically Southern women's society of the church that had been created in 1893 in spite of resistance from most of the all-male hierarchy.

Duncan's accomplishments represented ideals of womanhood for African Methodist church women, particularly Southern women. She was born into a known Alabama family and was well-educated, and she was a member of a prominent congregation in her town. A licensed schoolteacher, she married a respected African-American businessman and was foster mother to at least two children. In addition to the prestigious national position Duncan held in her denomination, she also founded a missionary newspaper, *Missionary Searchlight*, that was adopted by the church, and wrote *Progressive Missions in the South* (1906). She was active in almost every civic and social organization of African Americans in Alabama and was conferred an honorary M.A. by Alabama A&M College.

JUALYNNE E. DODSON

Duster, Alfreda (1904–1983)

Alfreda Barnett Duster will be remembered most for her successful resurrection of the works of her mother, **Ida B. Wells-Barnett,** from the dustbins of American history. Although the city of Chicago had named a public housing project for Wells-Barnett before World War II, outside the city limits only a handful of scholars had ever heard of her. For nearly thirty years, Duster painstakingly researched and edited an early first draft of her mother's moving autobiography, then cajoled a score of publishers before one finally agreed to publish it. Wells-Barnett now occupies an increasingly prominent place in history.

As the youngest daughter of Ida B. Wells-Barnett, from early childhood Alfreda had watched public life and the perpetual spotlight of notoriety consume much of her mother's energies. Even into her early teens, she was a constant companion at civic club meetings and public lectures, where her mother was much in demand. For the first half of her life, Duster avoided public life and laid no claim to her mother's legacy. Yet a series of forces moved her more and more onto the public stage, where she slowly emerged as an important public figure in her own right.

Alfreda Barnett was born on September 3, 1904, the daughter of Ferdinand L. Barnett and Ida B. Wells. Barnett was one of the first African-American attorneys in Chicago, in 1878, and the founder and publisher of the first black newspaper in the city, the *Conser-*

Alfreda Duster is best remembered for her successful resurrection of the works of her mother, Ida B. Wells-Barnett, from the dustbins of history. In this 1917 Barnett family portrait, she is shown as a young woman standing beside her mother. The family members are: (standing) Hulette D. Barnett (wife of Albert G. Barnett), Herman Kohlsaat Barnett, Ferdinand L. Barnett, Jr., Ida B. Barnett, Jr., Charles Aked Barnett, Alfreda M. Barnett, and Albert G. Barnett; (seated) Ferdinand L. Barnett, Sr., Beatrice Barnett, Audrey Barnett, Ida B. Wells-Barnett; (foreground) Hulette E. Barnett, Florence B. Barnett; the four little girls are the children of Albert and Hulette Barnett. (THE JOSEPH REGENSTEIN LIBRARY, THE UNIVERSITY OF CHICAGO)

vator. Wells is credited with pioneering investigative journalism and arousing the conscience of the nation to stop mob lynchings of African Americans. Alfreda therefore grew up in a household with a strong tradition of public service to the black community.

Alfreda attended Douglass Elementary School and Wendell Phillips High School on Chicago's South Side, then went on to earn a bachelor of philosophy degree from the University of Chicago in 1924. One of only four African Americans in her class, she would later reminisce about how she, a very talented swimmer and tennis player, was not allowed to play tennis or swim on campus. (Some forty years later, as a member of the Women's Board of the University of Chicago, she would monitor and influence policies to reduce gender and race discrimination.)

Alfreda then worked in her father's law offices, where, through her brother, Herman (also an attorney), she met and, on July 9, 1925, married Benjamin Cecil Duster of Mount Vernon, Indiana. Although a graduate of Indiana State Normal School, Ben Duster never pursued a career in education. During the trying years of the Great Depression, he withdrew from the world, seldom holding steady employment. Nevertheless, determined to raise a family and provide a nurturing home environment, the couple had five children. In 1945, Ben Duster died suddenly at the age of fifty-four, leaving Alfreda with the task of rearing the children, at that time ranging in age from nine to eighteen.

Having no savings, Duster joined the staff of the Southside Community Committee, an organization that sponsored youth programs ranging from entertainment activities to work with probation and parole officers. She supplemented her meager earnings of approximately $150 per month by using her clerical skills to fill out income tax forms for neighbors and friends and take on typing and mimeographing work for ministers and students. She routinely worked many hours into the night at such tasks.

Living in an environment hardly conducive to her children's academic achievement, she characteristically turned her adversity to advantage. She involved the children in helping perform her clerical tasks by assembling, stapling, and stamping, meanwhile employing a potpourri of home-based academic achievement strategies, such as word games and mathematical problems. She was a forceful presence in the Parent-Teacher Association (PTA), often serving as president, and, in 1950, became the first black woman to receive the PTA's Mother of the Year Award in Chicago.

Eventually, she was able to send all five children to college and see them become successful as: president of the National Association of Minority Enterprise Small Business Investment Corporation (Benjamin); architect and architectural engineer and participating associate at Skidmore, Owings & Merrill (Charles); Commonwealth Edison executive and member of the cabinet of Governor Thompson as director of business and economic development for the state of Illinois (Donald); special education administrator for Los Angeles County (Alfreda Duster Ferrell); and professor of sociology and director of the Institute for the Study of Social Change at the University of California, Berkeley (Troy).

The remarkable feat of successful child rearing in these unlikely circumstances was only one of her careers. Slowly, Duster found herself moving more and more into a public life. It was during this period that Duster worked late at night on her favorite personal project, completing her mother's unfinished autobiography. For the next quarter century, on weekends and during vacations, she followed leads to Mississippi and Tennessee, buttressing the facts with her own skillful research and carefully reediting the early draft. Initially, she had difficulty interesting a publisher in the project, but events of the 1960s led to demands for a fuller history of the Reconstruction era. Finally, in 1970, under the editorship of John Hope Franklin, the University of Chicago Press published *Crusade for Justice: The Autobiography of Ida B. Wells*, edited and with an introduction by Alfreda B. Duster.

Upon publication of the book, Duster began a decade of public speaking at universities and other public forums around the country. Much like her mother before her, she helped increase the consciousness of students and faculty alike about the economic and political strategies that were at the core of the "crusade for justice."

With the resurgence of interest in the life of Wells-Barnett, the book has been used as a standard reference work in classrooms and libraries across the country and in Europe. It was the basis of a Public Broadcasting Service (PBS) television documentary in 1989 and later served as a catalyst for the U.S. Postal Service's issuance of a commemorative stamp in early 1990, called Black Heritage U.S.A.

Duster likewise produced a legacy of her own. In 1973, the University of Chicago Alumni Association awarded her its prestigious Citation for Public Service. In 1978, for her life's work and public service, she was awarded a doctorate of humane letters by Chicago State University. She died the grandmother of fifteen and the grande dame of a distinguished family, who had helped rekindle and rejoin the legacy of Ida B. Wells-Barnett.

TROY DUSTER

F

Fearing, Maria (1838–1937)

At the age of fifty-six, with less than a high school education, Maria Fearing applied to the executive committee of Foreign Missions of the Southern Presbyterian Church (now Presbyterian Church in the United States) for an appointment as a missionary. Fearing had vowed as a young girl that she would go to Africa. The executive committee refused to subsidize her because of her advanced age. Undaunted, Fearing sold her home in Anniston, Alabama, took her savings and $100 pledged by the women of the Congregational Church in Talladega, Alabama, and for two years paid her own way as a missionary. Eventually, on October 7, 1896, the Southern Presbyterian Church appointed Fearing as a regularly stationed and salaried missionary.

Maria Fearing was born a slave on July 26, 1838, in Gainesville, Alabama. She completed the ninth grade at Talladega College and taught at a rural school in Anniston. She later returned to Talladega College and worked in the boarding department. In 1894, Stillman College (Tuscaloosa, Alabama) graduate William Sheppard, who was on furlough from the Presbyterian Congo Mission, spoke at Talladega and appealed for missionary volunteers.

Fearing sailed to the Congo Free State (now Zaire) on May 26, 1894. She was stationed at the Luebo station. There, she founded and directed the Pantops Home for Girls until 1915. In addition to her activities with the home, Fearing taught in the mission day school and Sunday School, and worked with women in surrounding villages.

Fearing took a furlough in 1915, but because of her age did not return to Africa. She died in Gainesville, Alabama, on May 23, 1937.

SYLVIA M. JACOBS

Fields, Mamie (1888–1987)

"I will *never* do it" was a favorite phrase of Mamie Elizabeth Garvin Fields whenever she spoke of the unwritten rules and customs of the Jim Crow order in South Carolina. In 1909, she began her professional career by disregarding the custom that African Americans present applications for teaching positions through the mayor's butler and, instead, presented her credentials in person to the superintendent of education in Charleston. To widespread astonishment, she got her first position, in a one-room school at Humbert Wood on John's Island in rural Charleston County. Testing the unwritten rules and contesting the written ones were concerns to which Fields returned often in speeches before the many civic, religious, and fraternal organizations to which she belonged and in her autobiography, *Lemon Swamp and Other Places: A Carolina Memoir* (1982).

Born in Charleston on August 13, 1888, and already rebellious by 1895, when South Carolina enacted its Jim Crow constitution, she claimed to have acquired "race pride" from her father, George Washington Garvin, a self-employed carpenter who made it possible for her mother, Rebecca Bellinger Garvin, never to "work out"; from her mother, who placed her education and energy at the service of church and community; from her father's father, Hannibal Garvin, who farmed independently after the Civil War on property near Bamberg, South Carolina, where he had previously been a slave; and from Middleton and Bellinger kin, whose education during slavery in clandestine schools prepared them for leadership after the Civil War. She began her education at the age of three in a private school operated by her cousin, Anna Eliza Izzard (who was in the first graduating class of Avery Normal Institute in Charleston), continued at the Robert Gould Shaw School, and earned a teaching certificate at Claflin Uni-

In 1909, Mamie Garvin Fields began her professional career as an educator by flouting the unwritten Jim Crow custom that black persons seeking teaching positions present their applications to the mayor's butler. Garvin, instead, presented her credentials directly to the superintendent of schools in Charleston, South Carolina, and was hired. In 1982, she published a memoir, Lemon Swamp and Other Places: A Carolina Memoir, *with her granddaughter, Karen Fields (left).* (WENDELL JOHNSON)

versity in 1908, boldly claiming her first job the following year.

In 1914, she married Robert Lucas Fields, a craftsman in brick and mortar and an active member of the first union local in South Carolina, Chapter No. 1 of the International Bricklayers, Masons, and Plasterers Union. The couple lived briefly in Charlotte, North Carolina, before returning to Charleston in 1917. They had two sons, Robert Lionel, who became an architect in Washington, D.C., and Alfred Benjamin, who became a social worker in Charleston. The family moved to New York City in 1923 but soon returned to Charleston.

In 1926, Fields returned to full-time work in rural Charleston County as head teacher of the Society Corner School on James Island. She and one assistant instructed 120 children, ages six to eighteen, in the daytime and at night conducted classes for adults, ranging from reading to canning. She established a "diet kitchen" at the school that was the forerunner of cafeterias in other Charleston County schools. During the Great Depression, her kitchen also served some 200 neighbors daily. Her other projects at the time included work in conjunction with **Mary McLeod Bethune**'s effort to gain National Youth Act projects for black youth and supplementary programs for the school through the Works Progress Administration (WPA). During World War II, she was appointed to the Selective Service Commission and joined a group that organized United Service Organizations (USO) facilities in Charleston for black soldiers. She retired from teaching in 1943.

Inspired in the 1920s by women like **Mary Church Terrell**, who lectured in Charleston about women's duty to organize and promote social uplift, Fields founded the Modern Priscilla Club, which eventually affiliated with the Federation of Colored Women's Clubs. Through simultaneous involvement with the Charleston Interracial Committee, she joined volunteers summoned by Susie Dart Butler to help conduct the urban surveys that laid the basis for public housing built in the city between 1936 and 1941. In the 1940s and 1950s, Fields served two terms as president of the state Federation of Women's Clubs and one term as statistician of the national federation. In the mid-1960s, she was resident director of the state federation's Marion Birnie Wilkinson Home for Girls.

In 1969, Fields took the lead in organizing the first public day-care center in Charleston; a center built in 1979 at the Sol Legare Homes bears her name. She was a member of Centenary United Methodist Church, the **National Association for the Advancement of Colored People** (NAACP), the **Young Women's Christian Association** (YWCA), and the Order of the Eastern Star for many years. In the 1960s, she became a member of the League of Women Voters, the Council of Democratic Women, and the South Carolina Council on Aging, which in 1972 named her Outstanding Senior Citizen of the Year.

KAREN E. FIELDS

Fleming, Louise Cecilia   (1862–1899)

On January 10, 1886, Lulu Fleming became the first black woman to be appointed and commissioned for career missionary service by the Woman's Baptist Foreign Missionary Society of the West, an auxiliary of the American Baptist Missionary Union (now American

Born into slavery, Louise "Lulu" Fleming courageously served her African heritage as a medical missionary in the Congo in the late 1880s and early 1890s. (SYLVIA JACOBS)

Baptist Churches in the U.S.A.). Louise (Lulu was a nickname) Cecilia Fleming was born a slave in Hibernia, Clay County, Florida, on January 28, 1862. She attended Shaw University (Raleigh, North Carolina), graduating as class valedictorian on May 27, 1885.

Fleming set sail from the United States on March 17, 1887, stopped in Europe on the way to the field, and reached Palabala, Congo (now Zaire) on May 16 of that year. Fleming taught the primary classes and the upper English classes. In an 1888 report to Dr. J. W. Murdock of the American Baptist Historical Society, she lamented: "All our converts thus far are men. Oh, how I long to see the women reached."

Fleming returned to the United States in 1891 to regain her health. While on furlough she studied medicine, first entering Shaw University's Leonard Medical School and then, in 1895, completing the full course at the Woman's Medical College of Philadelphia (now known as the Medical College of Pennsylvania). Fleming was transferred to the Woman's Baptist Foreign Missionary Society, which had headquarters in the East.

On October 2, 1895, Fleming again sailed from the United States and was stationed at Irebu in the Upper Congo, where she worked as a medical missionary. In 1898, when the Irebu station was closed, she was reassigned to the Bolengi station. Fleming was stricken with African sleeping sickness before the end of her second term and reluctantly returned to the United States. She died in Philadelphia on June 20, 1899.

SYLVIA M. JACOBS

Franciscan Handmaids of the Most Pure Heart of Mary

The Franciscan Handmaids of the Most Pure Heart of Mary is a religious congregation of women in the Catholic Church that was founded by a French priest and a black woman. In 1916, Ignatius Lissner, a priest of the Society of African Missions working among the black population of Georgia, sought to establish a community of black nuns to teach black children in the Catholic schools. Because the Georgia legislature was considering legislation to prohibit white nuns from teaching black children, black nuns for the black children became a necessity.

As superior of the Society of African Missions, which had been charged with the spiritual care of black Catholics in Georgia,

Lissner found a strong and capable leader in Elizabeth Barbara Williams. Williams was working for the Sisters of Notre Dame de Namur when she met Lissner and accepted his invitation. Lissner had the plans and the permission for a new congregation; Williams had the charisma, the courage, and the inspiration to found the congregation and to sustain it.

Elizabeth Barbara Williams was born on February 7, 1868, in Baton Rouge, Louisiana. She received her education from the Religious of the Sacred Heart and the **Sisters of the Holy Family**, a black religious community with its motherhouse in New Orleans. In 1887, at the age of 19, she joined a community of black sisters in Convent, Louisiana, who followed the Franciscan Rule. It was disbanded at the beginning of the twentieth century. Later, Elizabeth Williams became a novice for a short while with another congregation of black sisters, the **Oblate Sisters of Providence**, in Baltimore.

She was working as a receptionist at Trinity College in Washington, D.C., when she agreed to join Lissner in the founding of a community of black religious women. As founding superior of the community, she took her vows in 1916, taking Theodore as her religious name. The community was established in 1917.

Growth was slow and difficult. The threatened legislation to ban white religious sisters from the education of black children did not materialize. This left the black sisters without a mission except for one school. Father Lissner, unable to continue his work in Georgia, left Mother Theodore with the major responsibilities. In 1922, she moved the Handmaids from Savannah to Harlem in New York City. From the beginning, the sisters operated a day nursery to serve the needs of the working parents of Harlem and a soup kitchen for the indigent. Service to the poor and the education of children was their new mission. In 1929, Mother Theodore joined the congregation to the Franciscan Order, and it became known as the Franciscan Handmaids of the Most Pure Heart of Mary. On July 14, 1931, Mother Theodore died.

Primarily a community of black sisters, its membership has included women from the Caribbean and the Virgin Islands. In 1991, the community numbered thirty-three members, engaged mainly in educational and social work. The motherhouse is in Harlem, with a novitiate and summer camp on Staten Island and a mission in South Carolina.

CYPRIAN DAVIS, O.S.B.

G

Gaines, Irene McCoy (1892–1964)

Irene McCoy Gaines, noted Chicago social worker, prominent community, political, civil, children's, and woman's rights activist, and nationally known clubwoman, was born in Ocala, Florida, the daughter of Charles and Mamie Ellis McCoy, but grew up in Chicago. She graduated from Fisk

Dedicated social worker Irene Gaines led fellow Chicagoans on one of the earliest marches to protest discrimination in employment, in Washington, D.C., in 1941. (SCHOMBURG CENTER)

University and studied social service administration at the University of Chicago (1918–21) and Loyola University (1935–37). In 1914, she married Harris B. Gaines, a Chicago lawyer and Illinois legislator (1929–41). They had two children, Charles, born in 1922, and Harris, born in 1924.

Her social service career began during World War I in the Girl's Work Division of the War Camp Community Service. During World War II, she served in the Women's Division of the Illinois War Council. From the 1920s until 1947, when she retired as a social worker, Gaines held positions in Chicago's juvenile court, the Black **Young Women's Christian Association** (YWCA), the Urban League, the Cook County Bureau of Public Welfare, and the Parkway Community House.

Gaines was president of the Illinois Federation of Republican Colored Women's Clubs from 1924 to 1935 and, in 1940, became the first black woman to run for the office of Illinois state representative. In 1936, she helped found the Chicago Council of Negro Organizations, and, in 1941, led Chicagoans in a march on Washington to protest employment discrimination. From 1952 to 1958, Gaines was president of the **National Association of Colored Women** (NACW). Her platform—Unitedly We Work for a Better World—reflected her interest in international peace and human rights. Gaines also was active in the **National Association for the Advancement of Colored People** (NAACP), **Sigma Gamma Rho** sorority, Order of the Eastern Star, and the National Association of College Women.

JULIET E. K. WALKER

George, Zelma Watson (1903–1994)

You could say that, if Zelma Watson George could not override discrimination in one walk of life, she sidestepped the obstacle and moved upward in another field. But that is merely a guess as to why she filled so many roles—sociologist, educator, musicologist, opera singer, government official, diplomat, actress, lecturer, and consultant. Her own explanation was simply that many things interested her and the thread of communication united them.

The oldest of six children, Zelma Watson was born on December 8, 1903, in Hearne, Texas, to learned parents, Samuel Elbert and Lena Watson. Both musicians, they educated her at home until she entered public school in the sixth grade. Lena was by profession an educator, but Zelma would acknowledge Samuel, a boarding school principal and dynamic, wide-traveling minister, as her life's primary source of inspiration.

Young Zelma Watson was a remarkable singer, but there were virtually no opportunities in the world of opera for African Americans. It was not until 1930 that Caterina Jarboro became the first African American to sing with a major opera company, and that was in Italy. **Mary Cardwell Dawson** would found the National Negro Opera Company in 1941, and **Lillian Evanti** would receive raves for her performance

there in 1943 in *La Traviata*. But it was not until 1946 that Camilla Williams signed with the New York City Opera, becoming the first black woman to sign a contract with a major American opera company.

So Zelma Watson turned to scholarship. Even there, she met with resistance. In Topeka, Kansas, where young Zelma graduated from high school, she was discouraged by a white counselor from applying to the University of Chicago. She did anyway and was accepted.

She encountered considerable hostility from white students and was even physically assaulted, but she studied avidly and talked about those years as among her most rewarding. Earning a Ph.B. in 1924, she became a case worker, then a juvenile court probation officer, while continuing musical studies at Northwestern University and the American Conservatory of Music.

In 1932, she was working in Nashville as women's dean and personnel director of Tennessee Agricultural and Industrial State College. There, she forged links between the college and Fisk University and was president of a Fellowship of Reconciliation chapter that promoted social and civic education in Nashville.

Zelma Watson married Baxter Duke in 1937. In Los Angeles, where he was minister of Avalon Christian Church, she was executive director of the church's diversely staffed community center. She also began studying for a Ph.D. in education at the University of Southern California. Again, her love of music surfaced. Her field of interest was the sociological impact of black music in America. Her work at USC led to a two-year Rockefeller Foundation grant and, ultimately, to her ground-breaking 1954 Ph.D. dissertation for New York University, *A*

Guide to Negro Music: An Annotated Bibliography of Negro Folk Music and Art Music by Negro Composers or Based on Negro Thematic Material. She would continue to write on this subject in books and periodicals.

She moved to Cleveland upon her second marriage, to lawyer and Civil Service Commission Chairman Clayborne George, and was active in many city organizations. It was in Cleveland that her singing finally found a real outlet. In 1949, she sang the title role in Gian-Carlo Menotti's opera *The Medium* at Cleveland's Karamu Theatre. She reprised the role on Broadway in 1951 and later starred in Menotti's *The Consul* and Kurt Weill's *Three Penny Opera.*

Zelma George served the Eisenhower administration in various capacities through its second term, including service on the Defense Advisory Committee on Women in the Armed Services (1956–59), at the 1957 Minority Youth Training Incentives Conference and on the President's Committee to plan the 1960 White House Conference on Children and Youth.

A State Department grant sent her on a six-month, thirteen-nation goodwill lecture tour in 1959 that was widely praised. Appointed a U.S. alternate delegate to the United Nations the following year, she served on that organization's Economic and Finance Committee.

In great demand as a speaker, George was a full-time visiting lecturer for the Danforth Foundation between 1964 and 1967, visiting fifty-nine colleges. She continued this valuable work both through and beyond her tenure as executive director of the Cleveland Jobs Corps Center for Women (1966–71). In sub-

sequent years, she participated in numerous organizations and received many awards and honors.

Zelma Watson George died in Cleveland, after a life filled with good works and distinction, on July 3, 1994.

GARY HOUSTON

Gordon, Nora Antonia (1866–1901)
Nora Gordon was the first Spelman Seminary student to go to Africa. Her letters describing

Nora Gordon was one of many brave and dedicated black women who sacrificed their health and sometimes their lives to serve as missionaries in nineteenth-century Africa. (SYLVIA JACOBS)

her experiences kept Africa alive in the minds of Spelman students who sang "Give a thought to Africa, 'Neath the burning Sun." The song typified a spirit prevalent throughout the institution, that of the duty of African Americans to help Christianize and civilize their ancestral homeland.

Nora Antonia Gordon was born to former slaves in Columbus, Georgia, on August 25, 1866. In 1882, she entered Spelman Seminary (now **Spelman College**) in Atlanta, Georgia, graduating in 1888. She attended a missionary training institute in London before arriving at the Palabala mission in the Congo Free State (now Zaire) in 1889.

She was sent out by the Woman's Baptist Foreign Missionary Society of the West (today American Baptist Churches in the U.S.A.). At Palabala, Gordon worked with Lulu **Fleming**. Gordon taught classes in the day and Sunday school. In a report, Gordon echoed a recurring theme of women missionaries: "We very much need a girls' house. If we can save the women and the girls and have intelligent Christian wives and mothers, the atmosphere of the community will be greatly changed."

Gordon was transferred to the Lukunga mission station in 1891. There, she was in charge of the afternoon school and the printing office, where she set up type for printing the first arithmetic textbook in the local language. In 1893, Gordon took a furlough in the United States. Two years later, she married S. C. Gordon of Jamaica and the couple returned to the Congo under appointment by British Baptists. In 1900, she returned to the United States in poor health and died in Atlanta a year later, in January 1901, at the age of thirty-four.

SYLVIA M. JACOBS

At the age of fifty-six, Sarah Gorham became the first woman appointed by the African Methodist Episcopal Church to serve as a missionary in Africa or any other foreign country. (SYLVIA JACOBS)

Gorham, Sarah E. (1832–1894)

In Kissy Street Cemetery in Freetown, Sierra Leone, one tombstone has the following inscription: "She was early impressed that she should go to Africa as a missionary and that her life work should be there. She crossed the ocean five times, and ended her mission on the soil and among the people she so much desired to benefit." This was the message of Sarah Gorham's life.

Sarah E. Gorham was born on December 5, 1832, in Fredericktown, Maryland, or Fredericksburg, Virginia. Little is known of her life before 1880. In that year, she visited relatives who had emigrated to Liberia and she spent a year traveling throughout the country preaching and comforting the needy. It was on this trip that she became interested in African mission work.

In 1888, Gorham applied to the African Methodist Episcopal (AME) Church for appointment as a missionary. Gorham, fifty-six years old, became the first woman missionary of the AME Church appointed to a foreign field. Soon after her arrival in Freetown in September of 1888, Gorham traveled to the Magbele mission, where she was active in the Allen AME Church and worked among the Temne women and girls. It was at Magbele that she established the Sarah Gorham Mission School, which gave both religious and industrial training.

In 1891, Gorham traveled to the United States to recuperate and regain her health. She later returned to Sierra Leone. In July 1894, Gorham became bedridden with malaria. She died on August 10, 1894.

SYLVIA M. JACOBS

Guffey, Edith A. (1953–)

As the lay secretary of the United Church of Christ, Edith Guffey is an administrator in one of the largest religious organizations in the country. By choosing administration rather than direct ministry, Guffey has committed herself to her own sort of leadership and community service.

Born on September 16, 1953, in Kansas City, Kansas, Guffey is the daughter of Ernestine Marshall and John Marshall. She attended high school across the river in Kansas City, Missouri, graduating from Central High School in 1971. She went on to attend Baker University in nearby Baldwin City,

Kansas. She graduated in 1975 with a bachelor of arts degree in sociology.

Directly out of college, Guffey went to work for the State of Missouri as a social worker. By 1977, she was promoted to child support investigator. In 1979, she became a social worker/manager in Kansas, coordinating action on 250–300 child-support cases. She continued to supervise social work projects with the state of Kansas until 1984.

Meanwhile, Guffey became director of the Rape Victim Support Services of Douglas County, Kansas, in 1982, another social work position. She then decided to

Edith A. Guffey spent many years as a social worker and college administrator. In 1991, she became secretary of the United Church of Christ, one of the largest religious organizations in the country. (EDITH A. GUFFEY)

switch to school administration in May 1984. Guffey was an administrator for the University of Kansas at Lawrence from 1984 through September 1991. During this time she completed her masters in social welfare (MSW) at the University of Kansas, with an administrative concentration. She received her degree in 1987.

In 1991, Guffey left the University of Kansas to become secretary of the United Church of Christ. She had been active as a layperson in the United Church of Christ since the late 1970s, working in a variety of capacities. On the regional level, Guffey had been active in the Church of Christ Kansas-Oklahoma Conference since 1979. She was vice president of the Kansas-Oklahoma Conference in 1984 and 1985, and president in 1986 and 1987.

After years of experience working on many church boards, Guffey stepped into her present job of Secretary for the General Synod of the Church of Christ. Her duties include strengthening relationships with member churches, as well as participating in the management of the executive offices. As secretary, she also keeps the official record of the General Synod and Executive Council of the United Church of Christ.

Guffey believes in combining her background of social work with her love for the church and her natural aptitude for administration. While most people put emphasis on the minister in the pulpit, Guffey sees administrators as essential in furthering the goals of the church. As she puts it, ". . . a turning point for me was coming to recognize and value administration as a ministry that is important and valuable in the life of a religious institution. As a layperson, I use my skills in administration as a ministry that helps to connect my faith in a very concrete way to the work of the church."

ANDRA MEDEA

H

Hale, Clara McBride (1904–1992)

Clara McBride Hale, known as Mother Hale and the Mother Teresa of New York, was a Harlem housewife and licensed foster mother who for more than four decades devoted her life to caring for unwanted and drug-addicted black babies. Born in Philadelphia, Clara McBride was orphaned at sixteen. She finished high school and then became a domestic, the main work available for black women. She married Thomas Hale and moved to Brooklyn, where he started a floor-waxing business. After the birth of their third child in the 1940s, Thomas Hale died, leaving Clara Hale with three children (Lorraine, Nathan, and Kenneth). In need of employment, she started taking care of foster children.

Mother Hale (who earned that affectionate nickname from her children) loved talking about her work with her babies and her foster children. She took pride in having reared forty foster children and three natural children. Most of all, Mother Hale took pride in the accomplishments of her work with unwanted, drug-addicted babies.

Mother Hale's career of caring for drug-addicted babies started in 1969, when a young woman appeared at her door with a drug-addicted baby. The woman had a note from Mother Hale's daughter, Lorraine, and left the baby on the floor. A few days later, the mother reappeared with two more chil-dren. Thereafter, other young mothers brought their babies, and word spread quickly about Mother Hale opening her home. At the time, Mother Hale was sixty-five years old and looking forward to retirement.

In 1970, Mother Hale founded Hale House, a home for drug-addicted babies. She and a small staff have cared for nearly 1,000 babies born addicted to drugs and children with AIDS, with funds from private and public sources. Hale House, formally the Hale House Center for the Promotion of Human Potential, is not an institution but a home where infants live in a loving environment. As a result of her dedication, President Ronald Reagan in his 1985 State of the Union address hailed Mother Hale as an American hero. In addition, Mother Hale was awarded two of the Salvation Army's highest honors, the Booth Community Service Award and the Leonard H. Carter Humanitarian Award in 1987.

She died on December 18, 1992, in New York City of complications from a stroke. Her daughter, **Lorainne Hale**, is now the president of Hale House.

LAVONNE ROBERTS-JACKSON

Hale, Lorraine E. (1926?–)

Lorraine Hale was half the mother-daughter team that founded Hale House, the first home devoted to the care of children born

94

addicted to hard drugs. Hale House has grown to a multimillion-dollar project, with additional programs fostering the recovery of drug-addicted mothers, a hospice for mothers and children with AIDS, and a youth-peer program for troubled youngsters. Inspired by Mother **Clara Hale**, but planned, administered, and guided by Lorraine Hale, Hale House has continued to break new ground in the struggle against drug problems.

Hale was born in Philadelphia and moved with her family to Harlem before she was a year old. Her father owned a floor-waxing business. Her mother was a domestic. Her father died of cancer when Hale was only six years old, leaving her mother to provide for her and her two small brothers. Mother Hale continued to clean homes during the day, but also cleaned theaters at night. Meanwhile, she had to leave her own children in the care of others, who did not always treat them properly.

In order to solve the problem, Mother Hale stopped doing cleaning work and began taking in other people's children for $2 per week. By 1940, she had become a licensed foster parent, continuing this work until the late 1960s.

Lorraine Hale grew up among the foster children in her mother's household and knew that she wanted to help children as well. She worked during the day and took college classes at night at Fordham University and City College. She received her B.A. from Long Island University in 1960.

Hale began teaching with the New York Public School System and continued through a series of jobs within the public schools while she acquired more degrees at night. She earned an M.S. from City College of New York in 1964 and took courses at

Lorraine Hale grew up among the foster children in her mother, Clara Hale's, household. After getting degrees from City College of New York and Bank Street College of Education, Hale, her mother, and brothers raised the money to found Hale House, the haven for drug-addicted children and their families. (ANTONIO MARI)

the Bank Street College of Education from 1965 to 1967. She became, in turn, a first-grade teacher, a teacher for severely retarded children, a guidance counselor, and a school psychologist. Yet, she always felt limited by the city bureaucracy. None of these jobs satisfied her need to make a difference in the lives of children.

A chance encounter in 1969 changed all that. After talking with her mother one day, Hale was driving home when she saw a woman with a bundle sitting on a street corner. She realized the bundle was a child and discovered the mother was on drugs. Seeing that this was no place for a baby, she gave the mother a slip of paper with Mother Hale's name and address. Hale told the woman that Mother Hale cared about babies and she could leave the baby with her while she pulled herself together.

That day, Mother Hale telephoned her daughter, not pleased, saying that there was a junkie at her door who, apparently, Lorraine had sent. Hale explained, and after some confusion, the woman left her child in Mother Hale's care. When other addicted women learned that Mother Hale would take in their babies, the family soon had babies everywhere. Within three weeks, there were 22 babies in the apartment. Mother Hale informed her daughter

Legend has it that Hale House began when a young woman appeared at Clara Hale's door with a note from Lorraine Hale saying she could leave her drug-addicted baby there. Soon, other young mothers brought their babies and Hale House was born. Lorraine Hale has never looked back. (HALE HOUSE)

that she had better take a second job to help support them.

Hale did. Her brothers helped out financially as well. They managed to pay all the bills for the first 18 months, until they received their first grant from the New York Office of Economic Opportunity in 1971. The state money helped them to expand and, two years later, they incorporated into the Hale House Center for the Promotion of Human Potential. In 1975, they received a federal grant that enabled them to buy and renovate a five-story building on 122nd Street for their residential center.

In spite of her additional responsibilities, Hale continued her education. She earned a certificate in African history from the University of Ghana in 1970, then went on to get two advanced degrees—a Ph.D. from Western University in 1974, and a Ed.D. from New York University in 1977.

Even armed with so many degrees, Hale was venturing into uncharted territory. In the late Sixties and early Seventies, little was known about the effects of hard drugs on babies. Some medical experts did not wish to acknowledge that babies could be born addicted. Certainly, little was known about the special needs of such babies. Hale and the staff of Hale House sought to understand these needs, but always provided love first and foremost. New specialists were added to the staff, including a psychologist, a speech pathologist, and an occupational therapist. Three chiropractors were brought in to help enhance the children's growth and development.

The goal of Hale House was to reunite drug-addicted children with their families after the parents had completed a drug-rehabilitation program. In order to help the mothers toward addiction recovery, the group started a new program in 1985 called Homeward Bound. This program provided housing, education, and help while mothers learned a new drug-free lifestyle.

In 1985, the Hales were honored by President Ronald Reagan in his State of the Union Address. They subsequently traveled through every state in the union learning and educating others. This trip inspired a subsequent project, Children Helping Children, which uses a peer tribunal to help kids keep other kids out of trouble.

Still, the problems kept growing. By the 1980s, children were being born addicted to crack. Some were chronically ill, with what came to be known as AIDS. In response, the Hales opened The Respite, which was a facility for mothers and children seriously ill with HIV and AIDS.

Hale House encountered a setback in 1990 when New York State changed their funding regulations to support individual foster-care families over group-care homes. Undaunted, the Hales sought their funding from private sources and continued to operate. By the middle 1990s they expanded again, now to include Hale Haven, a home to protect and educate teenage mothers.

Mother Hale died in 1992, but Lorraine Hale continues as the administer and planner of the Hale House operations. Charting new courses against problems that have left others baffled, she continues to forge innovative projects to improve the lives of drug-addicted children and their families.

ANDRA MEDEA

Harris, Barbara (1930–)

Barbara Harris was the first black woman—indeed, the first woman—to become a bishop in the Episcopal church. She

At the end of her ordination ceremony (February 12, 1989), Bishop Barbara Harris blessed the congregation. The first female Episcopalian bishop, she has been outspoken in her support of the rights of black Americans, women, the poor, and other ethnic minorities. (EVAN RICHMAN)

was born on June 12, 1930, in Philadelphia, Pennsylvania, to Walter Harris and Beatrice Price Harris. She attended the Philadelphia High School for Girls and, as a teenager, started a young adults group at her local church, Saint Barnabas Church. It quickly became the largest church youth group in Philadelphia. Her friends from school remember her as charming, spirited, and carefree. After graduating from high school, Harris took a job with Joe Baker Associates, a public relations firm. One of her responsibilities there was to edit a publication promoting historically black colleges. At her church, she was active in the St. Dismas Society, a prison-visiting group, and belonged to the adult fellowship, which had grown out of her young adults group.

Harris went on to a position in public relations with Sun Oil Company and, back at her church, became a board member of the Pennsylvania Prison Society. She continued her volunteer work in prisons for fifteen years. In 1968, after Saint Barnabas merged with Saint Luke's, a primarily white parish, Harris decided that the resulting church was too sedate, and she became a member of the North Philadelphia Church of the Advocate. In that same year, a group of black Episcopal ministers formed the Union of Black Clergy. Harris was one of several women who lobbied for membership in the organization and were admitted, adding "and Laity" to the name. Eventually, the group became the Union of Black Episcopalians, and Barbara Harris was an active member.

It seems likely that if women had been accepted as part of the Episcopal clergy earlier, Harris would never have worked in public relations. As soon as the ordination of women was approved, she began to study for the ministry. She attended Villanova University from 1977 to 1979 and the Urban Theology Unit in Sheffield, England. She was ordained a deacon in 1979, served as deacon-in-training at her own church until 1980, and was ordained a priest in that year. From 1980 to 1984, she was priest-in-charge at Saint Augustine-of-Hippo in Norristown, and attended Hobart and William Smith Colleges in 1981. For the five years after she left Norristown, she was executive director of the Episcopal Church Publishing Company. She was serving as interim rector at the Church of the Advocate when she was elected suffragan bishop of the diocese of Massachusetts.

Harris' election was surrounded by controversy. There were those who objected because she was a woman. This objection was essentially futile because the General Convention of the Episcopal Church had opened all orders to women thirteen years earlier. There were those who complained she was divorced. However, there had been divorced male bishops before. Those who opposed her election then criticized her educational background. However, Harris had followed an educational route approved by the church as an alternate to the more traditional one. If it made her fit for ordination, her supporters argued, it made her fit for the bishopric.

What may have been at the heart of some of the objections was her social activisim. She has always been outspoken in her defense of the rights of black Americans, women, the poor, and other ethnic minorities. She has fiercely attacked, in print, the firebombing of abortion clinics and those who make excuses for it. She has spoken out on AIDS issues. Many people are uncomfortable with her stands, and with good reason. She is an uncommonly challenging choice as the first black woman bishop of the worldwide Anglican communion.

KATHLEEN THOMPSON

Height, Dorothy (1912–)

For nearly half a century, Dorothy Irene Height has given leadership to the struggle for equality and human rights for all people. Her life exemplifies her passionate commitment to a just society and her vision of a better world.

Born in Richmond, Virginia, on March 24, 1912, and educated in the public schools in Rankin, Pennsylvania, a small town near Pittsburgh where her family moved when she was four, Dorothy Irene Height established herself early as a dedicated student with exceptional oratorical skills. With a $1,000 scholarship for winning a national oratorical contest sponsored by the Elks and a record of scholastic excellence, she enrolled at New York University and earned bachelor's and master's degrees in four years. She did further postgraduate work at Columbia University and the New York School of Social Work.

Employed in many capacities by both government and social service associations, she is known primarily for her leadership role with the **Young Women's Christian Association** (YWCA) and the **National Council of Negro Women** (NCNW). While working as a caseworker for the New York welfare department, she was the first black American named to deal with the Harlem riots of 1935 and became one of the young leaders of the National Youth Movement of the New Deal era. It was during this period that Height's career as a civil rights advocate began to unfold, as she worked to prevent lynching, desegregate the armed forces, reform the criminal justice system, and guarantee free access to public accommodations. The turning point in the life of Dorothy Height came on November 7, 1937. That day, **Mary McLeod Bethune**, founder and president of the NCNW, noticed the assistant director of the Harlem YWCA, who was escorting Eleanor Roosevelt into an NCNW meeting. Height answered Bethune's call for help and joined

Bethune in her quest for women's right to full and equal employment, pay, and education.

This was the beginning of her dual role as YWCA staff and NCNW volunteer, integrating her training as a social worker and her commitment to rise above the limitations of race and sex.

A leader in the struggle for equality and human rights, Dorothy Irene Height is best known for her work with the Young Women's Christian Association, especially as a staff member of the National Board of the YWCA of the USA, and for her work with the National Council of Negro Women. As president of the latter organization since 1957, she has worked for justice for black women and has sought to strengthen the black family. (NATIONAL COUNCIL OF NEGRO WOMEN, INC.)

Height quickly rose through the ranks of the YWCA, from the Emma Ransom House in Harlem to the Phyllis Wheatley Branch in Washington, D.C. By 1944 and until 1977, Height was a staff member of the National Board of the YWCA of the USA, where she held several leadership positions and assumed responsibility for developing leadership training activities for volunteers and staff as well as programs to promote interracial and ecumenical education. In 1965, she inaugurated and became director of the Center for Racial Justice, a position she held until 1977, when she retired from the national YWCA.

Height was elected national president of **Delta Sigma Theta** sorority in 1947 and carried the sorority to a new level of organizational development throughout her term, which ended in 1956. Her leadership training skills, social work background, and knowledge of volunteerism benefited the sorority as it moved into a new era of activism on the national and international scenes. From the presidency of Delta Sigma Theta, Height assumed the presidency of the NCNW in 1957, a position she holds today.

As the fourth president of the NCNW, Height has led a crusade for justice for black women and since 1986 has worked to strengthen the black family. Under the leadership of Height, NCNW achieved tax-exempt status; raised funds from thousands of women in support of erecting a statue of Bethune in a federal park; developed several model national and community-based programs (ranging from teenage parenting to swine "banks" that address hunger in rural areas) that were replicated by other groups; established the Bethune Museum and Archives for Black Women, the first institution devoted to

black women's history; and established the Bethune Council House as a national historic site. In the 1960s, Height placed the organization on an action course of issue-oriented politics, sponsoring "Wednesdays in Mississippi," when interracial groups of women would help out at Freedom Schools; promoting voter education drives in the North and voter registration drives in the South; and establishing communication between black and white women.

Her international travels and studies throughout Africa, Asia, Europe, and Latin America began as early as 1937. As vice-chair of the United Christian Youth Movement of North America, she was chosen as one of ten American youth delegates to the World Conference on Life and Work of the Churches in Oxford, England. Two years later, Height was a YWCA representative to the World Conference of Christian Youth in Amsterdam, Holland. These early international experiences and activities as a leader of the youth movement left her with heightened confidence and the conviction that her goals and vision should be broadened to encompass international perspectives.

By the early 1950s, her leadership and understanding of the need to move the woman's agenda beyond the boundaries of the United States were evident. While she served as a YWCA staff member, she represented the NCNW at a meeting of the Congress of Women in Port-au-Prince, Haiti, in connection with Haiti's bicentennial exposition. While there, she arranged for the initiation of the first international chapter of Delta Sigma Theta. In 1952, Height arranged a four-month visiting professorship at the University of Delhi, India, in the Delhi School of Social Work, which was founded by the YWCA of India, Burma, and Ceylon to learn firsthand the needs of Indian women. Height became known for her internationalism and humanitarianism, and became the YWCA representative to conduct international studies and travel to expand the work of the YWCA. In 1958, she was one of a thirty-five-member Town Meeting of the World on a special people-to-people mission to five Latin American countries. Because of her expertise in training, she was sent to study the training needs of women's organizations in five West African countries. These early international and human relations experiences helped prepare her for moving the NCNW agenda into one of cooperation and collaboration in response to the needs of the people, both domestically and internationally.

Her experiences also caught the attention of the human rights community and the federal government. In 1966, Height served on the Council to the White House Conference "To Fulfill These Rights"; went to Israel to participate in a twelve-day study mission sponsored by the Institute on Human Relations of the American Jewish Committee; and attended an Anglo-American Conference on Problems of Minority Integration held by the Ditchley Foundation. In 1974, she was a delegate to the United Nations Educational, Scientific, and Cultural Organization (UNESCO) Conference on Woman and Her Rights held in Kingston, Jamaica. In 1975, she participated in the Tribunal at the International Women's Year Conference of the United Nations at Mexico City. As a result of this experience, under Height's leadership the NCNW was awarded a grant from the United States Agency for International Development to hold a conference for women

from the United States, Africa, South America, and the Caribbean in Mexico City, and to arrange a site visit with rural women in Mississippi. Under the auspices of the United States Information Agency, Height lectured in South Africa after addressing the National Convention of the Black Women's Federation of South Africa near Johannesburg in 1977.

Her distinguished service and contributions to making the world more just and humane have earned her over fifty awards and honors from local, state, and national organizations and the federal government. With Vice President Hubert H. Humphrey she received the John F. Kennedy Memorial Award of the National Council of Jewish Women in 1965; and in 1964, she was awarded the Myrtle Wreath of Achievement by Hadassah. For her contributions to the interfaith, interracial, and ecumenical movements for over thirty years, she was awarded the Ministerial Interfaith Association Award in 1969. She received the Lovejoy Award, the highest recognition by the Grand Lodge, I.B.P.O. Elks of the World for outstanding contribution to human relations in 1968. In 1974, *Ladies' Home Journal* named her "Woman of the Year" in human rights; and the Congressional Black Caucus presented Height the William L. Dawson Award for "Decades of public service to people of color and particularly women."

Working closely with Dr. Martin Luther King, Jr., Roy Wilkins, Whitney Young, A. Philip Randolph, and others, Height participated in virtually all the major civil and human rights events of the 1960s. For her tireless efforts on behalf of the less fortunate, President Ronald Reagan presented her with the Citizens Medal Award for distinguished service in 1989, the year she also received the Franklin Delano Roosevelt Freedom Medal from the Franklin and Eleanor Roosevelt Institute. Her awards also include the Essence Award, 1987; the Stellar Award, 1990; the Camille Cosby World of Children Award, 1990; the Caring Award by the Caring Institute, 1989; and the Olender Foundation's Generous Heart Award, 1990.

Dr. Height has received over twenty honorary degrees, from such institutions as **Spel**man College, Lincoln University (Pennsylvania), Central State University, and Princeton University.

As a result of her extraordinary leadership in advancing women's rights, her dedication to the liberation of black America, and her selfless determination, Height has carried out the dream of her friend and mentor, **Mary McLeod Bethune**, to leave no one behind. As a self-help advocate, she has been instrumental in the initiation of NCNW-sponsored food drives, child care and housing projects, and career and educational programs that embody the principles of self-reliance. She is proud that the NCNW established and maintains the **Fannie Lou Hamer** Day Care Center in Ruleville, Mississippi. As a promoter of positive black family life, Height conceived and organized the Black Family Reunion Celebration in 1986 to reinforce the historic strengths and traditional values of the African-American family. Now in seven cities, the Black Family Reunion Celebration has made a difference in the lives of millions of participants. Dorothy Height, too, has made a difference during her six decades of public life as dream giver, earth shaker, and crusader for human rights. In 1993, she received the Spingarn Medal from the **National Association for the Advancement of Colored People** (NAACP).

ELEANOR HINTON HOYTT

Hilyer, Amanda Gray   (1870–1957)

She was a prominent businesswoman and professional in Washington, D.C., and for sixty years a pillar of the black community. With her husband, she owned and operated a pharmacy in the heart of the black business district in the early years of the twentieth century. Many community institutions benefited from the support of Amanda Gray Hilyer.

Hilyer was born in Atchison, Kansas, on March 24, 1870, only five years after the end of the Civil War. She attended public schools, then married Arthur S. Gray in 1893. The couple moved to Washington, D.C., approximately four years later. Soon after arriving in Washington, Hilyer enrolled at the Hunter School of Kindergarten, a teacher training school, and then **Howard University**. In 1903, she earned her pharmaceutical graduate degree.

Hilyer and her husband owned and operated a pharmacy in what was then the center of the black business district. Like many prominent businesswomen and professionals, Hilyer became active in black women's clubs and other civic organizations. She was a life member of the **National Association for the Advancement of Colored People** (NAACP) and a life member of the Association for the Study of Negro Life and History, which later changed its name to the **Association for the Study of Afro-American Life and History.**

Through her association with the Booklovers Club, Hilyer was a founder of Washington's Phillis Wheatley YWCA, becoming its first recording secretary in 1905. The YWCA at this time was not just a place with a gym and a swimming pool. YWCAs provided important services that could not be found other places. For instance, at a time when higher education was prohibitively expensive for most black people—and when black people were not welcome at many public lectures—the local black YWCA could sponsor its own lectures on topics of concern to the black community.

YWCA hotels also provided a safe and inexpensive place to stay. This was extremely important, since many rural women moved to the cities for better opportunity, and they were often preyed upon by unscrupulous people who offered them lodging. White YWCAs provided a safe haven for white women, but black women were left to fend for themselves until Hilyer and others like her built their own facilities.

The Booklovers were active in other community issues. They joined together to protest the hanging of a black woman in 1911. In 1913, they opposed the opening of nickel theaters on Sunday, and, in 1914, they lobbied for the appointment of a matron to chaperon black youth at the public beach.

When her husband died in 1917, Hilyer decided to close the pharmacy. When the United States entered World War I, she became involved in the war effort, taking part in Hostess House activities for visiting black soldiers. The War Council later assigned her to Camp Sherman in Chillicothe, Ohio. After the end of the war, she became president of the Phyllis Wheatley YWCA in St. Louis.

Hilyer married her second husband, Andrew F. Hilyer, in 1923. He was another prominent Washington resident who had worked on many of the same committees as Hilyer and her late husband. Andrew Hilyer died two years later. Hilyer remained active in community service, becoming president of the Ionia Whipper Home for Unwed Mothers and president of the Peace Circle, which was organized to restore the home of Frederick Douglass.

Over the years Hilyer was honored for her service by the NAACP, the Community Chest, and the Afro-American Newspapers. After many years of devotion to the community, she died of a stroke in 1957.

Hope, Lugenia Burns (1871–1947)

"It is difficult for me to understand why my white sisters so strenuously object to this honest expression of colored women as put forth in the discarded preamble," Lugenia Burns Hope lamented in the 1920s, referring to the hesitation of white women to support antilynching legislation. "After all, when we yield to public opinion and make ourselves say only what we think the public can stand, is there not a danger that we may find ourselves with our larger view conceding what those with the narrow view demand?"

Lugenia Burns Hope was still a young woman when she became a community activist, work that would later distinguish her as one of the most effective African-American social reformers in the South. Born in 1871 to Louisa and Ferdinand Burns, Lugenia Burns spent her formative years in St. Louis, Missouri, and later Chicago, Illinois. The last of seven children, she was able to attend school, where she focused on photography, printing/drawing, sculpting, and business management. When her family's economic situation changed, however, she was forced to quit school and work full time. She worked with several charitable settlement groups for more than twelve years, including the Kings Daughters and Hull House in Chicago, which helped develop her interest in community building and public service.

Neighborhood Union founder Lugenia Burns Hope (center) and her husband, John Hope, pose with graduates of the Atlanta School of Social Work. The alliance with Atlanta University's sociology department helped Atlanta's Neighborhood Union develop scientific methods to determine community needs.
(ATLANTA UNIVERSITY ARCHIVES)

In 1893, she met John Hope, a native Georgian and a theological student at Brown University. They married during the Christmas holidays of 1897 and then moved to Nashville, Tennessee, where John Hope had accepted a professorship at Roger Williams University. During their one-year stay in Nashville, Lugenia Hope became involved in community activities through her relationship with families such as the Crosthwaits and the Napiers, and she taught physical education and arts and crafts classes to the female students at Roger Williams University. However, because of John Hope's desire to return to his native Georgia, the Hopes moved in 1898 to Atlanta, where he had accepted a position as an instructor in classics at Atlanta Baptist College (later to become Morehouse College).

For the next thirty-five years the Hopes lived on campus, beginning in Graves Hall, a dormitory, and ending in the president's house as John Hope's career took him from the classroom to the office of the presidency.

Lugenia Hope immediately became involved in the West Fair community as a result of the Conferences on African-American life that were hosted by Atlanta University and featured W. E. B. DuBois and Gertrude Ware. Spurred on by conference sessions on child welfare, Hope and a core group of women began to organize kindergartens and day care centers for working mothers of the West Fair community. The group persuaded Atlanta Baptist College to donate land for playgrounds for neighborhood children. Later, as their community work grew, the core group organized themselves into the **Neighborhood Union,** Hope's most important legacy.

For twenty-five years Hope led the Neighborhood Union—*her* organization—as it became an international model for community building and race/gender activism. Adopting the motto "Thy Neighbor as Thyself," the union offered services to Atlanta's African-American communities that were not provided by the state, county, or city. The union divided into zones, districts, and neighborhoods in order to ascertain the cultural, medical, educational, recreational, social, religious, and economic needs of the city. Students from the local black colleges, Morehouse, Spelman, and Atlanta University, were instrumental in organizing classes for young and elderly citizens. The union participated in the drive for equal education, instruction, and facilities, supporting black students as they produced community- and citywide rallies and confrontations. The union joined with many prominent male leaders, churches, and local organizations to fight the discrimination of separate-but-equal education. Their efforts to educate black Atlantans about the double and triple sessions of black schools, the shortage and low pay of black teachers, the poor physical condition of the school buildings, and the limited funds appropriated to black schools led to successful campaigns to block bond issues in municipal elections. Limited successes enabled the African-American community to appreciate the importance of being organized and united in order to overcome the odds.

As the Neighborhood Union grew, Hope acquired a national reputation as a social reformer and community leader. She took her place alongside **Mary Church Terrell, Mary McLeod Bethune, Charlotte Hawkins Brown, Margaret Murray Washington, Nannie Helen Burroughs,** and other African-American women fighting for equal rights and freedom. In the Southern network of African-American female activists, Hope was a major force in challenging racism and initiating interracial cooperation.

Hope's interracial work is best illustrated by two separate campaigns: the creation of African-American **Young Women's Christian Association** (YWCA) branches in the South, and the antilynching movement, especially her alliance with Southern Methodist women and the Association of Southern Women for the Prevention of Lynching (ASWPL). In both campaigns, Hope believed that she and her counterparts, representing more than 300,000 black Southern women, could speak without reservation in order to bring about immediate change. They first challenged the racist policies of the YWCA, which did not allow African-American autonomy, and threat-

ened to withdraw from the movement and return to their churches as bases of support. Hope worked for years to eliminate discriminatory practices and demand black women's participation in administrative functions. Her steadfastness often led to charges of inflexibility and hampering the progress of racial harmony and compromise, but Hope did not relent. She continued the struggle until the direction of black YWCAs in the South was controlled from the national office in New York and not the regional and state offices. Southern black women were soon able to determine the types of young women they would help and the areas where their services were most needed, a right that was not automatic prior to 1924.

While working on the second campaign, to outlaw lynching, Hope came to believe that Southern white women did not accept enough responsibility for the continued use of lynching in the region. Given the widespread assertion that lynching "protected white womanhood," Hope and her network expected enlightened Southern white women to do more than speak out against this so-called act of chivalry and merely hint at feminist jargon. They expected them to control their husbands, sons, brothers, uncles, and grandfathers, who were maliciously murdering black men. They also expected white women to include the rape of black women in their view of female liberation. The manner in which black domestics were treated in some white women's homes, and their low wages, were important issues for black Southern women who were determined to awaken Southern progressive white women to the fact of their own racism. Joining with such figures as Jessie D. Ames and the ASWPL, Hope tried to convince this group that the most expedient measure was a national bill to prohibit lynching, one that called for the prosecution of local law officials in towns where such acts occurred. Championing states rights, however, Ames and the ASWPL opposed federal intervention, believing that state laws prohibiting lynching would be more likely to pass local legislatures and to be enforced by local law enforcement officials. As a result, Hope came away with deep misgivings about Southern white women's commitment to equality and the elimination of racism, but she forced them to face their own role as participants and beneficiaries of racism.

Lugenia Hope was a member/official in several of the traditional race protest organizations. For example, she was first vice president of the Atlanta chapter of the **National Association for the Advancement of Colored People** (NAACP) in 1932. In this capacity she created citizenship schools, establishing six-week classes on voting, democracy, and the Constitution that were taught by professors of Atlanta University. The success of the Atlanta program triggered citizenship classes in other branches. That same year, Hope was nominated to receive the Spingarn Award, the NAACP's highest honor, but the award was not given.

The strategies developed by Hope were reused in the civil rights movement of the 1950s and 1960s. Representatives of the **Student Nonviolent Coordinating Committee** (SNCC) and the Congress of Racial Equality (CORE) canvassed the South, educating rural and urban African Americans about their rights and voting procedures, and enabling them to become politically active. The **Highlander School/Center** in Monteagle, Tennessee, used citizenship training to prepare many of the activists who led heroic efforts to repeal Jim Crow laws in the South. Although the connection is seldom made, the civil rights movement had its origin in the political activism of early-twentieth-century women such as Hope and those in the Neighborhood Union.

Hope the mother, wife, and "first lady" of Morehouse College had to balance Hope the social activist and reformer. She supported her husband's work as professor, college president, spokesman for the YWCA, race leader, and educator. She traveled with her husband nationally and abroad, especially on fund-raising trips. When the opportunity arose, she persuaded him to accept the position of president of Atlanta University. Having helped to establish Morehouse College, he could now help create new opportunities for more black students and at the same time build a major black higher educational center, the Atlanta University Center. Creating the country's first African-American graduate school, Atlanta University, was an opportunity of a lifetime, one that Hope believed her husband could not overlook or decline.

As a mother, Hope was not one to spare the rod, but she believed in negotiating and building expectations more than instilling fear as a means of establishing discipline. Although her community work often took her away from home, she sewed most of her children's clothing and ran her home herself. She instilled in her two sons respect and courage. She trained them to think independently, and not in terms of gender roles, when viewing themselves, women, and society.

In relation to the young men of Morehouse, Hope followed the African-American female tradition of the othermother, nurturing these young men as she took time to acquaint them with their different world. By forcing them to take lessons in etiquette and work with young children through the Neighborhood Union programs, Hope was instrumental in creating the mystique of the Morehouse man.

After John Hope's death in 1936, Lugenia moved to New York City, Chicago, and then to Nashville to be near relatives. She died in August 1947. In compliance with her wishes, her cremated ashes were thrown from the tower of Graves Hall over the campus of Morehouse College.

Lugenia Hope exemplified the strong-spirited race woman who worked for racial justice in the early years of the twentieth century. She was a determined woman who recognized and utilized her abilities and who expected the same from others. She succeeded as a leader because of her ability to work with diverse groups of people and because of her great executive skills. She was successful in African-American communities because of her access to the white power structure and her ability to use that access. Poor and voiceless black Atlantans expected her to be their voice at board and city council meetings. Thus, part of her appeal was her radical, undaunting activism; the other was her genuine love and concern for all children and her willingness to struggle to improve their lives. However, her radical style of activism made her far more outspoken than her peers, more demanding, and less willing to compromise on the issues of racial justice and gender equality. She was more accusatory, and more direct, in interracial meetings than were most of her colleagues. In fact, her voice spoke what other black women felt but could not risk saying. Her peers praised her courage, her frankness, and the forthright

manner in which she exposed deceit, prejudice, and injustice. Her refusal to allow misunderstandings and injustice to pass unchallenged sometimes cost her support and allies, but because of Hope the African-American women's agenda was always clear, its priorities always visible.

Lugenia Hope's dominating nature also cost her allies within the Neighborhood Union, but no one could produce the results she could. Oral and written accounts of the union's successes and failures reflect a respect and fear of Hope, for the group always deferred to her. Under her leadership, however, the community witnessed major reforms, including the establishment of the first African-American high school in 1924 and the first public housing for African Americans in the country.

Whether her steadfast and forthright leadership was politically correct is debatable. It did, however, take its toll on Hope's health, and it did put a strain on her family. Lugenia Hope was a product of Victorian America, and she worked to improve the image of her class versus those whose actions she viewed as immoral and a detriment to the race. She imparted and enforced her values on others so that they could use them to clean up their lives and uplift the race. At the same time, she presented an alternative to the Southern white view of conciliatory, conservative black Southerners. She openly opposed segregation and discrimination, and her efforts helped the growth of racial cooperation and intraracial solidarity in the New South of the late twentieth century. Without question, Hope's work was instrumental in improving the lives of African-American Atlantans during the early years of this century.

JACQUELINE A. ROUSE

Howard, Clara A. (1866–1935)

"My girls and women, you should live that the world may be better by your having lived in it," were words that Clara A. Howard heard in 1887 as valedictorian of the first graduating class of the Spelman Seminary in Atlanta, Georgia. As a member of a new generation of educated women in the post-slavery era, this moment marked a turning point in Howard's life. From that day forward she was inspired to dedicate her life to humanity, and she spent the next forty-eight years establishing a remarkable record as an educator, a missionary in foreign fields, and an inspirational advisor to countless numbers of young people whose lives she touched.

Born in Greenville, Georgia, on January 23, 1866, Howard was raised along with nine siblings in Atlanta by parents who held a deep commitment to Christian values and family. Howard also embraced these values and spent her life nurturing young people as a teacher, surrogate mother, advisor, and friend. Significant among Howard's contributions, however, was her pioneering work as a missionary in the French Congo from 1890 to 1895 and in Panama from 1896 to 1897. Totally committed to serving communities in dire need, Howard hazarded dangerous conditions as a woman traveling alone during this era. Howard was one of the very few women of her generation who held a missionary appointment in a foreign field in her own right rather than by means of a husband's appointment.

By 1897, Howard was forced to end her missionary career because of continuing bouts with malaria. Nevertheless, she left behind a legacy of international service, service as a long-term staff member of **Spel-man College** and as a member of the Atlanta community, in which she continued to be active until her death on May 3, 1935. On November 23, 1969, Spelman College dedicated a dormitory, Howard-Harreld, in honor of Clara A. Howard, its first seminary graduate, and Claudia White Harreld, its first college graduate, both of whom had distinguished themselves in their professions as well as in their daily lives.

JACQUELINE JONES ROYSTER

Hunter, Jane Edna (1882–1971)

I believe firmly in the philosophy of Booker T. Washington, namely, "to teach a man to do something and to do it well. To make him efficient in whatever he undertakes to do so no man coming after him can do the job any better."

Jane Hunter, 1945

Jane Edna Harris Hunter devoted her entire adult life to improving conditions for black women. Although the above quotation, from a letter she wrote to a white benefactor, refers to men, she applied the philosophy in every respect to her work as founder and executive director of the Phillis Wheatley Association in Cleveland, Ohio. The independent association, which opened its first home for black women in 1913, became the model for a network of clubs, residences, and employment services throughout the country, sponsored by the **National Association of Colored Women** (NACW). Between 1913 and 1950, Hunter was a major figure in the black women's club movement as well as in local politics and race relations. Her Phillis Wheatley Association was home to hundreds of women moving into the city for work opportunities, especially during World Wars I and II.

Jane Harris was born on December 13, 1882, on the Woodburn Plantation near Pendleton, South Carolina, the second of four siblings born to Edward and Harriet Milner Harris. Edward Harris, Jane's father, the son of a slave woman and the plantation overseer, named his first daughter after his English grandmother, Jane McCrary. According to her own account, young Jane, with her light complexion and keen features, resembled her father and felt a strong kinship with him and the grandmother she barely knew. Unfortunately, the same features alienated her from her dark-skinned mother. In her autobiography, she confessed that because she despised the "poverty, contempt, and subjugation of the race," she rejected her "racial heritage as a Negro." Later, after years of personal struggle, she dedicated her life to "give the world what [she] had failed to give her [mother]."

Jane was only able to attend school for a short time before her father's death when she was ten years old. However, when she was fourteen, she was invited by missionaries to attend a small Presbyterian school, Ferguson-Williams College, in Abbeville, South Carolina, where she could work in exchange for her education. In 1902, after a failed marriage, she enrolled at the Canon Street Hospital and Training School for Nurses in Charleston, South Carolina, and two years later she moved to the Dixie Hospital and Training School at Hampton Institute.

When Hunter arrived in Cleveland in 1905, she found that black nurses were not accepted in the hospitals and were barely tolerated for private duty. Even more devastating was the lack of available decent housing, especially for black women. She

Trained as a nurse, Jane Edna Hunter distinguished herself as the founder and executive director of the Phillis Wheatley Association in Cleveland, Ohio. The association opened its first home for black women in 1913, and became the model for a network of clubs, residences, and employment services throughout the United States. (PHILLIS WHEATLEY ASSOCIATION)

turned to the **Young Women's Christian Association** (YWCA) for help but was refused because of her race. As a result, she vowed to find a way to help other young black women avoid similar problems. After several years, she approached the YWCA again for help. This time, rather than ask them to allow black Americans into their facilities, she convinced the leadership to help her open a separate home. The white women eagerly embraced the idea.

The Phillis Wheatley Home, named in honor of the black slave poet, opened its doors in 1913. Jane Hunter was appointed secretary and manager by an interracial board of trustees, headed by the president of the YWCA. As director of the Phillis Wheatley Association, Hunter gained local and national attention as a master negotiator between the races. Although some black Americans denounced her servile manner with whites and her accommodationist ideology, none could deny her ability to maintain cordial relations with wealthy donors or her strength as head of the city's largest black institution. Under her leadership, the association grew from a twenty-three-room rented house to an eleven-story, half-million-dollar residence

Under Jane Edna Hunter's inspired leadership, the Phillis Wheatley Association in Cleveland grew from a twenty-three-room rented house to an eleven-story, half-million-dollar residence and training facility, the largest independent residence facility for black women in the country. (THE WESTERN RESERVE HISTORICAL SOCIETY, CLEVELAND, OHIO)

and training facility built in 1927—the largest independent facility for black women in the country.

Hunter remained executive director of the Phillis Wheatley Association until 1946, when she was forced to retire. During her tenure, the institution expanded its services to include a beauty school, fine dining room, gymnasium, music school, nursery school, large summer camp, three branch facilities, two training cottages, and the Booker T. Washington playground. The association was also well known for its controversial employment bureau, which emphasized placement for domestic workers. Hunter also established the Phillis Wheatley Department in the **National Association of Colored Women** (NACW). She served as state president and national vice president of the NACW during the 1930s and 1940s and edited its state organ, the *Queen's Garden*.

In addition to her activities as executive director of the Phillis Wheatley Association, Hunter also maintained active leadership in business and social service organizations. She was a founding member of the Board of the Colored Welfare Association of Cleveland, which later affiliated with the National Urban League; a founder of Saint Mark's Presbyterian Church; a trustee of Central State University; an active partner in the Empire Savings and Loan Association (a black banking organization); a member of the Progressive Business Alliance; a member of the **International Council of Women of the Darker Races**; and an officer and national figure with the Republican party's Colored Women's Committee. In addition, she was active in real estate as a director of the black-owned Union Realty Company and as a landlord with several properties in the city's central area.

Hunter also continued her education. She often participated in training events for black branch directors sponsored by the YWCA National Board, and she took courses in social work at the School of Social Work at Western Reserve University. She graduated from the Cleveland School of Law at Baldwin-Wallace College and passed the bar in 1926. Honorary degrees in recognition of her outstanding work were presented by Wilberforce, Fisk, and Allen universities and Tuskegee Institute. She was also nominated for the prestigious Spingarn Award of the **National Association for the Advancement of Colored People (NAACP)** in 1937.

After retirement, Hunter established the Phillis Wheatley Foundation, a scholarship fund for women. Although her yearly salary never exceeded $3,000, she left an estate at her death of nearly half a million dollars, most of which went to the foundation. According to her attorney, the money accumulated from real estate and stock investments. Tragically, after over fifty years of activism and service, she began to experience increasing periods of confusion and was judged to be mentally incompetent in 1960. She died of natural causes on January 19, 1971.

ADRIENNE LASH JONES

Hunton, Addie Waits (1866–1943)

Addie Waits Hunton described another woman as "gifted and favored by the gods" yet having "resolved to make her life full through work in this movement." Hunton's words could have described herself. The movement she referred to was the **National Association of Colored Women (NACW).** Through the NACW and the **Young Women's Christian Association** (YWCA), Addie Hunton challenged those who denigrated black women, worked for the uplift of all black people, primarily by uplifting black women, and fought for black women's suffrage, among other activities. Educated and cultured, she was also a teacher and a writer who used her pen to publicize, to educate, and to proselytize for black women.

Born in Norfolk, Virginia, on June 11, 1866, Addie D. Waits was the eldest of three children of Adeline Lawton and Jesse Waits. She graduated from Boston Girls Latin School and the Spencerian College of Commerce in Philadelphia, where she was the only black student in the 1889 class. She held several educational posts: teacher in the public schools of Portsmouth, Virginia; principal at the State Normal and Agricultural College in Normal, Alabama; and registrar and accountant at Clark University in Atlanta, Georgia (1905-06).

On July 19, 1893, in Norfolk she married William Alphaeus Hunton, the first black international secretary for the Young Men's Christian Association (YMCA). The couple moved to Atlanta in 1899 with high hopes for the future of black people, but their hopes were soon dashed with the brutal lynching near Atlanta of Sam Hose, a widely publicized murder that also deeply affected W. E. B. DuBois, who was living in Atlanta at the time. While her husband traveled, organizing college men for the YMCA, Addie Hunton combined motherhood, club work, and education. She bore four children. Only two lived, Eunice Roberta and William Alphaeus, Jr., both born in Atlanta.

During the 1900s and 1910s, her articles about the women's club movement and topics germane to black women appeared in the *Atlanta Independent*, the *Voice of the Negro*, the *Colored American Magazine*, and the *Crisis*. In one of her most important pieces, "Negro Womanhood Defended," she took to task those who accused black women of immorality:

> For centuries the Negro woman was forced by cruelty too diverse and appalling to mention to submit her body to those who bartered for it. She was voiceless, and there was no arm lifted in her defense. . . . In the face of all this ignominy—she has staggered up through the ages ladened with the double burden of excessive maternal care and physical toil, and she has, while climbing, thrown off much of the dross. . . . Work, pray and hope—this seems to be woman's part in the uplift of the race.

Hunton attended the NACW's 1895 founding convention in Boston and carried its mission to the Deep South, serving as president of the Atlanta and Georgia bodies and as board member of the Southern Federation. She organized in Southern states and later, during 1906-10, throughout the United States.

Referring to the work of Southern women she wrote, "About them the air is surcharged with the smoke of the battle. Around them they hear the heart-throbs and sighs of a people crying for right." Yet, unprepared for turn-of-the-century violence, the Huntons left the South after the 1906 Atlanta riot, never to live again "in the midst of the great racial conflict."

From 1907 to 1915, she was a national official for the YWCA, serving as city secretary and student secretary to black youth. During 1908–09, she studied at Kaiser Wilhelm University in Germany. The Huntons established their permanent home, which was to remain Addie Hunton's until her death, in Brooklyn, New York. However, William Hunton contracted tuberculosis, and after two years of treatment died in 1916. She stayed with him during most of his illness and later memorialized him in a loving biography, *William Alphaeus Hunton: A Pioneer Prophet of Young Men* (1938).

She once again returned to the civic and club life that motivated her. Under the auspices of the YWCA, she and two other women went to France to head the work with American black troops during the World War I years, 1917–18. She and **Kathryn Johnson** chronicled their experiences in *Two Colored Women with the American Expeditionary Forces* (1920).

Home from the war, in the early 1920s she worked as field secretary for the **National Association for the Advancement of Colored People** (NAACP) on behalf of black women who were being denied their suffrage rights. In particular, she confronted the National Woman's party and its leader, Alice Paul, to support voting rights for black women. In correspondence she wrote, "Five million [black] women in the United States can not be denied their rights without all the women of the United States feeling the effect of that denial. No women are free until all women are free."

In the 1920s, Hunton was also active on behalf of African peoples, observing the occupation of Haiti by the United States, writing of race relations in occupied Haiti (1926), and working as a principal organizer for the 1927 Pan-African Congress in New York City and as a member of the Women's

International League for Peace and Freedom. In the 1920s and 1930s, she also kept up her club work, serving for a time as president of the Empire State Federation of Women's Clubs and the **International Council of Women of the Darker Races**. At age seventy-seven she died of diabetes in Brooklyn on June 21, 1943, and was buried in Cypress Hills Cemetery.

Her daughter, **Eunice Hunton Carter** (1899–1970), was a lawyer and an active Republican and clubwoman, and was married to Lyle S. Carter. Addie Hunton's son, William Alphaeus Hunton, Jr. (1903–1970), taught at **Howard University,** was jailed for five years for refusing to cooperate with the McCarthy committee, and wrote *Decision in Africa* (1960).

GRETCHEN E. MACLACHLAN

I

International Council of Women of the Darker Races

> Our object is the dissemination of knowledge of peoples of color the world over, in order that there may be a larger appreciation of their history and accomplishments and so that they themselves may have a greater degree of race pride for their own achievements and touch a greater pride in themselves. The constitution declares that the membership shall be one hundred fifty American women of color and fifty foreign women of color. . . .
>
> A most interesting Committee of Seven . . . for the past year have been studying conditions on the West Coast of Africa paying special attention to Sierra Leone. Liberia and Ethiopia and also questions of India have come in for study as well as several books of great importance on conditions of American Colored people.

Margaret Murray Washington, 1924

The historical notes written in 1924 by **Margaret Murray Washington** (wife of Booker T. Washington) captured the essence of black women's commitment to the "racial uplift" movement of the late nineteenth and early twentieth century. Through their organizational life, the leaders of the black women's club movement created a powerful network of women of color. This historic movement began in Boston in 1895 when a convention of black women—organized at the urging of **Josephine St. Pierre Ruffin,** president of the **New Era Club**—resulted in the formation of a National Federation of Afro-American Women. In 1896, the **National Association of Colored Women (NACW)** was formed as a result of the merging of the Federation and **Mary Church Terrell**'s National League of Colored Women of Washington, D.C. Terrell was elected the first president of NACW and later held the position of second vice president of the International Council of Women of the Darker Races.

The council, an outgrowth of the black women's club movement, was created in the early 1920s to advance racial pride through the study and dissemination of information about people of color. Black clubwomen believed that their efforts to inform and be informed would lead to a greater appreciation and understanding of the races. The desire for connections to other women of color was articulated through this small, short-lived organization. Members of the council were among the former leaders of the NACW who understood the role education could play in liberation struggles throughout the world. The leadership of the council was in the hands of Margaret Murray Washington, its first president and the former president of NACW (1914–18).

Margaret Washington (1865–1925) was born in Macon, Georgia, to a poverty-stricken family that included ten children. She began teaching at age fourteen, graduated from Fisk University in 1889, and during the same year became the Director of Girls' Industries and later Dean of Women at Tuskegee Institute. She became Booker T. Washington's third wife in 1893, and was to be an important force, along with her husband, in the building of Tuskegee Women's Club. In addition to organizing the council, she was responsible for the development of a course at Tuskegee on the conditions of women in foreign lands.

Correspondence from some of the women on the council reveals Washington to have been the catalyst and sustaining force in the development of the council and its activities. A letter written by Addie Hunton of Brooklyn, New York, prominent clubwoman and later active in the **Young Women's Christian Association** (YWCA) and the **National Association for the Advancement of Colored People** (NAACP), praised Washington's persistent "efforts to stimulate interest in the Council for the study of race literature and the many books now being published on the subject of race." In the same letter Hunton admitted how difficult it was to be active in yet another organization. Study groups and other community and club work made major time demands on this select group of women, who had been very active during the previous two to three decades. However, most members shared the sentiments Hunton expressed in a letter to Washington in 1924: "I want you to know my heart is with you and that I will stand close beside you in whatever you undertake. As I study present day problems and touch them, I am more and more convinced that we need just such

an organization as you are fostering." She also expressed her desire for the council to send goods to Germany at Christmas. "If we are to be a part of the world's program and find favor for our needs we must also learn to share our little."

Lugenia Burns Hope, founder of the **Neighborhood Union** in 1908 and active clubwoman, also encouraged Washington's leadership while acknowledging the importance of the council. In an emotional appeal, Hope begged Washington not to permit the organization to function another year without her undivided attention. Having gained experience both locally and nationally, Hope realized that the council could be the vehicle through which to promote race literature in the public schools. The formation of study groups, which were called Committees of Seven, became the organizational strategy for curriculum integration projects in what we would now call Black Studies. Teachers were organized, recommended reading lists were distributed, discussions were held, and school boards were lobbied.

Understanding the conditions and status of women and children in West Africa, Haiti, Cuba, and India was also a concern addressed by the council's study groups through field trips to selected countries and fund-raising campaigns for international educational projects. One such project cooperated with the Chicago Women's Club in 1924 by supporting the efforts of Adelaide Casely-Hayford, wife of African nationalist Joseph Casely-Hayford, to build a school in Sierra Leone, West Africa.

The importance of this historic organization as part of the general history of the black women's club movement has not been determined. This is due in part to the paucity of information on the council. However, the historical evidence suggests a profound understanding on the part of these clubwomen of the importance of analyzing the intersection of race and gender on a global basis. According to Beverly Guy-Sheftall, "this forward looking organization is reminiscent of recent attempts by contemporary black feminists to establish linkages with other women of color throughout the world and to struggle for the elimination of sexism on a global level." The desire to understand and bond with other women of color across geographical boundaries is yet another manifestation of both feminist and Pan-African impulses on the part of earlier black women activists.

ELEANOR HINTON HOYTT

J

Jack and Jill of America, Inc.

For the young—a chance to see where life can go.

(Up the Hill 1988)

Jack and Jill of America, Inc., began as an African-American children's play group in Philadelphia. The club organizers were professional African-American mothers and the wives of professional African-American men. The goal was to provide their children with social, cultural, and educational programs in a time of de facto segregation in Northern cities. As the club grew into a national organization, the goals expanded to include service and charitable projects of an educational, literary, and scientific nature, financed through a nationally supported foundation.

Miriam Stubbs Thomas called the first meeting of sixteen women to her Philadelphia home in January 1938. A concert pianist during the 1930s, Thomas taught piano in her own studio while her children were young. Along with several women of the Philadelphia black elite, she agreed that most of the women who associated socially and professionally had children who did not know one another. Developing a mothers' club for children ages two to twenty-two, the women sponsored cultural events and opportunities for their children to meet and mingle. The club provided a network for parents and children. The black elite in Philadelphia extended to networks of black professionals in other cities, where plans to organize similar clubs were in the making. As a result, the New York chapter was founded in 1939. Like their Philadelphia friends, a group of New York City African-American mothers had been meeting and bringing their children together for activities. When Philadelphia named its group Jack and Jill, the New Yorkers decided to adopt this name also. By the time of the fiftieth anniversary in 1988, Jack and Jill of America had expanded to 187 chapters nationwide.

In less than a decade from the founding, the Jack and Jill concept had spread so quickly that a national organization was needed. The first national officers were selected in 1946, with Dorothy B. Wright of Philadelphia, president; Emilie B. Pickens of Brooklyn, vice president; Edna Seay of Buffalo, secretary-treasurer; Constance Bruce of Columbus, corresponding secretary; and Ida M. Smith Peters of Baltimore, editor of *Up the Hill,* the national journal. The chapters were organized into eight regions, with emphasis on building leadership opportunities for the children. Mothers remained in the club until their children had graduated from high school and then became Jack and Jill alumni. Teen groups were organized with a leadership structure similar to that of the parent organization. Teens met with mothers at the yearly regional meetings and at the biannual national conventions.

After thirty years, Jack and Jill became one of the first national organizations of African-American women to establish a foundation. In 1968, Jacqueline J. Robinson of Washington, D.C., chaired the foundation steering committee and became the first foundation president. Articles of incorporation were drafted and the foundation announced its purpose as a self-help organization designed to eliminate some of the contemporary obstacles that confront black youth. Many of the projects sponsored by the foundation are centered at historically black colleges around the nation. From 1968 to 1988, the foundation awarded $600,000 in grants to communities, serving thousands of youth, preschool to college in age. Among the projects funded in the late 1980s were the Saturday Academy at Central State University, Project "Get Smart" at Florida A & M University, the Saturday Academy at Kansas City Community College, and the Los Angeles Young Black Scholars program, cosponsored by Los Angeles chapters of Jack and Jill and 100 Black Men.

In reflecting upon the legacy of Jack and Jill over fifty years from the founding, Miriam Stubbs Thomas believes the organization has become an important link for black leaders today. Many Jack and Jill alumni became professionals who then joined Jack and Jill chapters to promote the social and cultural development of their children. This process has continued for three generations. The organization also provides a haven for African-American parents and youth who are confronted with the loneliness of working in integrated corporate America and living in upper-middle-class communities. For African-American professionals who are still connected to black institutions and communities, providing leadership in educational development for those in the community who are disadvantaged is a significant goal. Like the Greek organizations founded by African-American college women in the early 1900s for social reasons, Jack and Jill goals by the 1990s expanded to provide service to the larger black community.

ROSALYN TERBORG-PENN

Jones, Nancy (1860–?)

As she stated in a letter to E. M. Cravath, president of the American Board of Commissioners for Foreign Missions (ABCFM, now United Church of Christ), Nancy Jones contemplated mission work before applying to the ABCFM: "I have prayed to the Lord and asked Him what He would have me to do ever since I became a Christian and I believe He has given me the work of a missionary and He directs my mind and heart to Africa the land of my Forefathers." Jones had decided at the age of twelve that she wanted to become a missionary.

Nancy Jones was born in Christian County, Kentucky, on January 8, 1860, but her family moved to Memphis, Tennessee, during her childhood. Jones graduated from the normal department course at Fisk University (Nashville, Tennessee) in 1886. Although a Baptist, she applied to the Congregational American Board for a missionary appointment. Jones served the board in Mozambique from 1888 to 1893 and in Southern Rhodesia from 1893 to 1897.

In 1888, as the first unmarried black woman commissioned by the Congregational American Board, Jones joined Benjamin and Henrietta Ousley, an African-American couple, at the Kambini station in southeastern Mozambique. Jones and the Ousleys worked at the segregated station for five years. At Kambini, Jones began teaching and soon took charge of the school's primary department. She also visited nearby areas to work with the women and children. However, Jones never realized her dream of setting up a boarding school for girls and boys.

When the Ousleys retired in 1893, Jones was transferred to the new Gazaland mission in Southern Rhodesia (now Zimbabwe). At the Mt. Silinda station, Jones was the only black person. Initially, she worked as a teacher in the day school but eventually was relieved of that duty. Finally, in 1897, Jones resigned from the East Central African Mission stating that she was unable to work in harmony with the mission because of the prejudice against her by some of her white missionary coworkers. Jones returned to Memphis. Her date of death is unknown.

SYLVIA M. JACOBS

K

Kelly, Leontine T. C. (1920–)

The family of Leontine T. C. Kelly, the first black woman to become bishop of a major religious denomination in the United States, tells a story about her baptism: "The second black bishop elected in the Methodist church baptized me when I was three years old. The story goes that when he handed me back to my mother, he said, 'How I wish you were a boy, so that my mantle could fall on you.'" Kelly herself speculates that the bishop would turn over in his grave if he knew what happened to that little baby girl.

Leontine Turpeau was born on March 5, 1920, in the parsonage of Mount Zion Methodist Episcopal Church in Washington, D.C. Her father, David D. Turpeau, was minister of the church. Her mother, Ila Turpeau, was one of the cofounders of the Urban League in Cincinnati, Ohio, where the family moved in the late 1920s.

As a child, Kelly was constantly reminded of the richness of her heritage. At one point, while living in Cincinnati, she and her sister discovered a station of the Underground Railroad in the basement of their parsonage. Their father said that the real witness of that church was in the cellar. Kelly also remembered sitting on the floor playing, at the age of eight, while her mother talked with a visitor, **Mary McLeod Bethune**.

Kelly attended the Harriet Beecher Stowe School and Woodward High School in Cin-cinnati, then went to West Virginia State College. She did not receive a college degree until she graduated from Virginia Union University in 1960, when she was forty years old. She was early married and divorced from Gloster Current and then remarried, to James David Kelly. Her second husband was pastor of the Galilee United Methodist Church in Edwardsville, Virginia, until his death in 1969. One year later, the people of the church asked Kelly to become their minister.

Kelly, who had been a certified lay speaker in the church for twelve years, attended Union Theological Seminary in New York City and was ordained in the Methodist church. When the district superintendent asked Kelly's youngest son what he thought of his mother's going into the ministry, he said, "She's been preaching all my life."

Kelly served the Galilee church and later became a member of the staff of the Virginia Conference Council on Ministries. From 1976 to 1983, she was pastor of the Asbury United Methodist Church in Richmond, Virginia. She then became a member of the national staff of the United Methodist Church. In 1984, Kelly was elected bishop of the United Methodist Church in the San Francisco area. Her bishopric comprised nearly 400 churches and 100,000 members. She served as bishop until she retired in 1988, and then became a visiting professor at Pacific School of Religion in Berkeley, California.

Kelly has said, "For me, the crux of the gospel message is the way we share power. One of the things women bring to the situation in terms of sharing power is new styles of leadership. I am no less the bishop. I know where the buck stops and who is responsible. But that doesn't mean that I have to exert power in such a way that other people feel they are less than who they are because of who I am."

KATHLEEN THOMPSON

King, Bernice A. (1963–)

The youngest child of Dr. Martin Luther King, Bernice King is the only one to become a minister. As a classic Baptist preacher she is a fiery, passionate speaker. As her own woman, she is exploring new ways for the church to be relevant in the post-civil rights era.

King was born on March 28, 1963, in Atlanta, Georgia, to Dr. King and his activist wife, Coretta Scott King. She was born just after Dr. King left for his historic campaign in Birmingham, against the infamous "Bull" Connor. She was only five years old when her father was assassinated. A picture of her as a small child clinging to her mother at his funeral won a Pulitzer prize.

Young King grew up in Atlanta, where the King family is a virtual institution. She experienced both privilege and difficulty growing up in her father's shadow. Her mother encouraged her to be anything she wished to be. At different times King considered being a television anchor, the first black woman on the Supreme Court, or the first back female president of the United States. She did not consider becoming a minister.

It was not an easy decision for her to turn to the church. Her father's assassination caused her to think, "Forget God; forget the church." When she was sixteen, she was at a church youth retreat in Georgia, where she watched a documentary on the civil rights movement. She cried for two hours. King decided then to quit the church. A year later, she felt her call for the ministry. At seventeen, she delivered her first sermon at Ebenezer Baptist Church in Atlanta, the church where her father, grandfather, and great-grandfather had been ministers. From the beginning, listeners compared her sermons to her father's eloquent, fiery preaching style.

King entered **Spelman College**, graduating with a degree in psychology in 1985. She then entered a special program at Emory University, earning a double degree in law and divinity in 1990. While completing this program, she interned both at the Atlanta city attorney's office and as a student chaplain at the Georgia Retardation Center and Georgia Baptist Hospital.

The youngest child of Dr. Martin Luther King, Jr., Bernice is the only one to become a minister. As a classic Baptist preacher, she is a fiery, passionate speaker.
(ALAN S. WEINER/NYT PICTURES)

King spoke at St. Sabrina Church in Chicago, while she was still an undergraduate in 1983. Soon after, she addressed the U.N. General Assembly in New York.

After ordination, King maintained a dual career as both a law clerk in Georgia's Fulton County juvenile courts and assistant minister at Ebenezer Baptist Church. She spoke out against the Gulf War in 1991. King made the papers when she boldly criticized President Bush to his face at the 1992 Martin Luther King Day ceremonies.

Currently, King is an associate pastor at Greater Rising Star Baptist Church in Atlanta. Her focus is seeing that the church stays in touch with the modern needs of the community. "It is the only institution we still own, yet we function in mom-and-pop methods in a society that is high-tech." Looking at twenty-first-century realities, she is committed to developing a ministry to single people. She was also a founding member of AMEN, a group that councils juvenile offenders.

Like her parents before her, King is in great demand as a public speaker. She is also currently completing two books.

ANDRA MEDEA

L

(The) Links, Inc.

At the end of World War II, considerable racial tension and discrimination existed in the United States. Although large numbers of African Americans had fought and died to "make the world safe for democracy," they returned home to find that little had changed in the area of race relations. Nevertheless, many Americans began to view in a new light the age-old questions of civil rights, human rights, and social and racial injustice, which had been ignored for decades. It was in this atmosphere that The Links, Inc., a public service, nonpartisan, volunteer organization, was founded.

On November 9, 1946, Margaret Roselle Hawkins and Sarah Strickland Scott founded the organization in Philadelphia. The original members were Frances Atkinson, Katie Green, Margaret Hawkins, Marion Minton, Myrtle Manigault, Sarah Scott, Lillian Stanford, Lillian Wall, and Dorothy Wright. These women chose to "link" their friendship and resources in an attempt to improve the quality of life and provide hope for disadvantaged African Americans.

By 1949, fourteen groups of women had developed chapters and gathered in Philadelphia for their first national meeting. Delegates attended from various chapters in Delaware, Maryland, Missouri, New Jersey, North Carolina, Ohio, Pennsylvania, Virginia, and Washington, D.C. In 1951, the organization was incorporated, and in 1954 it was decentralized into four geographic areas: Central, Eastern, Southern, and Western. At present, The Links is an organization of approximately 8,000 women with over 240 chapters in 40 states, Washington, D.C., the Bahamas, and Frankfurt, Germany. The following have served as president: Sarah Strickland Scott, Margaret Roselle Hawkins, Pauline Weeden Maloney, Vivian J. Beamon, Helen Gray Edmonds, Pauline Allen Ellison, Julia Brogdon Purnell, Dolly Desselle Adams, and Regina Jolivette Frazier. Marion Schultz Sutherland was elected as the tenth president in 1990. The theme for the organization under her leadership is "Cherishing the Past, Cultivating the Present, Creating the Future."

The Links is committed to promoting educational, cultural, and civic activities. Over the years, the organization has adopted specific programs such as Service to Youth, the Arts, National Trends and Services, and International Trends and Services. All chapters initiate, support, and participate in programs designed to address the needs of their communities in these areas.

The Service to Youth program, adopted by the national group in 1958, was an outgrowth of a White House conference on the wasted potential of minority youth. The Links launched the program under the theme

"Educating for Democracy," with the purpose of supporting over 2,000 gifted minority youth. Over the years, programs in this area have been broadened and expanded to address issues in the following areas: teenage pregnancy, juvenile crime and delinquency, alcohol and drug abuse, mental and emotional disorders, breakdown of the family, unemployment, and education. Since 1982, a primary focus has been the development of programs in drug and alcohol abuse prevention. In an effort to empower youth to reject a variety of negative influences, the organization is spearheading Operation SEED (Self-Esteem Enrichment Day). It also is in partnership with the Library of Congress in its national literacy campaign.

National Trends and Services became a program facet in 1962 as a result of the organization's interest in public affairs, especially in promoting human rights, quality of life, and first-class citizenship for all. Links chapters across the country have developed programs concerning education, poverty, unemployment, spouse abuse, voter registration, crime, leadership, citizenship, civic concerns, consumer education, women, housing, nutrition, economics, the survival of black colleges, health education, and the black family. Local chapters and the national organization cooperate with other community groups to provide conferences, seminars, workshops, and funding in order to address these concerns. Recent programs include cancer prevention awareness for African Americans in partnership with the National Cancer Institute, wellness in the African-American family, a letter-writing campaign in support of the passage of the Civil Rights Act of 1991, and glaucoma screening in partnership with the Eye Institute.

In 1964, a program to encourage interest in the arts was added. Cultural enrichment programs have been developed throughout the United States. The Links provides scholarships for talented individuals, sponsors opportunities for the display of talent by new artists, supports the inclusion of African-American artists in public and private art institutions, and sponsors programs and projects for young people.

Originally a part of National Trends and Services, International Trends and Services became a separate facet in 1978. Its main goal is to involve Links in international events, affairs, and issues. The organization has provided more than $30,000 to support the African Water Wells Project through the International Drinking Water Supply and Sanitation Decade (1981–90). It also collaborates with other organizations in sponsoring international projects such as the Southern Africa Initiative in cooperation with AFRICARE. In recent years, it has been actively involved in initiating community support programs for the adjustment and rehabilitation of Haitian nationals. The organization also supports foreign students studying in the United States. The Links participated in the planning of the 1985 International Women's Decade Conference held in Nairobi, Kenya, supported the United States Commission on Women's Programs and Activities, and endorsed the goals of the International Women's Decade. The Links accepted status as a Non-Governmental Organization of the United Nations in May 1985.

In 1985, the organization developed the program entitled Project LEAD (Links Erase Alcohol and Drug Abuse): High Expectations!, funded in 1987 by the Office of

Substance Abuse Prevention; the Alcohol, Drug Abuse, and Mental Health Administration; and the Department of Health and Human Services. Targeted for high-risk African-American youth, Project LEAD seeks to provide field-tested, community-based educational outreach to prevent drug and alcohol abuse, premature sexual activity, unintended pregnancies, and sexually transmitted diseases. A sixty-hour, five-module curriculum was developed by Links chapters and other black fraternal, professional, and service organizations and was implemented in 107 cities and 139 sites.

A grant from the Lilly Foundation made it possible for The Links to join forces with fifteen of the nation's largest African-American women's organizations to form Black Women's Consultation. The purpose of this group was to address issues considered vital to the survival of African-Americans. Conferences were convened in 1980, 1982, 1983, and 1985, addressing topics such as "Black Women's Response to Global Concerns"; "Programming for Surviving in the New Federalism"; "Making History through Coalescence: Black Women's Organizations in Parallel Programming"; and "Black Women: Leadership, Responsibility, and Response."

The Links provides financial support for many organizations, educational institutions and programs throughout the United States through its Links' National Grants-in-Aid program. Since its creation, the organization and its chapters have made contributions of over $10 million, of which over $1 million has been donated to the United Negro College Fund. A similar amount has been pledged to the **National Association for the Advancement of Colored People** (NAACP) Legal Defense and Education Fund.

The national headquarters are located in Washington, D.C., and the chief administrative officer in 1992 was Mary Polly Douglass.

DOROTHY COWSER YANCY

M

Mason, Vivian Carter (1900–1982)

"I've never been afraid to speak my mind . . . and I don't back away from things, just because some people might consider them controversial." In her many roles as a clubwoman, social worker, and social activist, Vivian Carter Mason lived up to her words. The daughter of a Methodist minister, George Cook Carter, and Florence Williams Carter, a music teacher, she credited her parents with instilling values that inspired her social concerns. Born in Wilkes-Barre, Pennsylvania, on February 10, 1900, Vivian Carter received her early education in the public schools of Auburn, New York, and graduated from the University of Chicago, where she studied political economy and social welfare. She later pursued graduate course work at Fordham University and New York University.

While a student at the University of Chicago, Vivian Carter met her future husband, William T. Mason, a native of Trinidad, West Indies. They married in Brooklyn, New York, where Vivian Carter Mason worked as a **Young Women's Christian Association** (YWCA) program director. Their only child, William T. Mason, Jr., was born in 1926 in Norfolk, Virginia, where his father established a lucrative real estate and insurance business. William Mason, Sr., was an astute businessman who weathered the Great Depression and amassed a considerable fortune before his death in 1976.

Unwilling to place her son in poorly equipped schools in segregated Norfolk, Mason moved with her son to New York City in 1931. In New York, she worked her way through the ranks to establish herself professionally as the first black woman administrator in the city's Department of Welfare, and also gained prominence in a number of local and national organizations. A member of the **National Association for the Advancement of Colored People** (NAACP), Mason sat on the national board of the YWCA and on the executive board of the **National Council of Negro Women** (NCNW). She also founded the NCNW Committee of 100 Women, an organization that sent poor New York City children to camp.

In the mid-1940s, she returned to Norfolk, where she continued to devote herself to social and political reform. Mason represented the NCNW at the inaugural meeting of the International Women's Democratic Federation (IWDF) in Paris in 1945. She served on the executive board of the IWDF and as vice president of its American affiliate, the Congress of American Women. From 1949 to 1953, Mason served as president of the Norfolk chapter of the NCNW and founded the Norfolk Women's Council for Interracial Cooperation. In 1953, she was elected to the first of two terms as president of the NCNW. During her term of office, she steered the council through the

The third president of the National Council of Negro Women, Vivian Carter Mason helped the organization devise strategies to work toward implementation of the Brown v. Board of Education Supreme Court decision. She is shown here standing between Eleanor Roosevelt and Ed Sullivan (Mary McLeod Bethune is second to her right). (BETHUNE MUSEUM AND ARCHIVES)

tumultuous years following the Supreme Court's historic ruling in *Brown* v. *Board of Education*. As the organization's leader, she emphasized interracial coalition building and support for grassroots efforts to bring about racial justice.

Following her tenure as NCNW president, Mason turned her attention to local politics. She urged women to become involved. "We have to educate women to realize that they have a right to share in the legislative process," she said. She challenged women not only to vote but to run for office themselves. As she put it, "Any governing body is better for having women on it." She led the way. In 1968, she was the only black

woman on Virginia's Democratic central committee.

Long an outspoken critic of local school administration, Mason was nonetheless appointed to the Norfolk City School Board in 1971—the first black woman to serve on the board. In 1971, Virginia Press Women named Mason "Newsmaker of 1971," citing "her work with black and white women to achieve equality" and "her demonstrated belief in the American political system." Yet, Mason saw perhaps more clearly than those who honored her that although black and white women might find common cause, the agenda of black women sometimes differed from that of white women: "Black women realize that to get ahead they have to work with the black man because he has been so beaten down it would be a form of self-destruction to do otherwise." Still, she believed, "Black women have unique capabilities, tempered by decades of oppression and indignities. . . . they have the qualities of endurance, determination, and foresight."

Her own involvement in conventional party politics toward the end of her life did not prevent Mason from supporting the more radical choices other black women made. In 1972, for example, Mason risked her reputation and political standing to defend the rights of Communist party member **Angela Davis**. It also did not alter her course—one that always sought new avenues for social change and social justice. In 1978, Mason resigned from the Norfolk school board to focus attention on founding a local chapter of the National Urban League, feeling that the need for direct support to black economic enterprise was pressing. Vivian Carter Mason died in Norfolk, Virginia, on May 10, 1982.

VIRGINIA SHADRON

McCabe, Jewell Jackson (1945–)

Businesswoman Jewell Jackson McCabe is president of her own management consulting firm, a distinguished spokesperson for professional black women, and founder and chair of the **National Coalition of 100 Black Women,** an organization designed to meet the needs of professional black women and facilitate their access to mainstream America. Notable not only for her successful career in the world of business, McCabe's dedication to the advancement of women and minorities has been described as "impressive and much to be admired."

Jewell Jackson McCabe, daughter of broadcast pioneer Harold "Hal" B. Jackson and Julia O. (Hawkins) Jackson, was born on August 2, 1945, in Washington, D.C. She graduated from Bard College in 1966. She married her first husband, Frederick Ward, at age nineteen and later married Eugene McCabe. Twice divorced, she has no children.

McCabe served as director of public affairs for the New York Urban Coalition from 1970 to 1973 and as public relations officer for the Special Service for Children, New York City, from 1973 to 1975. She then held a position as associate director of public information for the women's division of the Office of the Governor, New York, for two years. In 1977, McCabe became director of the government and community affairs department of WNET-TV, a public broadcasting station in New York City. As director, she helped maintain and improve the station's relationship with federal, state, and city governments for the purpose of securing tens of millions of dollars in financial assistance. More recently, McCabe has served as president of Jewell Jackson McCabe Associates, a consulting firm specializing in government relations, minority marketing, and establishing links between government and the private sector.

The National Coalition of 100 Black Women, an extension of the New York Coalition of 100 Black Women, was founded by McCabe in 1981. The coalition has a membership of 7,000 women in twenty-two states and is organized along lines similar to its counterpart, 100 Black Men. Described as "a coalition of high achievers combined with highly energetic women," the group provides a leadership forum for professional women, places important emphasis on the concept of alliance, and sets special priorities in the areas of voter registration and mobilization. The coalition also serves as a resource network for young people. Every year, the coalition honors ten black women for achievement in the arts, science, technology, and business through the presentation of the Candace Award. The title of the award (pronounced Can-day-say) is the Ethiopian word for "queen."

McCabe has served on numerous corporate boards, including Reliance Group Holdings. Her gubernatorial appointments range from chair of the New York State Jobs Training Partnership to member of the New York State Council on Fiscal and Economic Priorities and the New York State Council on Families, where her assigned committee was teen pregnancy prevention. McCabe's affiliations have spanned a broad spectrum of business and community groups, such as the National Alliance of Business, United Way of America, the Association for a Better New York, and the United Hospital Fund.

Honored by several national organizations, McCabe has received tributes from the Women's Equity Action League, a leading advocacy group for women, and the national **Young Women's Christian Association** (YWCA) for her endeavors on behalf of women in business. In 1980, she served as deputy grand marshal in the annual Martin Luther King, Jr., parade in New York City; that same year she was awarded the Outstanding Community Leadership Award by Malcolm/King College. McCabe has received two honorary doctorates. Her published works, or works composed under her direction, include *Commemorative Book: Motown Returns to the Apollo* (fiftieth anniversary) (1984); *Women in New York* (1975–77), a newsletter published by New York State; and *Give a Damn* (1970–73), published by the New York Urban Coalition.

With a wide range of experience in both the public and private sectors, Jewell Jackson McCabe has been both an influential and a dedicated force in the business world.

FENELLA MACFARLANE

McCrorey, Mary Jackson (1869–1944)

Mary Jackson McCrorey became one of the first African-American women to run for public office in the South when she sought a seat on the Charlotte, North Carolina, school board in 1937. McCrorey's pursuit of elective office, which came toward the end of her long career as a political activist, reflected her commitment to black education and accomplishments.

Mary Jackson was born in 1869, the first child in her large family to be born a free person. Her parents, Alfred and Louise Jackson, had been the slaves of a professor at the University of Georgia at Athens who taught them how to read and write. The Jacksons emphasized the value of education to their eighth child, Mary, who graduated from Atlanta University. Mary Jackson later pursued graduate courses at Harvard University and the University of Chicago.

From the late 1880s through the mid-1890s, Mary Jackson taught in Georgia and Florida. In 1895, she joined Lucy Laney, another Atlanta University graduate, at the Haines Institute, Laney's school in Augusta, Georgia. Jackson was the assistant principal at Haines until 1916, when she became the second wife of Henry Lawrence McCrorey, president of Biddle University in Charlotte, North Carolina. (During their marriage, Biddle became Johnson C. Smith University.) McCrorey taught at Biddle part-time and, after the admission of women to the university, served as an advisor to women students and supervised their campus conduct.

After moving to Charlotte, McCrorey became involved in civic affairs. In 1916, she founded a **Young Women's Christian Association** (YWCA) for African Americans, one of the first in the South. She served as chairperson of the **Phyllis Wheatley YWCA** branch from 1916 to 1929, reporting to a committee of local YWCA white women. She became president of the African-American auxiliary of the Charlotte Associated Charities, serving from 1916 until 1944. When Methodists founded the Bethlehem Center, a settlement house for African Americans, they named McCrorey to the board. A Presbyterian, McCrorey served on regional and national denominational boards. She also joined the Priscilla Art and Literary Club, a leading women's organization in Charlotte, and worked with the North Carolina Federation of Colored Women's Clubs.

McCrorey's abilities quickly became apparent to state and national leaders. A member of the regional and the North Carolina Commission on Interracial Cooperation from 1920 to 1944, she also held a seat on the advisory board of the State Commission of Welfare and Public Charity from 1924 to 1944. She served on the executive board of the **National Council of Negro Women** (NCNW), an organization founded by her friend **Mary McLeod Bethune** to give African-American women a greater voice in politics. From 1922 to 1944, McCrorey was corresponding secretary of the **International Council of Women of the Darker Races.**

Although McCrorey did not succeed in her 1937 bid for a Charlotte school board seat, her campaign was well received and created a precedent for the participation of African-American women in local government. In 1941, Benedict College in Columbia, South Carolina, recognized her contributions to African-American education with the honorary degree of Doctor of Pedagogy. Mary Jackson McCrorey died in 1944 in a fire at her home, the president's residence at Johnson C. Smith University.

GLENDA ELIZABETH GILMORE

Moon, Mollie (1908–1990)

Two months to the day before her death on June 24, 1990, the *New York Times* described Mollie Moon as "an organization unto herself." The occasion was a presidential award ceremony marking National Volunteer Week and honoring Mollie Moon's career of civic volunteerism. The description was apt; Moon had devoted nearly half a century to the presidency of the **National Urban League Guild.** Since 1942, the organization she helped found had grown to eighty-three affiliates nationwide. Moon remains best known, however, as the guiding force behind the guild's famous Beaux Arts Ball, which, since 1942, has contributed millions of dollars to the National Urban League.

Working in an admittedly elite milieu, Moon was nonetheless a pioneer of the civil rights movement. Her vision was modest, yet it proved far reaching: to foster cooperation and understanding among black and white individuals while they worked together to advance the cause of racial equality and social justice in America. She accomplished this goal by bringing black and white middle-class people together for social, cultural, and educational activities. Unlike other interracial organizations, the guild's focus was always social—doing good while having a good time. In the 1940s and 1950s, racial segregation by law and by custom discouraged black and white people from interacting socially. In cities across America, however, **National Urban League Guild** activities brought black and white people into each other's homes and offices, fostering personal friendships and underscoring common interests. Consequently, the guild cemented important bonds between black and white urban, middle-class Americans, helping to build a solid foundation for the burgeoning civil rights movement.

Mollie Moon's proudest single achievement, however, was breaking the color line at Rockefeller Center's Rainbow Room. Naming Winthrop Rockefeller her cohost for a 1948 guild event, Moon quashed any attempt to bar black patrons from the posh nightclub. "Nobody was going to buck the landlord," she declared.

Moon served for many years as secretary to the National Urban League's board of trustees. In addition, she was a board member of the Dance Theatre of Harlem, one of the Coalition of 100 Black Women, and a leader in several Catholic women's organizations. After her husband's death in 1985, she raised money to establish the Henry Lee Moon Civil Rights Library and Archives at the headquarters of the **National Association for the Advancement of Colored People** (NAACP) in Baltimore. A pharmacist by training, she served as an advisor to the U.S. Food and Drug Administration. In addition to her volunteer work, Moon owned and operated a public relations firm on New York's Fifth Avenue.

Born July 31, 1908, in Hattiesburg, Mississippi, Mollie Lewis Moon was educated

Mollie Moon sought to foster cooperation and understanding among individuals by bringing black and white middle-class people together for social, cultural, and educational activities. She devoted nearly half a century to furthering this goal through the National Urban League Guild and its famous Beaux Arts Ball.
(NATIONAL URBAN LEAGUE GUILD)

at Meharry Medical College, Columbia University Teachers College, the University of Berlin, and the New School for Social Research. She spent her adult life at the center of black America's civic, social, and cultural life. In 1932, she traveled with poet Langston Hughes, future husband Henry Lee Moon, and others to the Soviet Union to make a film about race relations in America. This youthful adventure, however, turned into a political and artistic debacle; the film was never made. In 1938, she married Moon, a respected journalist, scholar, *Crisis* editor, and NAACP official. Their daughter, Mollie Lee Moon Elliot, a mother of five who is also committed to the guild and the Henry Lee Moon Library, lives in Manhattan with her husband, film producer Stephen Elliot.

Mollie Moon's imprint on the National Urban League Guild and America's urban middle class remains an important yet over-

A *"freedom rider" in the 1940s and a student leader of sit-ins in Washington D.C. restaurants, attorney Pauli Murray was also a founding member of the National Organization for Women.* (SCHOMBURG CENTER)

looked part of the history of American race relations in the twentieth century.

LINDA NIEMAN

Murray, Pauli (1910–1985)

Pauli Murray, lawyer, teacher, poet, and minister, was also a strong advocate of women's rights. She once remarked, "I entered law school preoccupied with the racial struggle and single-mindedly bent upon becoming a civil rights lawyer but I graduated an unabashed feminist as well." She was nominated by the **National Council of Negro Women** (NCNW) as one of the twelve outstanding women in American life for the year 1945 and was named Woman of the Year by *Mademoiselle* magazine in 1947. Murray was a founding member of the National Organization for Women (NOW), formed in 1966.

Anna Pauline (Pauli was a nickname) Murray was born on November 20, 1910, in Baltimore, Maryland. Her parents, William Henry and Agnes Georgianna Fitzgerald Murray, were middle class and of mixed ancestry. In late March 1914, when she was three years old, Anna Murray's mother died. Since her father was unable to care for all six of his children, Anna Murray's mother's oldest sister, Pauline Fitzgerald Dame, adopted her and took her to live in North Carolina. Three years after her mother's death, her father was committed to a mental institution, where he remained until his death in 1923.

Murray attended public school in Durham, North Carolina. After graduation from Hillside High School in Durham in 1926, she attended Richmond Hill High School in New York City for one year in order to meet college entrance requirements. In September 1928, she entered Hunter College in New York City. Her years at Hunter were interrupted by the Great Depression and a brief marriage. She eventually earned an A.B. degree from Hunter College, graduating in January 1933.

In 1938, Murray unsuccessfully attempted to break the color line by applying for admission to graduate school at the University of North Carolina at Chapel Hill. She later was accepted at the **Howard University** Law School, where she graduated in June 1944 with an LL.B. degree. She was first in her class and the only woman. Also in 1944, Murray applied to Harvard University Law School to study for an advanced law degree but was denied because the law school was not open to women. Instead, she did a year of graduate study at the Boalt Hall of Law at the University of California at Berkeley, where she earned an LL.M. degree in 1945.

In 1965, Murray was the first black person to be awarded a Doctor of Juridical Science degree from the Yale University Law School, with a dissertation entitled "Roots of the Racial Crisis: Prologue to Policy." She also received many honorary degrees.

Pauli Murray was a crusading human rights attorney, a teacher, a civil rights and women's rights activist, a poet and writer, and a priest. She was admitted to practice law in California, New York, and the U.S. Supreme Court. For nine months in 1946, she practiced law with the Commission on Law and Social Action, an agency of the American Jewish Congress. She later opened a private law practice in New York City, where she worked until 1960. From 1960 to 1961, she was a senior lecturer (the equivalent of a full professor) and taught the first course in constitutional and administrative law at the Ghana Law School in Accra. While in Accra, she coauthored (with Leslie Rubin, a senior lecturer in law at the University College of Ghana) the first textbook in a series of books on law in Africa, *The Constitution and Government of Ghana* (1961). An earlier book, *States' Law on Race and Color* (1951), became an invaluable reference for civil rights lawyers. She served as vice president of Benedict College in South Carolina and a professor of law at Brandeis University in Waltham, Massachusetts.

Murray became active in the early civil rights movement during the New Deal. She was a freedom rider in the early 1940s and was arrested for protesting segregated seating on interstate buses. While at Howard University Law School, she was one of the student leaders of the sit-ins in Washington, D.C., restaurants.

In 1972, at the age of sixty-two, Murray had a call to the Episcopal ministry and applied for admission to holy orders. She completed an M.Div. degree from General Theological Seminary in 1976 and was consecrated and ordained the first black female priest of the Episcopal Church in 1977 at the National Cathedral in Washington, D.C.

In addition to her other achievements, Pauli Murray was a poet and writer. She authored an autobiography, *Song in a Weary Throat: An American Pilgrimage* (1987), *Proud Shoes: The Story of an American Family* (1956), *Dark Testament and Other Poems* (1970), and numerous monographs and articles.

Pauli Murray died of cancer on July 8, 1985, in Pittsburgh, Pennsylvania.

SYLVIA M. JACOBS

Muslim Women

Any discussion of black women who are Muslim must encompass their Islamic identity and situate their activities within the understandings of Muslim women in general. The primary belief of Muslims is based in the revelation of the Qur'an (Koran, the Glorious Recitation), which asserts that Islam is the way that God has given for the welfare of humanity. Muslims believe the Qur'an to be the last revelation, spoken to the Prophet Muhammad by God for the guidance of humanity. The Qur'an sits at the center of Islamic intellectual activity, from philosophy and jurisprudence to art and music. The first Muslim community is the paradigm for all Muslim communities.

Some of the principles of Islam are: (1) the belief that there is only one God; (2) the belief that God has provided every human community with guidance through prophets and scriptures (the Qur'an lists at least twenty-five prophets, including Jesus, in a line from Adam to Muhammad); (3) the belief that there will be a final accounting for earthly life; and (4) the belief that all Muslims are in a constant struggle (Jihad) within themselves to be Muslim. Believing in one God, praying five times daily, fasting, sharing wealth, and a possible once-a-lifetime pilgrimage become central in the continual remembrance of God.

The worldview of Muslim women anywhere in the world has at its center Islamic legal injunctions regarding women, which are focused primarily on marriage, divorce, inheritance, and ownership of property. Dress, although not a legal situation, is a cultural consideration whose social affirmation is rooted in theological tradition. In addition to these concerns, all Muslim women spend a great amount of time in spiritual practice. Common concerns for Muslim women include the practice of Islam, marriage, divorce, dress, the home, health, and travel.

Estimates of the number of Muslims (immigrant and indigenous) in the United States range from 3 million to 9 million, depending on which source is consulted. In this article, the range of possibilities is used. Given this range, Muslims of African descent are said to account for between 30 percent and 50 percent of all Muslims in America. From this estimate, we can approximate the number of black women who are Muslim to be between 200,000 and 900,000 on the lower end and 300,000 to 1.5 million on the higher end. There are at least 17 distinct Islamic communities in the United States to which these women belong. Because communities of Muslims of African descent have existed since the turn of the century, by 1970 there were, in some communities, families with three generations present. Contrary to popular understanding, many of these black women who are Muslim did not belong to the Nation of Islam, and the communities to which they did belong have grown in large numbers in subsequent decades. Truly, black women who are Muslim represent the diversity of Islam. They belong to Sunni, Shi'i, and Sufi communities, more specifically, Ansar, Ahmadi, Moorish Science, Sufi, Twelver Shi'i, Nation of Islam, American Muslim Mission, Fuqra, and university communities to name a few.

Women's Islamic practice differs little from that of men. Islam is very clear and specific about behaviors that are prohibited and practices that are obligatory. Women pray five times daily beginning before sunrise; they are exempted only during their menstrual cycles and immediately after childbirth for a period of up to forty days. Fasting during the month of Rahmadan (the month during which the Qur'an was revealed to Prophet Muhammad) is an obligation on all Muslims. Fasting during pregnancy is not encouraged and, in some communities, is actively discouraged. Women generally organize the providing of charity and set up the network for acknowledging need. They direct, along with men, the educational networks. The Hajj, the pilgrimage to Mecca, is an act of worship in which women participate if they are financially able and can secure a male escort, usually a husband or other male family member. Women go to the Friday congregational prayers at a Masjid (mosque), usually near their homes. Although separated from men, most women do not find this to be a subjugating experience because they are not there to socialize but to pray.

Women's lives are lived inside a network of women, studying Islam, performing their religious obligations, working at careers, pursuing education, tending husbands and children. Islam places the greatest stress on the individual's accountability to God. Older women or those with infirmities are generally cared for by the community as a whole, as are widows. At the time of death, the body of a deceased woman is attended (washed, perfumed, and prayed over) by women. Muslims are not embalmed (this is Islamic law); they are wrapped in a shroud and placed in a wooden casket and buried within three days of death. In some cities, Muslims have burial grounds; in others, their families contract with cemeteries for plain or unmarked graves.

It is this core of concerns that forms the framework around which the lives of black women who are Muslim are structured and their experiences explained. Muslim girls are introduced early on to the traditional gender separation in Islam. Whether in the Masjid, Muslim schools, or at social events, gender separation is the norm. Girls learn quickly that their primary social contacts, their models for behavior and their teachers, will be women. At seven years of age, Muslim girls generally are encouraged to dress modestly, as this is the age when their training in making formal prayers and fasting begins. Black mothers who are Muslim generally keep their daughters close to them and accompany them in play or on outings. Most Muslim girls attend weekend Islamic studies classes taught by women, where they learn how to perform prayers, read the Qur'an, and speak and read Arabic. The weekend schools (rarely composed of only one nationality) also provide an opportunity for women's community.

Puberty is a significant time in the lives of black girls who are Muslim. They have learned their prayers, fasted for several years, and are now considered young women, accountable for their actions. Mothers are even more vigilant about their daughters' associations and, in some instances, begin to look around the community for a potential future husband. Casual social mixing of boys and girls is prohibited in order to safeguard the integrity of both. At puberty, girls are taught to exercise propriety in conversation, appearance, and behavior.

Morality emerges as a key issue and marriage as its testimony. The Qur'an asserts that marriage is foundational, and tradition asserts that marriage is half of faith. Marital age patterns among black women who are Muslim follow those in the general black community—young women and men marry soon after high school. There is, however, a stronger inclination for marriage in the black Muslim community primarily because of prohibitions against dating and premarital sex. Black women who are Muslim generally marry using two traditions—Islamic and secular. Islamically, marriage is a contract that requires some negotiations prior to agreement. Women usually draw up their contracts in consultation with mothers and/or women from the community. Contracts include the request and stipulations of a dowry (a gift given to the bride, ranging from money to houses), the couple's living arrangements, educational and career considerations, and so on. After a contract is agreed upon and a date set, the accompanying ceremony can be held either in a home or at a Masjid with witnesses. Generally, couples go to city hall to get a marriage license, either prior to or immediately following the religious ceremony.

Black women who are Muslim marry from all over the Muslim world in significant numbers. Among black women who are Muslim, arranged marriages are rarely if ever enacted. Education and careers are actively sought by most black women who are Muslim, but not to the exclusion of marriage. There are no limits on the type of career a woman can pursue, except those generally thought to intrude upon the Islamic understanding of modesty. The problems that black women who are Muslim have encountered in seeking an education or a career have, for the most part, been generated by the larger American community. Black women who are Muslim generally have been discriminated against both in educational institutions and the workplace because of their dress and refusal to participate in social events.

Dress for Muslim women has several fundamental criteria; first and foremost it must be modest—loose-fitting garments that do not expose legs, chest area, and arms. The hair, by tradition, is covered in a variety of ways, usually depending on taste, from scarves to the more traditional veil that covers the breast as well as the hair. Black women who are Muslim feel that their modest dress protects them from unwanted advances from males and also, and perhaps more significantly, that it marks off their personal space. Most Muslim women in America create their dress by arranging Western styles, but they also purchase modest clothing from numerous Muslim stores owned by Muslims from other countries. Although there is definitely an American Muslim woman's dress, black women who are Muslim are just as likely to wear clothes from Pakistan, Saudi Arabia, or Senegal.

The homes of black women who are Muslim also reveal the centrality of Islam in their lives. Generally, there is a great deal of framed Arabic calligraphy on the walls instead of pictures; bookcases are filled with Qur'ans and Hadith, texts on the sayings and actions of the Prophet Muhammad; and floors are covered in oriental rugs. Space is important in the Muslim home because the family is constantly making prayers. In some homes, a room is set aside for this purpose, while in others, there is a minimal amount of furniture so that prayers can be made anywhere. Shoe stands and baskets are kept near the door because outside shoes are not worn in the house. Cleaning is done continuously, also primarily because of formal prayers. Grocery shopping is a serious matter for Muslim women because they cannot buy food that contains pork or any of its by-products. Usually, a group of women in the community makes and updates lists of which products contain pork and then distributes the lists at the Masjid.

Black women who are Muslim travel extensively throughout the Muslim world, as they have an expanded sense of community. With male guardians, they have made the pilgrimage to Mecca in increasing numbers since the 1970s. Some have taken their educational skills to Muslim countries in Africa to teach in schools, practice medicine, and study Islamic sciences. All Muslim countries welcome them and their families, often providing financial support. Women engaged in import/export businesses travel to buy materials and artifacts. In an effort to get their children out of the drug culture of America, several black women who are Muslim have opened schools specifically for black American Muslim children in countries such as Senegal and the Sudan. Marriage to foreign Muslims also has significantly increased travel for black women who are Muslim. Women work in all areas of U.S. industry, from television broadcasting, to medicine, education, business, and engineering.

Health care elicits a variety of concerns among black women who are Muslim. They prefer Muslim female physicians first and then female physicians who are at least willing to understand the cultural difference. Generally, black women who are Muslim prefer homeopathic medicines and home remedies, and they are users of midwives and birthing centers. Hospital stays are accompanied by the normal anxieties, plus the additional apprehension of being different.

BEVERLY McCLOUD

Mutual Benefit Societies

Theory and practice neatly converge in explaining the critical presence of women among the ubiquitous mutual benefit societies in African-American history. In theory, the millions of black women who organized and participated in these societies were giving institutional life to traditional gender roles associated with religion, sickness, death, education, household economies, social welfare, and above all, family and kinship—what Herbert Gutman identified as a web of social obligations reaching back to family and gender responsibilities in Africa. In practice, these obligations became a social fortress against the crushing weight of American racism and slavery, producing a symbolic, but nonetheless protective, African-American kinship system that embraced non-related, fictive kin who turned to one another as brothers and sisters in need of mutual assistance. Family became community and vice versa—the perfect precondition for the vast array of voluntary associations that freedwomen and freedmen would usher in after emancipation.

Before emancipation, organized mutual aid, like organized religion, took place in two worlds: the visible and the invisible, the world the free blacks made, and the world the slaves made. Given the importance of women in African mutual aid, it is inconceivable that first-generation African-American slave women did not transfer these social assignments to the New World, where the need was all the more urgent and extensive. The African connection may have been lost from consciousness over time, but the "female slave network," emphasized by Deborah Gray White as a cultural mainstay on American plantations, evolved pragmatically as a less formal but widespread system of community cooperation, especially in regard to collective care for children, the sick, and the elderly.

In the meantime, free black men and women could afford to organize a more visible infrastructure of mutual aid. As a rule, mutual benefit societies, like most other black institutions, came out of the church. Sometimes it was the other way around, with the mutual benefit society, an institution nearly as basic as the family, taking the lead. The African Methodist Episcopal Church, for example, evolved out of the Free African Society, a mutual assistance organization founded in 1787 by the free black citizens of Philadelphia to provide their community the rudiments of social welfare. In 1793, the welfare functions of the Free African Society were absorbed by the Female Benevolent Society of St. Thomas, one of hundreds of such societies organized by free black women in antebellum cities. By 1838, there were 119 mutual aid societies in Philadelphia alone, more than half of which were female associations, and women made up nearly two-thirds of the membership of all benefit societies. A sample of the earliest established female societies in Philadelphia would include the Benevolent Daughters (1796), the Daughters of Africa (1812), the American Female Bond Benevolent Society of Bethel (1817), the Female Benezet (1818), and the Daughters of Aaron (1819).

In general, benefit societies collected dues, which they distributed among their members to relieve the sick and bury the dead. Just as often, especially in church-related societies, their activities embraced a larger commitment to community uplift and moral reform. Surely this was the case with the Female Wesleyan Association of Baltimore, or New York City's Abyssinian Benevolent Daughters of Esther, as well as another New York society, the African Dorcas Association, founded in 1827 for the expressed purpose of providing clothing for black school children. The Colored Female Charitable Society of Boston (1832) pledged itself to "mitigate [the] sufferings" of widows and orphans. The African Female Benevolent Society of Newport, Rhode Island, sponsored that city's school for black children from 1809 until 1842 when Newport finally opened a public school. In neighboring Massachusetts, the Colored Female Religious and Moral Society of Salem (for dues of 52¢ per year) offered weekly prayer, religious conversation, profitable reading, and friendly advice along with sickness and death benefits to members who would "resolve to be charitably watchful over each other" and not "commit any scandalous sin, or walk unruly." The 1846 charter of the New Orleans Colored Female Benevolent Society of Louisiana, in addition to providing insurance benefits, called for the "suppression of vice and inculcation of virtue among the colored class." The Female Lundy Society in Albany and its sister institution in Cincinnati, both founded in the 1840s, combined antislavery with social welfare. Indeed, with the rapid expansion in the number and variety of black organizations, especially after 1830, the lines of demarcation among moral reform movements, political protest groups, mutual benefit societies, secret lodges, insurance associations, credit unions, orphanages, schools, library companies, and literary societies became difficult to discern. There existed at once a division of labor and a melding of functions—the sa-

The Independent Order of St. Luke is the classic example of a mutual benefit society. By 1920, it had more than 100,000 members in twenty-eight states. This photograph shows the headquarters building. (NATIONAL PARK SERVICE)

cred, the secular, and the sororal—in order to serve the all-encompassing purpose of racial deliverance.

This distinctive mission widened into a war for survival after emancipation. The invisible became visible; self-help and racial solidarity coincided with the advancing career of Jim Crow; hence, as four million ex-slaves sought institutional support and expression, voluntary associations among black women multiplied by the thousands. At the turn of the twentieth century, W. E. B. DuBois' pioneering studies in sociology uncovered so many mutual aid societies that he found it "impractical to catalog them." Among women in the black belt of Alabama, DuBois concluded that "The woman who is not a member of one of these [benevolent societies] is pitied and considered rather out of date." In Petersburg, Virginia, DuBois gave up after listing twenty-two mutual benefit societies, at least half of which were women's associations like the Sisters of Friendship, the Ladies Union, the Ladies Working Club, the Daughters of Zion, the Daughters of Bethlehem, the Loving Sisters, and the Sisters of Rebeccah. It was in nearby Richmond, however, that the mutual benefit society among black women assumed its highest stage of development in a century-long evolution from folk networks among female slaves to national organizations among professional women.

By the close of Reconstruction, black women in Richmond had organized twenty-five "female benevolent orders." Doubtless, the most important among these was the Independent Order of St. Luke, which had expanded to Richmond from Baltimore, where it had been founded in 1867 by an ex-slave, **Mary Prout**. By 1899, the order had fallen on hard times, and might have expired had it not come under the leadership of **Maggie Lena Walker**. Born in Richmond (1867), Walker had been active in the Order of St. Luke since the age of fourteen, while also teaching in Richmond's public schools and helping to found an insurance company, the Woman's Union. It was the Order of St. Luke, however, that became the instrument of her vision for community development. By 1920, with more than 100,000 members in twenty-eight states, the order had created the St. Luke Penny Savings Bank; a weekly newspaper, the *St. Luke Herald*; a department store, the St. Luke Emporium; and generally had emerged as a collective force to reckon with in Richmond. Walker and St. Luke women, for example, funded scholar-ships, helped to found a school for delinquent girls, fought for women's suffrage, protested racial disfranchisement, denounced lynching, and took the lead in the 1904 boycott against Richmond's segregated streetcars. The Order of St. Luke (which included men) represented a holistic movement guided by Walker's "womanist" consciousness, wherein "dichotomous thinking" about domestic vs. public, male vs. female, and black vs. female had little meaning in a historic struggle that subsumed antithetical notions of race and gender.

The Order of St. Luke symbolized a major transition in the evolution of African-American institutions. By the turn of the twentieth century, the functions of the benefit society increasingly passed into the more modern and secular hands of black insurance companies, savings banks, settlement houses, hospitals, civil rights organizations, and government agencies. However, many of these functions passed into the caring hands of black clubwomen who, as descendants of the mutual aid tradition, continued to offer substance and hope in the vast spaces where modern institutions seldom reached. The connection between the Daughters of Africa and the **National Association of Colored Women** (NACW) may not have been direct, nor perfectly aligned across the social strata, but it was nonetheless linear and ran through the Independent Order of St. Luke and thousands of earlier such societies that also liftedas they climbed.

WALTER WEARE

N

National Association of Colored Women

The national club movement developed as a response to increasingly complicated social welfare demands on community resources, a reaction to the growing racism of the late nineteenth century, a need to build a national reform network, and a mission to demonstrate the abilities of black women. Reflecting the spirit of progressive reform, black women subordinated denominational, regional, and ideological identities to forge a national club movement dedicated to racial betterment. The northeastern urban areas dominated the early years of national organization, influencing the direction and leadership during the formative years. As a result of these efforts, the National Association of Colored Women (NACW), through its regional, state, and city federations, developed institutions to serve the race for generations.

The groundwork for successful club work emerged from experiences in beneficial, church, and literary societies in northern urban areas, where black women used their relative freedom to develop social organizations for serving the race. Philadelphia, the city with the largest nineteenth-century black population in the North, was a leading city for mutual aid societies by 1890. Church-related missionary societies, often called Dorcas societies after the biblical Dorcas who dedicated her life to good deeds, maintained several organizations to provide aid to ill and dependent women and children. The African Dorcas Association in New York City provided clothing, hats, and shoes for children attending the African Free School. Other women held fairs in New York City to support the Colored Orphan Asylum.

Literary societies, primarily social improvement associations meeting in a member's home, provided a structure through which women became informed about issues and skilled in effecting change. The literary societies provided poetry readings and musical performances, experience with parliamentary procedures, opportunities to develop leadership skills unhampered by either male or white dominance, and increased educational awareness of racial issues, which included segregation in transportation, lynching, debt peonage, and voting rights. Such literary societies often adopted projects to benefit the race. Their fund-raising skills supported local homes for the aged, colored schools, or orphanages.

Responding to specific community needs, these early club efforts were narrow in scope, limited to a particular denomination or social clique, and short-lived because of lack of administrative knowledge or finances. By the late nineteenth century, the potential for organized action increased as the black population gained education, settled in urban areas, developed organizations to respond to local needs, and faced intensified racial discrimination and violence. During the last decade of the nineteenth century, all these preconditions came together and resulted in the national club movement to improve life for black Americans.

The national club movement emerged from three centers of club life in the North and East: Washington, D.C., New York, and Boston. Washington, D.C., a center of the black elite, attracted a national audience through conventions, conferences, and a forum, the Bethel Literary and Historical Association (founded in 1881). This public platform engaged the intellectual elite, including **Mary Ann Shadd Cary**, the first black female editor of *Provincial Freeman*; **Hallie Q. Brown**, lecturer for the British and American temperance movements; **Mary Church Terrell**, daughter of the first black

In the spirit of progressive reform, black women subordinated denominational, regional, and ideological identities to forge a national club movement dedicated to racial betterment. The National Association of Colored Women, through its regional, state, and city federations, developed institutions to serve the race for generations. Among the distinguished women who served as president were (left to right) Mary McLeod Bethune (1924–28), Mary Church Terrell (1896–1901), Mary Waring (1933-37), and Elizabeth C. Brooks (1908–12). (BETHUNE MUSEUM AND ARCHIVES)

millionaire; **Fannie Barrier Williams**, Chicago community leader, and **Anna Cooper**, leader in black secondary education. Most of the Washington women were teachers, aware of children's problems. Many were volunteers at the Home for Friendless Girls, founded in 1886 by Caroline Taylor. Leaders in education, benevolence, and literary societies, these women joined together during the summer of 1892 to form the Colored Woman's League of Washington, D.C.

Black women in New York City were also involved in a variety of activities. On October 5, 1892, the black female leadership from the New York-Brooklyn community held a testimonial dinner to honor the antilynching crusader, **Ida B. Wells**. Organized by **Victoria Earle Matthews**, a contributor to several New York dailies; Maritcha Lyons, a public school teacher; Sarah Smith Garnet, principal of a Manhattan grammar school; **Susan Smith McKinney [Steward]**, a Brooklyn physician; and others, the testimonial dinner recognized Wells for her courage in researching, writing, and lecturing about lynching, one of the major injustices experienced by black men. This dinner stimulated the formation of two important women's clubs: the **Woman's Loyal Union**, organized by Matthews and Lyons later that month, and the Woman's Era Club of Boston, founded by **Josephine St. Pierre Ruffin** in January 1893.

The Boston women reflected the town's educational and community activism. Ruffin had served on the Sanitary Commission and in the Kansas Relief Association, Women's Industrial and Educational Union, and Moral Education Society. With her daughter, **Florida Ridley [Ruffin]**, and **Maria Baldwin**, principal of Agassiz School, one of the most prestigious white schools in

Cambridge, she met to collect data, publish and disseminate tracts and leaflets, and develop any other service to improve the image of black women through example.

While these three centers were developing services for their communities, several events soon drew these women together in a national collective effort. In preparation for the **World's Columbian Exposition** in Chicago, a Board of Lady Managers encouraged women from other countries to participate in this international demonstration of progress commemorating the discovery of America. When black women's groups from Washington, D.C., and Chicago petitioned for inclusion in the planning process, they were rejected since they had no national organization to represent them. The Colored Woman's League of Washington, D.C., attempted to organize a convention to become a national group, but lack of cooperation from other centers resulted in failure to gain exposition participation. Soon after, the Washington League invited women in all parts of the country to affiliate for racial advancement. Women's clubs from Kansas City, Denver, Norfolk, Philadelphia, and South Carolina responded. Black women in Chicago also responded to the rejection from the Columbian Exposition. In September 1893, the Chicago Women's Club was formed to take leadership in civic and community reform.

The move to develop a national representative body quickened. In January 1894, the Colored Woman's League incorporated with affiliated leagues. Two months later, the Boston Woman's Era Club launched the first monthly magazine published by black women, the *Woman's Era*, which informed subscribers about fashion, health, family life, and legislation. Women from Chicago,

Kansas City, Washington, Denver, New Orleans, and New York contributed to the magazine and served as heads of the magazine's departments. In October 1894, the National Council of Women invited the Colored Woman's League to become a member and send delegates to the spring 1895 convention. Eligibility required the Colored Woman's League to call itself a national organization. Through the columns of the *Woman's Era*, the league requested delegates from other clubs, but only a few accepted. Even though the announcement appeared in the *Woman's Era*, the Woman's Era Club sent no delegates since the Boston leadership was seeking a similar national role. Although the league behaved as a national organization at the spring 1895 National Council of Women's convention, no national convention of black women had yet taken place.

The catalyst for calling a national convention was a slanderous letter sent by a Southern journalist to a British reformer. The British reformer sent the letter to Josephine Ruffin, editor of the *Woman's Era,* who included a copy in a communication to subscribers. The black elite reacted with moral outrage, leading to Ruffin's call for a national conference in Boston. The newly elected leaders of the First National Conference of Colored Women of America represented an alliance of competing groups: Ruffin (Boston) as president, Helen Cook (Washington, D.C.) and **Margaret Murray Washington** of the newly formed Tuskegee Woman's Club as vice presidents, and Elizabeth Carter (New Bedford, Massachusetts) as secretary. Before leaving the conference, the delegates voted to form a permanent organization, the National Federation of Afro-American Women

(NFAAW) to correct the image of black women. The conference's 104 delegates and fifty-four clubs represented fourteen states and Washington, D.C., and reflected the middle-class interest in home life and racial uplift. The women sought to lead the masses to the social righteousness that these leaders embodied.

As a result of this meeting, NFAAW was invited to participate in the Women's Congress at the 1895 Cotton States and International Exposition in Atlanta, Georgia. Prominent black women from twenty-five states attended to demonstrate the race's skills, culture, and talents. The separate black exhibition provoked conflict among the women. Josephine St. Pierre Ruffin expressed the northern integrationist opinion when she declined the invitation because of the racial segregation of contributions. She did not speak for all northern women. Victoria Matthews attended and gathered information for the New York women. The participating group declared itself the Colored Women's Congress of the United States. The group met once more in Nashville during the Tennessee centennial (1897), during which time members disbanded to strengthen the national aspirations of black women threatened by the proliferation of so-called national organizations.

To strengthen these aspirations, the National League of Colored Women and the National Federation of Afro-American Women had to clarify their interrelationships as national organizations. The women realized that competition for members, financial resources, and the attention of the white press could endanger the emerging club movement. Both groups held their national conventions in Washington, D.C., during July 1896, a duplication of effort that made their organizational quest seem ridiculous. The leadership of both groups sought unity. Therefore, a representative body of seven women from each organization deliberated together to overcome the factionalism and conflicts that historically had constrained the effectiveness of these black women's clubs. The joint committee elected Mary Church Terrell as chair, and recommended the two organizations merge to form the National Association of Colored Women (NACW). For self-protection, self-advancement, and social interaction, the NACW gradually lessened the city and/or class divisions that had historically prevented national unity.

Mary Church Terrell became the first president of the NACW, aided by vice presidents from Boston, Philadelphia, Kansas City, and New Orleans. The strength of the NACW remained in the Northeast with Washington, D.C., and the Boston area predominating. These women valued self-help, protection of women, honesty, and justice. They honored past and present black leadership with organizations named the Sojourner Truth Club, **Phyllis Wheatley Club**, Lucy Thurman WCTU Club, Ada Sweet Club, and **Ida B. Wells** Club. Religious roots appeared in clubs such as the Calvary Circle and Christian League. Joining heroines of the past with younger, ambitious women filled with hopes for the future, merging old traditions with new scientific methods of social organization, the NACW became a major vehicle through which black women attempted reform during the next four decades.

After founding the NACW, the women responded to the general reform context. As educated, elite women, they actively supported the major women's reform movements seeking moral purity, temperance, self-improvement, and suffrage. Their racial identity, however, complicated participation in national organizations that included the National Congress of Mothers, the Women's Christian Temperance Union, the National Council of Women, the General Federation of Women's Clubs, the National American Woman Suffrage Association, and the **Young Women's Christian Association** (YWCA). Black women had different perspectives on the women's issues; they possessed a triple consciousness because they were American, black, and women.

They reassembled in Nashville (1897) to formalize the organizational structure of the NACW and to demonstrate black female worth and capabilities. Held during the Nashville centennial, the first annual conference (the first biennial was held in Chicago in 1899) became a platform for racial self-defense. Unlike the Chicago exposition, the Nashville centennial's woman's department recognized the NACW, a national organization representing about five thousand members.

The leadership wanted to develop and protect women. They wanted less criticism and more emphasis on the progress of the race. Self-help and racial solidarity appeared in every speech.

The defensive nature of the NACW was evident in the organization's mission to furnish evidence of the moral, mental, and material progress made by people of color. The present status of the race required black women's leadership in self-help beginning in the home and through mothers' congresses, kindergartens, and schools to develop the intellect and prepare for jobs. The elite leaders were duty bound to protect and sympathize with their fallen sisters, not only preaching but also practicing race unity and race pride. By the end of the Nashville meeting, the NACW had gained both a formal structure and a communications network in the publication of the *National Notes*, a means through which local, reform-minded black women could disseminate information, discuss issues, and stimulate further organization.

The strength of the North in leadership, conference locations, and issues appeared in the biennials of the NACW during the pre-World War I period, a time when 90 percent of the black population resided in the South. During these early years, regional, personal, and ideological conflict threatened to halt the precarious unity of the national club movement. At the first biennial in Chicago (1899), all three types of conflict were present. Mary Church Terrell had to rely on the local Chicago women for assistance in planning and executing this meeting. The Chicago clubwomen warned Terrell that the participation of Ida B. Wells-Barnett would result in their lack of cooperation.

Since Terrell had to rely upon the local women for the planning and program, she decided to omit Wells-Barnett during these stages. Wells-Barnett, offended by the exclusion, charged that Terrell feared losing her position to her. Terrell, however, was more a practical politician than a jealous competitor. Terrell did not include Wells-Barnett in the planning stages for many reasons. First, since the convention took place in Chicago, Terrell could not offend the leading clubwomen who specifically disliked working with Wells-Barnett. Second, Wells-Barnett, as the secretary to the Afro-American Council, which was holding its annual meeting in Chicago during the same week, would be involved in other activities. Third, Wells-Barnett's reputation for creating controversy was not a desirable commodity in an organization attempting to unite factions of black women and provide a public image of reserved, ladylike leadership. Terrell personally admired Wells-Barnett's courage and direct approach to many issues, but that very style of interaction could threaten the loosely organized, infant federation. Terrell was an excellent judge of the politically expedient. She understood the need to build a structure with which black women could then effectively attack racial injustices.

A second conflict emphasized regional jealousies. When the organization began to function with the recognition of credentials, selection of officers, and parliamentary procedures, disagreements developed. Some of the delegates arrived with no credentials. To avoid setting a negative precedent for the NACW, Mary Church Terrell ruled that those delegates lacking proper credentials could not take part in the proceedings. When Josephine St. Pierre Ruffin attempted to speak on a subject, Terrell ruled her out of order. The past rivalry of the Boston-Washington clubs was reinforced by the credential/parliamentary procedure difficulties.

The regional rivalries erupted again during the election process. The NACW constitution prevented a president from serving more than two consecutive terms. Since Terrell had served as the head of the joint committee and as president of the NACW when formally organized at Nashville in 1897, many delegates thought Terrell ineligible. The constitutional issue was resolved and Terrell won reelection. The position of first vice president had Ruffin, Libby Anthony, and Josephine Bruce in competition. Ruffin and Anthony withdrew, giving that office to Bruce. The position of recording secretary, too, produced conflicts. Chicago's Connie A. Curl, New Bedford's Elizabeth C. Carter, and Pittsburgh's Mary Sutton vied for the position. Even though the South had won only three of the eleven offices, Carter withdrew, charging the NACW with playing power politics in using the Northeast for money and influence to help the expansion of the NACW. Because of the election conflicts, Carter announced the withdrawal of the Northeast federation, the only regional federation. The Woman's Era Club of Boston and the Northeast federation took its complaints to the press. The NACW responded with public refutations of the charges and persuaded the northern women to remain for the sake of unity.

The next seven biennials deliberately attempted to balance the centers of club activity in biennial location and leadership to lessen the regional conflicts. Hence, the northern interests received four biennials: 1901 Buffalo, 1906 Detroit, 1908 Brooklyn, and 1914 Wilberforce, Ohio. Centers of club activity received recognition in the election of their leaders to the presidency: Josephine Silone Yates (1901–06) of the Kansas City league, Lucy Thurman (1906–08) of the Michigan State federation, Elizabeth Carter (1908–12) of the Northeast federation, and Margaret Murray Washington (1912–16) of the Tuskegee Women's Club and the National Federation of Afro-American Women. The clubs of the North were satisfied, but conflict did not cease. The election of the darkest-skinned candidate, Lucy Thurman, demonstrated the color consciousness of the black female network, which was seeking to prove that leadership skills had no relationship to the percentage of white ancestry. The publication of *National Notes* at Tuskegee provoked charges of "Tuskegee machine" censorship from Ida B. Wells-Barnett at the Louisville meeting. More a personal than ideological conflict, the charges failed to gain adherents, and Tuskegee continued publishing the newsletter through 1922.

The clubwomen shared more in common as the decades progressed. During the pre–World War I years, the NACW expanded in numbers, regions, and interests. Only one regional and six state federations existed in 1901, yet by 1909, the Southern federation and twenty state federations had developed. By 1916, 300 new clubs had joined the NACW since the last biennial. The departments within the NACW grew and changed from social science, domestic science, juvenile court, humane and rescue work, religion, temperance, music, literature, and publication to include mothers' clubs, kindergartens, and business/professional women. The expansion and increased specificity of interests responded to the participation of educated women in business, social work, and the professions while still showing interest in women's issues and the family. The clubwomen stressed the responsibility of the privileged to help their social inferiors, since white Americans increasingly judged the race by its lowest elements. By training the lower classes to adopt attitudes, manners, and other behavior acceptable to the middle class, these "missionaries" hoped to improve the white perceptions of the race. The self-help method fit the careers of the overwhelming majority of the NACW leaders and was the most acceptable path to advancement supported by white reformers and philanthropists alike.

These self-help efforts to uplift and serve the community are best seen in the local club activities in the North. Typically, care for the race's aged was the first type of organized reform initiated by clubwomen. Lack of programs to care for aging ex-slaves mobilized groups of women to organize, charge membership fees, hold socials, and solicit county funds to raise money to cover services, purchase facilities, and hire qualified personnel to manage these homes for the aged. The Alpha Home in Indianapolis, the Cleveland Home for Aged Colored People, and similar services in Chicago, Brooklyn, New Bedford, Newark, and Philadelphia emerged from the efforts of individual women joined by clubs that adopted the project. For example, Gabrella Smith of Chicago founded the Home for Aged and Infirm Colored People by taking homeless elderly into her house. She interested other women in her project, and soon, Anna Hudlin organized a club for the placement of aged in the home. The club raised funds, obtained other properties, provided furnishings, and managed an endowment for the home's operation. Many of the daily responsibilities were assumed by clubwomen through a network of volunteers. The Woman's Loyal Union established a Home for Aged Colored People. The same group provided the support for a venture started by clubwoman Elizabeth Carter. Her New Bedford Home for the Aged soon received recognition from the NACW as the greatest such enterprise established by the race. Soon, clubs accepted responsibility for the aged in their communities. New Haven's Twentieth Century Club assumed the financial obligations for the Hannah Gray Home. Detroit's club with the same name developed the Phyllis Wheatley Home for Aged Colored Women

under the leadership of **Mary E. McCoy**, wife of the inventor Elijah McCoy and founder of the Detroit club.

Closely related to care for the aged were the local programs to aid the infirm and dependent populations. Women's clubs aided the colored departments or wards in hospitals, created medical facilities for black communities, and developed specialized medical services. The New York clubwomen contributed food, clothing, and services in the form of lectures and performances to the Lincoln Hospital and Home. New Jersey women formed the Charity Club to assist Christ Hospital in Jersey City. Berean Church clubwomen helped Dr. **Caroline Still Anderson** establish a dispensary in Philadelphia, while the Yates Women's Club supported a small black hospital in Cairo, Illinois. The need for health care for tuberculosis patients led the Indianapolis Woman's Improvement Club to establish the Oak Hill Tuberculosis Camp, the first of its kind in the nation. Gradually, these health care efforts emerged from their charity roots to reflect the general trends in progressive reform calling for investigation, planning, and alteration of the environment rather than the patient.

Such mixtures of charity and social welfare approaches were also evident in the clubwomen's efforts for youth. As with homes for the aged, many of the orphanages started out with one woman's concern for dependent children. **Amanda Smith**, international evangelist and temperance lecturer, used her own money to start a children's home in Harvey, Illinois. Joined by the Illinois clubwomen and aided by the State of Illinois, the home expanded to care for over sixty children by 1908. Smith was over sixty at the time she began the effort, but her dream prospered and continued after her death through the organized efforts of the clubwomen. Chicago clubwomen aided the Louise Children's Home and Home for Dependent Children. The New Bedford Women's Club supported a children's home founded in 1904. As with homes for the aged, the segregated facilities did not provoke conflict because of their charitable nature and belief that the race could better care for its own.

Black clubwomen thought that the most efficient way to reform society was to care for and instruct the young. As a result of that belief, clubwomen developed day nurseries and kindergartens that required little expenditure for facilities or staff. Provided in a church basement, clubwoman's home, or rented house, day nurseries needed only to rely on the women as volunteers. Kindergartens (a concept imported from German liberals) were usually established by the educated leadership in clubs. In many kindergartens, the clubwomen provided instruction for mothers in child care, health, and hygiene. The Chicago clubwomen helped Wells-Barnett establish a kindergarten at Bethel Church in 1897. The Women's Christian, Social and Literary Club of Peoria, plus several others in the Illinois Federation, supported similar kindergarten/day nursery projects. Because of the integration of social services in Boston, the clubwomen there supported a kindergarten for black children in Atlanta through their Georgia Educational League. Before the Great Migration of black Americans came from the South to these Northern cities, women had developed self-help services for the aged, infirm, and/or dependent populations from New York to Chicago to Detroit.

The seeds for the development of urban multiservice centers grew out of the homes or missions for the protection of women coming to the northern population centers. The travelers' aid services could not or did not meet the expanding needs of black women migrating in search of better wages, working conditions, or opportunities. Victoria Earle Matthews, president of the Brooklyn Women's Club and **Woman's Loyal Union**, had been concerned about young women since her trip to attend the Atlanta Exposition. Upon her return, she gathered clubwomen together to develop a social service for young working girls: the White Rose Home. These clubwomen had served as founders, administrators, and teachers and/or volunteers in kindergartens and industrial training programs in cooking, laundry, sewing, chair caning, and wood burnishing. The White Rose Home in New York City became a model settlement house for other institutions in the North.

The National League for the Protection of Colored Women, one of three organizations that merged to form the National Urban League, was directly influenced by the White Rose Home. Soon, such homes for working women as the **Phyllis Wheatley Home** in Evanston and Chicago, Lincoln Settlement in Brooklyn, and the **Phyllis Wheatley Association** in Cleveland expanded as community needs grew with the Great Migration.

As jobs opened during World War I, black Americans left the South for northern opportunities. Between the 1910 census and the 1920 census, Detroit's black population expanded by 623 percent, Cleveland's by 308 percent, and Gary, Indiana's, by 1,284 percent. New York gained the highest urban black population, while Chicago went from eighth place to fourth place in similar population growth. By 1920, 85 percent of black Americans outside the South were urban residents. These numbers exacerbated the conditions that black women had been trying to improve through their self-help efforts. These centers filled the needs for lodging, job placement, night classes, industrial training, day nurseries, kindergartens, libraries, boys and girls clubs, savings clubs, choir and music programs, and social gatherings. They became the training ground for black visiting nurses and social workers graduating from the newly formed educational programs. These multiservice community centers cooperated with the National Urban League through affiliation, and laid the foundation for major social services in black communities for generations. As these services changed, so too did the women.

The biennials of the NACW demonstrated the growth of competence and confidence among club workers. The 1916 Baltimore biennial highlighted trends toward racial pride and interorganizational cooperation. By the time the women reconvened, the NACW had passed formal resolutions to support the woman suffrage amendment, to cooperate with the YWCA, National Urban League, and the **National Association for the Advancement of Colored People** (NAACP), and to support federal antilynching legislation. The newly elected president, Buffalo clubwoman **Mary B. Talbert**, directed the NACW to assume financial obligations for the redemption and restoration of the Frederick Douglass home. Talbert's creative fund-raising and participation techniques appealed to racial identity, to female pride, and to individual needs for recognition. All ages, regions, and institutions assisted. The campaign was so successful that the 1918 Denver biennial held a ceremonial burning of the mortgage on the Frederick Douglass home, which came to symbolize the success of one black man and the triumph of organized black clubwomen.

While rescuing the Douglass home, international conflict influenced the American homefront. The First World War provided the occasion for clubwomen to prove their patriotism, their abilities, and their solidarity. The war meant an end to laissez-faire social policy as the government guided national health campaigns, mobilized housing and urban development, and encouraged reforms such as industrial education, social insurance, and community activism. This surge in organizational activity created a growth in confidence and self-image because women felt needed. They proved their abilities, performed nontraditional jobs, and increased their expectations for postwar progress. The clubwomen raised money through Liberty Loans, War Savings Stamps, and United War Work campaigns. Many club leaders served in the six black base hospitals and hostess houses. The Circle for Negro War Relief called on the national club movement for help. The clubwomen used the war years to garner services for their communities and to demonstrate racial pride.

As the war ended, demobilization produced thousands of returning soldiers, unemployment caused by reversion to peacetime economy, and readjustment to civilian life. Economic and social tensions exploded in the Red Summer of 1919. By year's end, seventy-seven lynchings included eleven soldiers, and twenty-six cities suffered race riots killing hundreds. The postwar period provided the context in which rising expectations collided with reality. Black clubwomen armed with better training, interorganizational connections, and confidence sought less charity and more justice. They embodied both the New Negro and the New Woman as they attacked the chronic injustice of lynching.

Mary Talbert built on wartime networks to mobilize women against lynching. She utilized women's imagination, money, and volunteer time to spread the information and raise the funds to cooperate with the NAACP in the national campaign against lynching. Talbert formed an ad hoc group for fund-raising and publicity that became known in 1922 as the Anti-Lynching Crusaders. Broader based than the NAACP, the crusaders directed religious fervor into their attempt to unite one million women to suppress lynching and pass the Dyer Anti-Lynching Bill. Although federal legislation was never achieved, the public and political awareness of lynching injustices changed and lynchings declined. Talbert completed her term of office with the NACW and became a board member of the NAACP. The clubwomen approached the 1920s as activists in the NACW, NAACP, and National Urban League. These multilayered commitments modified the clubwomen and the NACW.

The change in the NACW was gradual at first. The biennials of 1920 and 1922 were held in the South (Tuskegee and Richmond) under the leadership of a northern clubwoman, **Hallie Q. Brown**, of Wilberforce, Ohio. With the NAACP fighting the legal and political battles, and the National Urban League negotiating and investigating social and economic problems in the communities, the NACW had to carve out a special niche for itself. Brown's leadership started to shape that role in education through what came to be known as the Hallie Quinn Brown Scholarship Loan Fund.

Ohio clubwomen honored Brown by leading the states in contributions to the fund. The letters that the NACW came to stand for were National pride, Achievement, Cooperation, and Willingness to serve. The publication of *National Notes* was turned over to Myrtle Foster Cook of Kansas City, Missouri, who developed the newsletter into a magazine with reports, comments, and items of interest to clubwomen. The departments of the NACW had changed to include the Frederick Douglass Memorial and Historical Association, Education, Child Welfare, Health and Hygiene, Social Service, Legislation and Law Enforcement, Big Sisters Movement, Fine Arts, Business, and Interracial Cooperation.

The biennial attempts to balance location of meeting and national presidency continued under the leadership of the Southeast federation's leader, **Mary McLeod Bethune**, president of the NACW from 1924–28. The biennials during her leadership took place in Chicago and Oakland, a recognition of the regional and numerical expansion of the NACW, which in 1924 included over 100,000 members. The NACW, now in the consolidation phase of its growth, gave Bethune authority to establish a national headquarters in the nation's capital and to compile the first official directory.

A generational transition was also in progress. The founding leaders of the NACW were dead or aging; thus, the organization initiated plans to attract younger women into membership through a junior division. The younger generation had its own interests that reflected the social life of the 1920s. The NACW adapted to these changes.

When the clubwomen came to the fifteenth biennial in Washington, D.C. (1928), the NACW dedicated the national headquarters at Twelfth and O streets and the caretaker's cottage at the Frederick Douglass home, both physical examples of achievement. The new president, **Sallie W. Stewart** of the Indiana federation, reported that the junior division work was growing rapidly. The women memorialized past leaders and looked to the future, not knowing that this would be their last, great celebration of club work.

The Great Depression modified the optimism. The women met for the next biennial in Hot Springs, Arkansas (1930). Two days of executive sessions focused on the financial problems confronting the organization. As if to escape the unpleasant realities surrounding them, the clubwomen toured a model house, viewed exhibits of beautiful homes and fine art, and expressed optimism about the scholarship fund, expansion, and the nation's future. The departments merged to form the Board of Control (a financial monitor), a National Association of Colored Girls, and Women in Industry, Mother, Home, and Child.

The NACW did not meet again in biennial until 1933, when clubwomen came to celebrate the Chicago Exposition. Dr. Mary Waring, one of the original clubwomen in Chicago, became president. The discussions, although permeated with references to the causes of and solutions to the Depression, focused on traditional women's issues: standardize the home; create a good environment for the child; train girls to be industrious, artistic, and gracious; improve working conditions for women and girls;

and increase community service. At the 1935 Cleveland biennial, Waring informed members about threatened court action against the NACW for the printing costs of the official history compiled by **Elizabeth L. Davis**. Past president **Mary McLeod Bethune**, director of the National Youth Administration's Division of Negro Affairs, reported on the financial condition of the NACW headquarters.

Bethune's position in the Roosevelt administration had demonstrated to her a need for a united coalition of all black women's organizations able to pressure the political system into action to help the race. Criticized by many of the older leaders of the NACW for attempting to weaken or destroy the national club movement, Bethune nevertheless organized the **National Council of Negro Women** (NCNW) in 1935. With this united coalition, Bethune continued to influence the national direction of black women through national political structures. Her efforts in the National Youth Administration provided work experience for over 400,000 blacks and used over 700 to administer these programs. Self-help could make no such claims. Just as some years earlier, local clubwomen united to form a national club movement, now Bethune saw a need to influence national politics through a united coalition of all black women's groups.

With the creation of the NCNW in 1935, the NACW declined in its original importance. With the NACW's cooperation and support, other organizations had taken over responsibilities to the black community by specializing in goals and tactics. City, state, and private organizations provided institutional support for many of the services started by the clubwomen. The Depression brought economic devastation to black communities and a changing political context through which reform was directed. The younger generation joined the NACW more as a social outlet than as a means to serve the community. They sought means to effect their personal mobility, not to uplift their sisters.

As the political and ideological contexts changed, the NACW persisted with fewer members and a different direction after 1935. It was during the period of the club movement's greatest growth, 1890–1920s, that the NACW achieved its legacy—shaping the leadership, the institutions, and the identity of a people through its women.

DOROTHY SALEM

National Black Sisters' Conference

The civil rights movement gave the U.S. Roman Catholic Church a singular opportunity to witness concretely the meaning of unity in faith and diversity in race, culture, and ethnicity. While individual Catholic lay men and women, sisters, and priests participated in marches and sit-ins, and while individual bishops denounced the sin of racism, the Catholic Church as a whole made no substantial contribution to this organized effort. While liberal faintheartedness and indifference dismayed black Catholics, it did not prevent them from resourceful and programmatic activity. In fact, the resurgence of their one-hundred-year-old struggle for justice and equality within the Roman Catholic Church coincides with their engagement in the civil rights movement. The National Black Sisters' Conference, an organization of black Roman Catholic nuns, is a product of this effort.

The National Black Sisters' Conference (NBSC) was founded in August 1968 by an international gathering of 155 black Roman Catholic nuns from 79 different religious congregations, 45 U.S. cities, the Caribbean, and the continent of Africa. The conference's position paper pledged to work unceasingly for the liberation of black people. Since then, the NBSC has been the chief means through which black nuns have cooperated across congregational lines to confront individual and institutional racism in the Roman Catholic Church and in U.S. society; maintain a network for personal and communal support, self-criticism, study, and prayer; and develop initiatives to promote systemic change in religious life. The founding president and executive director of the conference was (former) Religious Sister of Mercy, Mary Martin de Porres Grey (now Dr. Patricia Grey Tyree).

Since the organization's founding, NBSC leadership, staff, and members have sponsored annual meetings; conducted spiritual retreats and workshops for black laity, vowed members of Catholic religious orders, and clergy; provided consultative services to parochial and community schools, Catholic and Protestant parishes, and dioceses; published a quarterly newsletter, *Signs of Soul*, as well as four monographs; and developed and implemented workshops on the training and preparation of black sisters. From 1973 to 1975, the conference provided technical and personnel assistance to the Roman Catholic bishop of Benin City, Nigeria, in the founding of an indigenous order of Roman Catholic sisters. In the early 1980s, the conference founded Sojourner House in Detroit, Michigan. Sojourner House is a national facility grounded in African-American values, spirituality, and culture. It is a place for prayer, counseling, spiritual discernment, training, and support for black lay women and lay sisters in ministry.

During the 1970s, the NBSC sponsored or contributed to several projects aimed directly at the cultural, social, and economic conditions of African Americans. Two important collaborative projects included a tutorial and recreational program for the children of Louisiana sugar-cane workers and formal participation in the National Black Political Assembly, a grass-roots organization that sought to create a national political agenda responsive to the conditions of the black poor. To address the crisis of education in the black community, the NBSC developed and maintained for five years Project DESIGN (Development of Educational Strategies in the Growing Nation). This consulting agency prepared diagnostic evaluations of schools, provided curriculum and pedagogical assistance to instructors, lent organizational support to community school boards, trained parents in curriculum assessment and teacher evaluation, and cosponsored a graduate degree program in education with Antioch-Putnam Graduate School of Education, Washington, D.C., and Carlow College, Pittsburgh, Pennsylvania.

The national office of the NBSC is located in Washington, D.C.

M. SHAWN COPELAND

National Coalition of 100 Black Women

In 1970, a small group of women met in New York City to address the problems and opportunities facing black women in the wake of the civil rights and women's movements. Calling themselves the Coalition of 100 Black Women, they initiated programs that dealt with the crisis of the black family;

career advancement, especially in the corporate sector; and political and economic empowerment. Through these programs, the women also were able to identify and develop their leadership potential and encourage the use of their leadership skills.

The group's efforts were so successful that the number of members in the coalition soon surpassed the "100" in its name. In 1981, under the leadership of its president, **Jewell Jackson McCabe** of New York, the coalition expanded into a national organization, the National Coalition of 100 Black Women (NCBW). By 1991, under McCabe's leadership as president and then chair of the NCBW board of directors, fifty-nine chapters in twenty-two states and Washington, D.C. had become NCBW affiliates—with a membership of 7,000 women.

Chapters, the basic organizational units of NCBW, are governed by the national board of directors, which consists of national officers, directors appointed by the national president, and members elected by chapter delegates at biannual meetings.

A volunteer, nonprofit organization, NCBW seeks to empower African-American women through programs that meet their diverse needs. These programs enable NCBW (1) to provide effective networks among black female leaders and establish links between NCBW and the corporate and political sectors; (2) to make black women a visible force in the socioeconomic and political arenas and, through role modeling and mentoring, expose the next generation to new career opportunities, especially in the corporate arena; (3) to develop and position the leadership talent within the community of black women; and (4) to recognize the

This formal portrait was taken at the NCNW's 1940 annual convention. (BETHUNE MUSEUM AND ARCHIVES)

historic and current achievements of black women.

Since its inception, NCBW has secured $550,000 for its Women in Partnership program, a role-modeling project for pregnant teenagers being carried out by approximately half the NCBW chapters; generated $750,000 for a career exploration program for high school students, which included a summer internship with major businesses and corporations and a career education course at Hunter College in New York City; established a model mentoring program, in conjunction with **Spelman College** in Atlanta and City College in New York, that has been replicated by the Alabama, New Jersey, Texas, California, and Indiana chapters; presented the annual Candace Awards, a program established in 1982 to recognize black women of achievement nationally; held an NCBW Colloquy in 1986, supported by a Louis Harris study of leadership values among high-ranking black women and by eminent black female scholars who presented research papers at the colloquy establishing a twenty-year blueprint for NCBW action in the areas of education,

economic development, and society governance; launched, in 1989, a nationwide reproductive health rights education program; and became, in 1991, a partner with Time-Warner in sponsoring Time-Warner's Time to Read program at NCBW chapters in Atlanta, Los Angeles, Houston, Richmond, and Washington, D.C.

SHIRLEY POOLE

National Council of Negro Women

The National Council of Negro Women (NCNW), the first black organization of organizations, and the first national coalition of black women's organizations, was founded on December 5, 1935, by **Mary McLeod Bethune**. Since its inception, it has had four presidents:, **Mary McLeod Bethune** (1935–49); **Dorothy Bolden Ferebee** (1949–53), **Vivian Carter Mason** (1953–57), and **Dorothy Irene Height** (1957–). Modeled after the National Council of Women (NCW), a white association that included few black women's organizations, the NCNW was proposed by Bethune as an effective structure to "harness the great power of nearly a million women into a force for constructive action."

Prior to 1935, the **National Association of Colored Women** (NACW) was the foremost national organization of African-American women. Founded in 1896 as a national coalition of black women's clubs, many of which were of local and regional significance, it had established an enviable record of achievement and attracted a significant number of black women leaders. As a young woman seeking national support and visibility for her fledgling school, the Daytona Normal and Industrial Institute, Bethune affiliated with the NACW (1912). Moving through the ranks, Bethune served as president of the Florida Federation of Colored Women's Clubs (1917–1924), founder and president of the **Southeastern Association of Colored Women** (1920–25), and as the eighth president of the NACW (1924–28). It was the latter experience that convinced Bethune of the need for a National Council of Negro Women.

Between 1896 and 1935, over thirty national organizations of African-American women were founded. In addition to the NACW, there were college-based professional sororities and a number of religious, political, and professional organizations. The effectiveness of these organizations was frequently undermined by program duplication and competitiveness. Although a number of their members joined the NACW, few national organizations affiliated. It was Bethune's perception that the NACW's membership structure in some ways prevented it from affirming the level of power that the NCW wielded. When asserting their right to speak for black women, NACW presidents frequently quoted membership numbers. With the exception of Bethune,

presidents serving between 1900 and 1934 cited a membership of 50,000. In 1927, Bethune laid claim to an organizational base of 250,000 members. The NCW, an umbrella organization for national women's organizations, claimed to represent millions of women, members of its diverse affiliates.

Beyond the issue of structure, as president of the NACW, Bethune had experienced significant opposition to the promotion and implementation of her organizational agenda. Her primary goal was to have black women fully represented in national public affairs. Achievement of this purpose required establishing a headquarters in the nation's capital and employing an executive secretary. She was also concerned about the lack of a clear feminist focus and commitment in NACW to women's issues, and especially to working-class and poor black women. While Bethune was an ardent supporter, and frequently a part of the black leadership that defined key race issues and strategies, by 1928 she was extremely concerned about the lack of financial support NACW members and African-American women gave to causes and issues specifically related to the NACW and to black women. Bethune noted that black women spent an inordinate amount of time and effort raising money for male-dominated organizations and male-defined causes. Bethune's focus on securing and maintaining a national headquarters brought her and her program into direct conflict with the old guard NACW leadership, which for years had made retrieval, restoration, and maintenance of the Frederick Douglass home a major fund-raising and organizational priority.

Bethune's decision to found the NCNW was based on an astute analysis of the issues of the time, the weaknesses of the NACW, and her personal need for continued recognition as the leader of a major organization of black women. In 1928, at the end of her tenure as NACW president, Bethune began to recruit supporters for the development of a new organization. In December 1929, she invited the heads of all national black women's organizations to meet in Daytona Beach, Florida, to discuss the development of a "National Council of Colored Women." Bethune argued that women's organizations were "more numerous and diversified and more keenly alive to the needs of the group" and "in a better position to make use of the Negro's purchasing power as an effective instrument to keep open the doors that have remained closed." She stated that the proposed meeting would forge new relationships among black women, and that the new organization would provide an unprecedented base of power for black women.

Between 1929 and 1935, Bethune held a number of planning meetings attended by key black women leaders. A national promotion committee, chaired by Bethune, was authorized to contact and inform every national organization of the purpose of the national council plan. Organizations were asked to consider the idea at their annual conventions, or in executive committee meetings, and to send representatives to the council planning meetings.

After six years of recruitment, discussion, and planning, Bethune had garnered the support of the fourteen black women's organizations represented at the 1935 founding meeting, held in New York City at the 137th Street Branch of the **Young Women's Christian Association** (YWCA). Although NACW did not affiliate with the National Council of Negro Women, a number of its prominent members, including **Mary Church Terrell** and **Charlotte Hawkins Brown**, attended the founding meeting. Both Terrell and Brown argued against the founding of the NCNW. Brown, the president of the North Carolina Federation of Colored Women's Clubs, a supporter of Bethune and the national council concept, anticipated that NACW president Mary F. Waring would accuse Bethune of splitting the NACW; thus, for political expediency she contested a permanent organization. Terrell, the venerable first president of the NACW, had mixed feelings about the new organization. She told the gathering that "Theoretically I believe everything that has been said. But I can't see how this organization can help. I do not see how the mistakes made by other groups will not be made by this one."

Charlotte Hawkins Brown accurately gauged the NACW response, immediately delivered by Waring. Waring criticized and impugned the motives of Bethune and the founding members of the NCNW. Responding to Waring's criticism, Brown stated that the NACW had "so devoted itself to politics that it could do nothing constructive. The main idea has been to elect a president." Brown argued that the NACW had become "a political machine, a ballyhoo for section[alism]." She pointed out that there was no discussion of issues related to the place and problem of women in American life, and that no committees were appointed to investigate issues concerning African-American women.

THE BETHUNE YEARS (1935–49)

The founding of the NCNW was controversial, and effectively split the black women's

The National Council of Negro Women actively cooperated with the YWCA, the NAACP, the League of Women Voters, and other groups to eliminate racism and sexism. The council was an active participant in and planner of several conferences called by President Franklin D. Roosevelt and Eleanor Roosevelt. Here, Mary McLeod Bethune, Mary Church Terrell (center), and other NCNW *members stand at the White House gate in 1946.* (BETHUNE MUSEUM AND ARCHIVES)

club movement, leading to the eventual decline of the NACW. Unanimously elected as president, Mary McLeod Bethune set about the difficult task of unifying the divergent national groups into a national council that could at once tap the expertise of member organizations and harness their memberships and spheres of influence. The founding organizations were widely differentiated in purpose, membership, and organizational strength. Several organizations required that members be college educated; others required that members possess professional training in specified occupations; one group focused primarily on problems of organized labor; another had no requirements other than the payment of dues. Some organizations had extensive programs and received

wide recognition. Thousands of black women throughout the United States belonged to one or more of these associations.

The National Council of Negro Women was clearly an ambitious undertaking. Beginning as a national organization that proposed to carry out activities on a national level, the council, by virtue of its constitution, theoretically co-opted the membership of the affiliate organizations. The initial success of the organization depended upon unconditional support from member organizations, a well-trained volunteer staff, a cadre of highly articulate and visible volunteers, and carefully chosen projects and interpretations that could justify the council's existence to the general public and the constituent membership. The election of Charlotte Hawkins Brown, Mary Church Terrell, **Lucy D. Slowe,** and several other key women to serve as NCNW officers helped to quell some of the criticism and projected an image of unity to thousands of black women who closely scrutinized the public actions of their leaders.

The NCNW constitution defined the national council concept and the role of the organization in rather broad terms. The specific purpose of the council was to unite national organizations in a powerful bloc that could function as an instrument for distributing information from the leadership to the constituent memberships, and as a vehicle through which black womanhood could cooperate with national or international movements affecting questions of peculiar interest to women.

During the first year of operation, the NCNW consisted of national women's organizations (affiliates) and life members. Within a short period of time, it became apparent that this structure was inadequate for implementing a national program. In 1937, local councils, known as metropolitan councils, were established in communities where five or more affiliated branches were located. Affiliates were asked to urge their local chapters to work with the metropolitan councils. Registered councils were set up in rural areas, and junior councils were authorized for youth. During the 1940s, regional directors were elected to aid in the coordination of programming with affiliates and local councils. Regional directors were seen as the lifeline between the national and the regional and local communities because the national office could not directly address the need for field services. In the early 1950s, the regional director's broad powers were expanded by both constitutional redefinition and common practice. Under Dorothy Height, local councils became known as sections, and the regional system was supplanted by the state mechanism.

During the early years, the council was administered by a board of directors consisting of twelve officers, four members-at-large, and the chairpersons of thirteen standing committees. The board was comprised of the president and affiliate representatives. During the 1970s and 1980s, as affiliate representation became more *pro forma* and their attendance and involvement more sporadic, the board was expanded to include nonaffiliated women and additional sectional leaders. The national office was operated by a series of volunteer executive secretaries. The council had no paid staff until 1942, when Jeanetta Welch Brown became the first paid executive secretary. She was assisted by a stenographer, a clerk, and a team of volunteers. The addition of paid staff and the purchase of a national headquarters in 1943 provided the base necessary to propel the organization toward becoming a clearinghouse for information related to black women's organizations and projecting the NCNW's national agenda.

During Bethune's administration, the NCNW's national program, administered through thirteen committees, was carefully designed to achieve credibility for the council through affiliation and collaboration with organizations and associations in every area of American life. In addition to national women's organizations, the NCNW extended its contacts to every major social, educational, governmental, and community organization. Focusing upon public affairs, employment, citizenship, family life, religion, postwar planning, consumer education, rural life, membership, personnel, and the publication of the *Aframerican Woman's Journal*, the committees successfully used the media and collaborated with key national organizations, governmental agencies, educational institutions, and individuals to educate and effect change.

Working with the Young Men's Christian Association (YMCA), labor unions, and other organizations, the NCNW collected, analyzed, and distributed data regarding the employment of black Americans on federal jobs, particularly in the Civilian Conservation Corps and the National Youth Administration. The NCNW exposed the discriminatory practices of local communities that excluded black workers from government training programs. During World War II, the council systematically documented black employment in plants engaged in war work and, as a result of pressures brought to bear from many sources, the Fair Employment Practices Committee was established.

At the NCNW's annual meeting in 1947 at Shiloh Baptist Church, Washington, D.C., president Mary McLeod Bethune (far right) posed with Daisy Lampkin (second from left), Dorothy Ferebee (far left), and an unidentified woman. (BETHUNE MUSEUM AND ARCHIVES)

While the NCNW exposed discriminatory practices, it also impressed upon black workers their responsibility to maintain a professional attitude and appearance and to develop job-related skills. Taking advantage of public meetings nationwide, contacts with employees and employers, newspaper articles, and the dissemination of materials, the NCNW conducted a "Hold Your Job" campaign.

The NCNW campaigned for integration of black Americans into the military and fought for the admission of women into the women's divisions of the army, navy, and air force. As a result of a series of conferences between Bethune and army leaders, black women were accepted into the Women's Army Corps (WACS). Bethune personally recruited many of the first thirty-nine WACS. She inspected training camps and, when necessary, lodged complaints against discriminatory practices. The metropolitan councils sponsored programs for the WACS and took a special interest in their activities.

While the NCNW closely monitored the government, it also gave strong support to government programs. By sponsoring "We Serve America" programs, encouraging local councils to "Buy Bonds and Be Free," and launching the **Harriet Tubman** Liberty Ship, the NCNW membership stressed its patriotism.

The council did not limit its associations to black women's organizations. It actively worked with the national board of the YWCA, the **National Association for the Advancement of Colored People** (NAACP), the NCW, the National Urban League, the League of Women Voters, the National Council of Church Women, the National Council of Jewish Women, and the National Council of Catholic Women to educate and effect programs targeting the elimination of racism and sexism. In 1944, the council sponsored a conference to address the status of minorities in the United States. The council was an active participant and planner in numerous conferences called by President Roosevelt and Eleanor Roosevelt. Conferences on employment, child care, and women's participation in the war were attended by black women representing diverse organizations. Black women were appointed to serve on boards and conference committees for the War Manpower Commission, the Women's and Children's Bureau, the Department of Labor, and other government bureaus.

Bethune possessed a worldview. She felt that people must be aware of and become actively involved in the struggles for peace throughout the world. Her concern led her to join the Moral Rearmament Movement and support the idea of a United Nations.

Accompanied by **Dorothy Boulding Ferebee** and **Edith Sampson, Mary McLeod Bethune** traveled to San Francisco to witness the founding of the United Nations. As one of two consultants to the NAACP, she was able to attend this historic meeting and project the image and program of the NCNW. The NCNW was the only national black woman's organization represented at that meeting. The NCNW sent representatives and observers to meetings throughout the world, and since that time has maintained an official observer at the United Nations.

At the end of Bethune's tenure, the National Council of Negro Women was recognized as the major advocate for black women. Its advocacy was well articulated in the pages of the *Aframerican Woman's Journal.* Edited by Sue Bailey Thurman, the journal informed black women of the major issues concerning women, targeted legislation that affected women and black Americans, highlighted the accomplishments of individual women, and projected the work of the NCNW. In 1949, the name of the journal was changed to *Women United.* The council also published *Telefact,* a newsletter that informed members of the council and its affiliates of news and important issues and events relevant to legislation, international affairs, and economic developments.

DOROTHY BOULDING FEREBEE 1949–53

In November 1949, at the fourteenth annual convention, Dorothy Boulding Ferebee was elected the second national president of the National Council of Negro Women. Ferebee was one of several young women whom Bethune had groomed and identified as a possible successor. Ferebee was a physician who came from a distinguished family of organizers and club leaders. She was the grandniece of **Josephine St. Pierre Ruffin,** the founder of the Boston **New Era Club** and a founder of the NACW. Prior to her election as president of NCNW, Dr. Ferebee had served as tenth national president of **Alpha Kappa Alpha** sorority and national treasurer of the NCNW. Earlier in her career, she had founded the Southeast Settlement House in Washington, D.C.

Dr. Ferebee served as NCNW president from November 1949 to November 1953. By supporting the United Nation's policies of human rights and peace, and through more focused programmatic thrusts aimed at eliminating the segregation of and discrimination against blacks and women in health care, education, housing, and the armed forces, Dr. Ferebee's administration succeeded in maintaining the established NCNW program of advocacy and in expanding the understanding of the national council concept. Ferebee began by immediately announcing a "Nine Point Program" that affirmed NCNW goals and set forth a few new specific programmatic approaches. She proposed to address most problems through brochures and pamphlets informing the membership of the issues, and to collaborate and cooperate with federal agencies and nonprofit organizations in sponsoring conferences and distributing data. In particular, she proposed that the council implement its commitment to basic civil rights through education and legislation by conducting voter-registration campaigns for local and national elections, recommending the appointment of qualified black citizens to high level government positions, and promoting the passage of legislation that would address lynching, the poll tax, genocide, federal aid to education, women's status, national health, and the establishment of a Fair Employment Practices Commission.

Dorothy Ferebee's job was not easy. It was difficult to fill Mary McLeod Bethune's shoes, and although Bethune had relinquished the presidency, she was constantly sought as the official representative of the NCNW. She graciously helped to smooth the path for Ferebee, but as founder and president emeritus, she outshone all the existing and aspiring black female leadership. It took at least a year or more before Ferebee received the recognition associated with her position. Hampered by a limited budget and staff, and having to maintain a full-time job while being a full-time president, was no easy task. However, Ferebee, highly motivated, success-oriented, and committed, was able to guide the council smoothly through the transitional period.

Still, the need for a clearly defined program was a major issue until the late 1960s. Dorothy Ferebee and her successor, Vivian Carter Mason, understood the problem, but with a limited financial base were unable to solve it. The delivery of tangible program services was not realized until the administration of Dorothy Irene Height, the fourth president of NCNW. Yet, though the NCNW lacked the traditional programming associated with voluntary organizations, it continued to diversify its activities and address issues of major significance.

VIVIAN CARTER MASON 1953–57

At the first biennial convention, held in 1953, the National Council of Negro Women elected its third president, **Vivian Carter Mason**. Having served as vice president under Ferebee, and having worked closely with Bethune, she was well known to the membership. During Ferebee's extended trips to represent the council at conferences and meetings, both within the United States and abroad, it was Vivian Carter Mason who had chaired the meetings and addressed crucial organizational issues.

Vivian Carter Mason served as NCNW president from November 1953 to November 1957. By 1953, basic program activities were broadly defined under eleven national departments whose titles differed little from the original committees established in the late 1930s. The departments included Archives and Museum, Citizenship Education, Education, Human Relations, International Relations, Labor and Industry, Public Relations, Religious Education, Social Welfare, Youth Conservation, and Fine Arts. The NCNW's special projects and programs tended to reflect the apparent needs of its national affiliates and local councils, and during Mason's administration there was a special emphasis on interracial cooperation.

The NCNW had grown in stature, membership, and influence. Its structure incorporated a rather comprehensive program emphasis; its internal composition included local councils and national affiliates; and its cooperative endeavors, extending to every major program affecting black people, required a national office with the professional expertise and physical resources necessary for administering what had become a large organization. It was the scope of the NCNW's work, not the size of the membership, that defined the necessary level of administration.

Vivian Carter Mason introduced a tighter and more sophisticated administration, and further interpreted the organization's program. The national headquarters became the center in which the council greeted national leaders, hosted social functions, and built coalitions with other national organizations. The building was painted, refurbished, and physically realigned to provide additional office space, privacy, and improved working conditions.

Mason understood constitutional law and the importance of developing an instrument that could govern the organization effectively. Under Mason's administration, the constitution was amended to include additional membership categories such as the Life Members Guild, and to incorporate specific items aimed at curtailing the freewheeling activities of some local councils and individuals who were acquiring property, soliciting funds, and engaging in partisan political activities not sanctioned by the national office. The NCNW began to require that local councils hold annual elections. Local councils were permitted to structure their own constitutions, with the stipulations that the constitutions conform to the legal scope of the national organization, and that a copy of the document be forwarded to the national office. In 1955 and 1957, revised local council manuals and handbooks for regional directors were distributed to the membership. Mason felt that these materials both explained and enhanced the administrative process.

Vivian Carter Mason was thrust into leadership during one of the most critical and historic periods in American history: on May 17, 1954, the U.S. Supreme Court struck at the heart of the "separate but equal" dictum by ruling that segregation in public schools was unconstitutional. Mason's administration was dominated by the civil rights struggle that emerged in the 1950s. The NCNW joined with the NAACP and other national organizations to devise strategies to implement the 1954 Supreme Court decision. Following the court decision, the NCNW met with affiliate presidents and experts in education and group relations to discuss program development throughout the nation. In October 1954, the heads of eighteen national organizations of women met to share information concerning both implementation of the Supreme Court decision and educational programs. Two years later, the twenty-first annual convention was an interracial conference of women. This conference explored how women of all colors and all persuasions could work to surmount barriers to human and civil rights. Other activities included public programs supportive of **Rosa Parks**, Autherine Lucy, and the Birmingham bus boycott. Mason visited Alabama to acquire first-hand information on the situation there.

During her four years as NCNW president, Vivian Carter Mason succeeded in moving the council to another level. Assessing her administration, she said that many of the goals had not been reached. In her recommendations for the future, she cited a number of areas that needed the immediate attention of the next president. She suggested that the NCNW develop more local councils and strengthen existing ones by continuing to hold the leadership conferences begun in 1952 and by extensively promoting programs; that the NCNW sponsor at least two meetings per year with national affiliates to ensure greater participation and cooperation; and that the council

In 1974, a seventeen-foot statue of Mary McLeod Bethune (with two children) was placed a short distance from the Capitol. Shown here admiring the model are the three women who succeeded Bethune as president of the National Council of Negro Women (left to right): Vivian Carter Mason, Dorothy Height, and Dorothy Ferebee. (BETHUNE MUSEUM AND ARCHIVES)

build a strong public relations program. After twenty-two years of operation under three administrations, the NCNW had built a solid base of credibility, had developed an extensive network of contacts and supporters, and had created a sound constitution and operational structure that could easily be amended and expanded. The organization still needed money and clearly defined program service areas.

DOROTHY IRENE HEIGHT   1957–

In 1957, **Dorothy Irene Height** became the fourth president of the National Council of Negro Women. Introduced to Bethune and the council in 1937, she had served for twenty years in a number of appointive positions that provided her a unique opportunity to understand every aspect of the NCNW. Prior to her election as NCNW

president, she served for thirteen years as a member of the YWCA National Board staff and for eight years as the president of **Delta Sigma Theta Sorority.** By 1957, she understood the many dimensions of a national organization and was ready to assume the leadership of the major national black women's organization. She had several mentors, but none had more impact than **Mary McLeod Bethune.**

Coming to power on the eve of the civil rights revolution of the 1960s, Dorothy Height was determined to make the National Council of Negro Women the organization Bethune intended it to be. The groundwork necessary to achieve this goal was laid between 1958 and 1965; between 1966 and 1980, the growth of the organization was little less than phenomenal. The election of Ronald Reagan as president of the United States in 1980 effectively checked the NCNW's growth and to some extent the growth of other major black organizations that had become dependent on the federal government's largess. The NCNW had in the 1980s received a number of government and foundation grants that allowed it to enlarge the national staff and relocate its headquarters. Struggling to maintain the large staff and NCNW offices catapulted the organization into debt and forced it to scale back its national staff. While it continues to maintain a high profile and a commitment to international programs, it has not been able to mount major domestic programs.

During the late 1960s and 1970s, Height developed the NCNW into an international corporation with a highly trained professional staff, and with capabilities for program delivery and advocacy seldom realized by voluntary organizations. In spite of many contradictions and problems,

Dorothy Height has been able to maintain the illusion of power that Bethune affected during the early years. During the late 1930s, Bethune frequently stated that the NCNW represented 500,000 women, which was the collective membership of the fourteen NCNW affiliates. In the 1940s, the figure was adjusted to one million. Until the late 1980s, Height maximized this image of power and gained political capital by stating that she represented four million women. Bethune and Height were accurate in their projections of the number of black women represented through the membership of affiliate organizations; however, the public, particularly white Americans, perceived the NCNW, Bethune, and Height as more powerful than they actually were. The idea of NCNW's representative power has been particularly attractive to predominantly white, politically oriented governmental agencies or organizations seeking to identify one representative of a diverse constituency for a variety of purposes, including sponsorship of government-funded community service projects.

Dorothy Height during her tenure has moved the NCNW to a new level. Following her election, the NCNW began to move in new directions to solve a number of old problems, introduce program initiatives more tailored to the times, and find new ways to institutionalize the legacy of Mary McLeod Bethune and the national council concept. Questions regarding finances, membership development, public relations, interpretation of the national council concept, and the functioning of local councils and regions were candidly addressed by Dorothy Height and the board of directors.

In particular, Dorothy Height saw the acquisition of tax-exempt status as the key to solving many financial problems, for it would make the NCNW more attractive to philanthropists, foundations, and other potential donors who were reluctant to give large sums of money for which they would be taxed. Because of the council's emphasis on legislative and political activities, this status had been consistently denied to the council under Bethune. Under Height's direction, the Articles of Incorporation were revised and the base of the NCNW's educational and charitable programs broadened. In 1966, the Internal Revenue Service ruled that NCNW was tax-exempt.

Acquiring tax-exempt status was viewed by many as the biggest news in NCNW's history because it paved the way for grants and contributions that made growth and expansion possible. The simultaneous announcement of two major grants for programs to recruit and train African-American women for volunteer community service was cause for great celebration. Grants of $300,000 from the Ford Foundation and $154,193 from the Department of Health, Education and Welfare meant that for the first time in its thirty-one-year history, the NCNW would be able to expand its quarters and staff and develop more effective community service programs. Height announced that the grants provided the NCNW with resources to mobilize a nationwide network to work within a variety of communities, middle-class and poor, Negro and white, to carry out needed community service and social action programs.

After 1965, major program priorities focused on issues related to youth, employment, housing, health, consumerism, hunger and malnutrition, civil rights, volunteerism, women's issues, international problems, and family life. From 1965 to 1980, they sponsored at least forty national projects; about one-fourth were related to youth; another fourth targeted women's issues. Operation Sisters United, Youth Career Development, Health Careers, National Collaboration for Children and Youth, New Roles for Volunteers, the National Immunization Program, the **Fannie Lou Hamer** Day Care Center, Volunteers Unlimited, and Ujamma are some of the programs designed to respond to problems concerning youth unemployment, delinquency, teenage pregnancy and parenthood, and health care, and to stress the need for education in areas where black professionals are underrepresented. Operation Cope, Women's Rights and Housing, Women's Opportunity, Project Woman Power, the NCNW Leadership Development Project, and the Women's Learning Center explored problems related to lower-income women, single heads of households, sexism, employment, the acquisition of management skills, education, household workers, and affirmative action.

Under Height's direction, the NCNW's historic concern for working with women in the African-American diaspora and maintaining advocacy on international issues has been a key focus. Following forty years of international program emphasis, in 1975, the NCNW, with a grant from the Agency for International Development, established an international division. The division formalized ongoing NCNW work in this area and provided a unique opportunity for black American women to work with women in Africa, the Caribbean, and other parts of the world. In 1979, this division concluded an agreement with the director for educational and cultural affairs of the International Communication Agency for a "Twinning" program involving the NCNW and the na-

tional women's organizations of Senegal and Togo.

Employment issues have been central to the NCNW's efforts to advance the economic status of black women and their families. With the "Hold Your Job" campaigns of the 1940s, the NCNW had sponsored seminars and conferences and developed extensive program materials on this topic. The 1970 opening of the Women's Center for Education and Career Advancement for Minority Women extended the NCNW's commitment to minority women employed at all levels of business. The center, located in New York City, now offers a variety of programs and services. Education and career consultation and an educational program geared toward gaining and keeping employment are features of the center. In cooperation with Pace University, the center sponsors an associate degree program that emphasizes the skills and knowledge necessary for advancement in business. In 1976, the center published a detailed curriculum guide that offered all NCNW sections and affiliates, government agencies, and business training programs an instructional package useful for the development of educational programs for women employed in entry-level positions in large corporations and financial institutions.

In the last five years, the NCNW's domestic program has focused largely on Black Family Reunion celebrations. To address the many negative images of the black family, in 1986 the NCNW launched a culturally based event emphasizing the historic strengths and traditional values of the black family. The celebrations are reminiscent of the large state fairs and festivals of the past. The events consist of workshops, issue forums, exhibits, and demonstrations anchored by extensive entertainment. They have helped to renew the NCNW's public role, and signify its reentry into national public policy discussions.

CONCLUSION

The development of the national council concept was a stroke of genius. Mary McLeod Bethune conceived the idea and founded the organization, **Dorothy Ferebee** and **Vivian Carter Mason** sustained the idea, and Dorothy I. Height implemented important elements of the concept. Handicapped by a lack of resources, Ferebee and Mason were unable to develop and maintain clearly identifiable programs that could be replicated and sustained at the local level. Bethune brought to the council talented women representative of diverse affiliates and other national organizations, using their skills and personal resources to expand the understanding of the national council concept and provide a level of advocacy unknown to black women of that time. They spoke for women and they spoke for black America in such a forceful manner that within a short period of time, NCNW was able to mobilize thousands of black women through its affiliate and organizational network.

By 1960, the most profound changes in the status of black Americans since Emancipation were well under way. As the Southern Christian Leadership Conference (SCLC), the **Student Nonviolent Coordinating Committee**, and other civil rights groups began to utilize the techniques of nonviolence to force social and political change, violence erupted in Alabama, Mississippi, and other Southern cities. The NCNW, through its volunteer network, which included a

number of militant young black women, moved into rural communities and urban areas and immediately began to set up workshops to define problems and develop strategies for addressing the needs of black Americans. The NCNW identified local, state, and national resources that were available for program development in these areas. The NCNW was one of the first national organizations of black women to be recognized by the federal government as possessing the capabilities for coordinating and implementing major government-sponsored programs.

Beginning with President John F. Kennedy and continuing with President Lyndon B. Johnson, there seemed to be a solid commitment to providing opportunities for black Americans and women. As the Great Society and War on Poverty programs were launched, the federal government sought organizations and institutions capable of implementing programs at the local level. They turned to the NAACP, the Urban League, the NCNW, the SCLC and several other organizations for guidance and direction in defining the needs and programs that would serve the poor and dispossessed. The NCNW, using the skills of both educated and uneducated black women, developed self-help programs such as Wednesdays in Mississippi, the Okolona Day Care Center, Project Homes, and Operation Daily Bread.

Mary McLeod Bethune understood the nature and function of power, and believed that if black women could be united in purpose they could be a potent force for effecting economic, political, and social change. She knew that they could not be as effective as individuals and separate organizations as through an organization of organizations. In effect, Bethune was asking black women's organizations to give up a little power to acquire great power. Some heads of black women's organizations interpreted unification as a threat to their personal power bases, frequently defined by their leadership in a national organization.

Prior to the 1940s, there had been many black female leaders, but Mary McLeod Bethune became the first to function as an equal with black male leaders. The NCNW records demonstrate that W. E. B. DuBois, Walter White, Carter G. Woodson, and others had immense respect for her. Indeed, she frequently opened new doors by taking the views of the black leadership into areas unknown and inaccessible to even the most prominent race leaders. Yet, even though Bethune had immense personal power and was able to build respect and credibility for her new organization, she was not able to build the kind of financial and administrative capability necessary to sustain the national council concept.

The accomplishments of Dorothy Height's administration have enhanced NCNW's prominence and recognition. Achievements notwithstanding, the NCNW has yet to realize the goal of unifying national black women's organizations. The goal is as elusive today as it was when the council first formed. The growth in numbers and power of the major sororities, Alpha Kappa Alpha and Delta Sigma Theta, and the advent of new organizations, such as the **National Coalition of 100 Black Women,** present powerful challenges to the NCNW's goal of unification. Many national black women's organizations have become disillusioned with the NCNW's leadership and its fiscal instability. Some maintain a *pro forma* relationship with the NCNW—they pay the annual affiliate membership fee to keep a

place on the board. Many are concerned about the lack of new leadership and are looking forward to the identification of Height's successor. Members of many affiliate groups feel that their organizations are more viable than the NCNW. Nonetheless, in less than half a century the National Council of Negro Women achieved many of the goals articulated by Mary McLeod Bethune. Collaboration and coalition building have proven key to harnessing the power of 4 million women.

BETTYE COLLIER-THOMAS

National Urban League Guild

Best known for its annual sponsorship of New York's legendary Beaux Arts Ball, the National Urban League Guild is a nonpartisan, nonprofit, interracial service organization. As an independent fund-raising auxiliary to the National Urban League, the guild shares the league's dedication to improving the quality of life for urban minorities. Changing over time to reflect contemporary exigencies, the issues and goals both groups embrace demonstrate a deep concern for social justice and equal opportunity: racism, employment, housing, health care, economic development, criminal justice, social welfare, and education are major areas of commitment.

The National Urban League was organized in 1910 to provide assistance and guidance to the large numbers of African Americans migrating to northern industrial cities form the rural South. Guided by the standards, objectives, and methods of professional social work, the organization has been an effective national force for improving the lives of urban racial minorities and fostering cooperation and understanding among racial and ethnic groups. Today, the

The National Urban League Guild is an interracial fund-raising auxiliary to the National Urban League. The goals it embraces demonstrate a deep concern for social justice and equal opportunity. This group photograph includes guild founder Alta Taylor (seated, center), president Mollie Moon (left foreground), and vice president Helen Harden (seated on floor, right, wearing white blouse). (NATIONAL URBAN LEAGUE GUILD)

Urban League's activities include researching how blacks and other minorities live and work in urban communities across the nation, analyzing policies affecting urban life, consulting with government agencies and community groups, providing direct services to disadvantaged city dwellers, disseminating educational information about all aspects of the changing conditions of urban life, and advocating policies and programs to improve and enrich the quality of urban life.

To support the league's research, policy, and program initiatives, the guild conducts its own fund-raising, publicity, and educational projects. Over the years, its art exhibitions, literary evenings with famous authors, membership drives, public relations campaigns, and educational forums have supported the league's work in a variety of ways. In addition, by attracting the participation and support of black and white middle-class people, guild activities have helped foster interracial cooperation and understanding.

Fund-raising, however, remains the organization's primary focus. Since 1942, the Beaux Arts Ball has been its major annual project. At this star-studded gala—held until 1958 at Harlem's famed Savoy Ballroom and subsequently at the Waldorf-Astoria Hotel—celebrities and guests come together for an all-night extravaganza of dancing, dining, and entertainment. Elaborately costumed according to each year's theme, guests celebrate the Urban League's achievements while contributing thousands of dollars toward its ongoing work.

A small group of young New York City professionals—blacks, whites, women, and men—began meeting in members' homes in June 1942. Their desire to promote racial harmony through organized action led them to initiate a program of educational, cultural, and social activities aimed at improving race relations. In an era when racial segregation was widely practiced by both custom and law, these visionaries developed a successful and highly visible model for interracial cooperation as they undertook programs aimed at enriching community life while calling attention to the concerns and work of the Urban League. This fledgling group grew quickly into a national organization. Today, guild officers and committees conduct the organization's business from a volunteer-staffed office in the National Urban League's headquarters in New York City.

The guild's membership has always included men and women of both races. In the early years, most members were social workers and teachers, while others were artists, journalists, librarians, and medical professionals. Some of the women were homemakers whose husbands were profes-

sionals and businessmen. At a time when fewer women worked outside the home and when racial prejudice discouraged the participation of African-American women in many civic groups, the Urban League Guild proved an important outlet for middle-class women's talents and energies.

Indeed, the dynamic force behind the founding of the group was a committed nucleus of Harlem women. Well connected in the arts, professions, and civic organizations, they brought together an impressive array of professional expertise, leadership skills, and influence. Mollie Moon presided over the organization for nearly half a century, from its founding in 1942 until her death in 1990. Co-founder Helen E. Harden, a teacher in the New York public schools, served until 1991 as the organization's first vice president. In 1991, Sylvia Hughes became the group's second elected president.

Soon after the guild's founding in 1942, its leaders began receiving requests to help organize affiliate groups in other cities. In its first fifty years, the guild chartered eighty-three chapters throughout the United States. Today, local guild chapters in cities across America promote the National Urban League's goals within their own communities, adapting them to local circumstances and concerns. Affiliates serve as auxiliaries to their own local Urban Leagues, patterning many of their activities after those originated by the national guild. Ten years after its founding, the National Urban League Guild group joined with its affiliates in forming the National Council of Guilds, a confederation of autonomous organizations. In 1952, Mollie Moon was elected the first of many council presidents; today Anita Marina of Carrollton, Texas, presides over the confederation.

As successful as the guild's efforts have been throughout its history, two significant contributions to African-American life merit recognition. Among national organizations whose membership includes women and men of all races and creeds, the guild is unique in affording urban middle-class black women a half-century of leadership and control of a national organization. While leadership posts are filled without regard to race or sex, black women as a group have consistently enjoyed unlimited leadership opportunities. By establishing a separate organizational entity, the guild's founders ensured that its members would control their own leadership. Moreover, because its financial contributions to the league have been considerable, the guild has become a significant voice within the National Urban League's historically male-dominated leadership hierarchy. At least one guild official traditionally sits on the league's board of trustees. President Mollie Moon, for example, served for many years as an Urban League officer. The league's formal recognition of the guild also includes providing office space in its national headquarters in New York City and appointing staff liaisons to work with the National Urban League Guild and the National Council of Guilds.

A second guild achievement—rooted in the days of segregation—has remained unrecognized despite its significance. As it expanded to cities across America, the National Urban League Guild's organizational network became an invaluable social and professional resource for members of the black middle class. In a racially segregated America, middle-class blacks had to rely heavily on personal and organizational contacts for social entree wherever they moved or traveled. Like affiliation with a historically black college or university or membership in a national

black fraternity or sorority, league and guild connections proved an important social credential, recommending members to prominent social circles wherever they traveled. There was a practical side to this as well, for blacks of every class risked humiliation and rebuff when seeking dining or lodging accommodations in unfamiliar areas. Consequently, the hospitality and guidance of prominent locals helped middle-class black travelers to insulate themselves from potentially unpleasant—and possibly dangerous—situations. Because the guild was interracial, this important network extended into parts of the white community as well. Thus, guild affiliation formed an important thread in the tapestry of black middle-class social identity, enabling its members to manipulate Jim Crow America within the comfort and security of their class.

Like the National Urban League, the guild has been criticized for being elitist and conservative. A broad historical evaluation, however, must take into account each group's accomplishments, both in terms of its own goals and in terms of what was possible at the time. By these criteria, both organizations made important and lasting contributions to America's urban masses and its middle class.

LINDA NIEMAN

Neighborhood Union, Atlanta

On Thursday, July 8, 1908, community activist **Lugenia Burns Hope** assembled her neighbors to discuss the need for settlement work on Atlanta's West Side. Out of this meeting evolved the Neighborhood Union, a community service organization designed to improve the moral, social, intellectual, and religious life of black Atlantans. Adopting the motto "Thy Neighbor as Thyself," the union sought to build playgrounds, clubs, and neighborhood centers; develop a spirit of helpfulness among neighbors; promote child welfare; impart a sense of cultural heritage; abolish slums and houses of prostitution; and improve the overall moral quality of the community. Toward this end, Atlanta was divided into zones, districts, and neighborhoods led by neighborhood presidents and district directors, and supervised by a board of directors and a board of managers. By 1915, branches of the union were stretched across the city.

The union's legacy is one of varied civic service. It hosted medical fairs, bazaars, clinics, and carnivals in order to provide much needed medical attention to the black residents of Atlanta; it set up kindergartens and day care centers; its settlement house provided temporary shelter for homeless families; it offered classes in motherhood training, child care, and care for the elderly, vocational training in the arts for boys, and sewing and millinery for girls. Its most outstanding and ongoing project, however, was the union's drive for quality education for Atlanta's African-American children. For decades, the group petitioned Atlanta's board of education, the mayor, and the city council, asking for additional schools, the restoration of dilapidated facilities, and the elimination of double (sometimes triple) sessions in order to increase the pay of African-American teachers. It protested the lack of a high school for black students, and the lack of special education classes, vocational arts classes, and literary classes beyond the sixth grade. Joining with other groups and leaders, the union was able to work for or against the passage of school bonds in special and municipal elections.

However, because funds appropriated for black schools were not always forthcoming, even after elections, the union often found itself rallying and protesting in order to ensure that black schools actually received the funds budgeted to them. The Neighborhood Union also helped realize a long-held dream—the opening of Booker T. Washington High School in 1924, the first high school in Atlanta for African-American students.

The female members of the union viewed their organization as an experiment in community cooperation designed to enhance ethnic pride, promote citizenship, and strengthen families. For more than seven decades, the union served Atlanta's most neglected population. Financially reliant on fund-raisers and membership fees, the Neighborhood Union received very little county and municipal support until 1920, when the city made the union responsible for the health care of African-American preschoolers. For the next fifty years the agency did indeed serve "Thy Neighbor as Thyself." From the early years of the century until the Neighborhood Union disbanded in the 1970s, it was a continuous voice of protest against social and racial injustice.

JACQUELINE A. ROUSE

New Era Club

The New Era Club was founded in 1893 in Boston, Massachusetts, by **Josephine St. Pierre Ruffin**, a prominent African-American community worker; her daughter, **Florida Ruffin Ridley**; and **Maria Louise Baldwin**, the first African-American female principal in a Massachusetts public school. As one of the first African-American women's civic organizations in the country, the New Era

Club enabled African-American women to organize and devote themselves to their own needs as well as those of the larger African-American community.

The membership of the New Era Club was typical of emerging African-American women's organizations. As middle-class educated women, these clubwomen had distanced themselves from the larger African-American urban community. They did not see their involvement in the African-American clubwomen's movement as a reaction against American middle-class values; indeed, these values were upheld as the goal for all African Americans, and they emphasized education and social advancement as the means of solving the problems of the urban environment.

The club movement borrowed from women's involvement in church-related work. Participation in church activities had introduced women to community service work and raised their consciousness and understanding of larger social issues. In the club network, such activities provided women with a strong sense of sisterhood. African-American clubwomen organized their own movement in support of voluntary efforts to ameliorate urban problems during the Progressive era. They enlarged the scope of their movement, and their interest in the urban environment was informed by a combined perspective of race and gender.

The emergence of the New Era Club signaled the efforts of African-American women to break away from the white women's club movement and form their own clubs in order to place middle-class African-American women in positions of power and leadership. Ruffin, the first and only president of the New Era Club, considered the club's importance to be its ability to guarantee African-American women an autonomous role in the efforts of Progressive reformers. A primary goal of the African-American club movement was to demonstrate to white clubwomen, and to society at large, the capabilities of African-American women, and to demonstrate to African-American women the opportunities that were available to them.

The two most significant achievements of the New Era Club were its involvement in forming the first national African-American women's organization and its creation of the *Woman's Era*, the club's journal. Together, these accomplishments demonstrated the ability of African-American women to organize successfully—without the assistance of white women.

In July 1895, Ruffin convened a conference in Boston, assembling representatives from thirty-six African-American women's organizations from twelve states. The meeting was held to increase the visibility of African-American women and the efforts of their club movement. A second motive for the conference was to protest charges of immorality that had been lodged against African-American women by the male editor of a Missouri newspaper in a letter to a British suffragist. At the three-day conference held from July 29 to 31, conference members organized the National Federation of Afro-American Women. The formation of this national organization, spurred by the efforts of the New Era Club, gives a strong indication of the cooperation that existed among the various African-American women's clubs.

The New Era Club became a charter member of the **National Association of Colored Women** (NACW) the following year, when the National Federation of Afro-

American Women joined with the National League of Colored Women at a meeting held in Washington, D.C. By helping to effect the union of these two national organizations, the New Era Club secured greater awareness for the African-American clubwomen's movement.

First issued on March 24, 1894, the *Woman's Era* reported the organization's activities, but its greatest service was as a source of news about the activities of a growing network of African-American women's clubs throughout the country. The publication further expanded its influence when it became the official organ of the NACW in 1896. Devoted to social and political issues of interest to the African-American community, the *Woman's Era* acted as a powerful instrument for the New Era Club. In addition, the New Era Club maintained a prominent position in the newly formed national organization because the *Woman's Era* continued to report the local concerns of the Boston club but reserved space for the more national concerns of the NACW. As a result, the local activities of the New Era Club were nationally known to African-American clubwomen. In November 1897, the *Woman's Era* shifted focus from reporting local and national club activities to calling attention to the need for prison reform in the South. The journal ceased publication in 1898.

The New Era Club continued to struggle against discrimination of African-American women's clubs by white clubwomen. Initially accepted into the Massachusetts Federation of Women's Clubs, the New Era Club attempted to increase its influence in the white clubwomen's movement by gaining membership in the General Federation of Women's Clubs, and, in 1900, the federation's executive committee granted provisional membership to the club. The same year, however, Ruffin, as the official representative of the New Era Club, attempted to secure membership into the Milwaukee Convention of the General Federation of Women's Clubs, but conference organizers, all white women, denied admission to Ruffin as the representative of an African-American women's club and refused to ratify the membership of the New Era Club in the General Federation of Women's Clubs. Despite her failure to gain entrance into the national convention, the New Era Club brought into full view the discriminatory practices of the white clubwomen's movement, which limited the effectiveness of the movement as a whole.

The New Era Club disbanded in 1903, but left a legacy of achievement of African-American women in the Progressive era.

SHELAGH REBECCA KENNEDY

O

Oblate Sisters of Providence

Twenty-two vessels from the island of Saint-Domingue anchored off Fell's Point near Baltimore, Maryland, on July 9, 1793, with more than 500 black and white people on board. All were fleeing the Haitian Revolution. The well-to-do French-speaking black Haitians would join the 15,800 black Roman Catholics already in Maryland and bring new life to black Catholicism in America. That new life began with a Sulpician priest, Father Jacques Hector Nicholas Joubert, and **Elizabeth Lange**, a Haitian refugee.

Joubert, who had been assigned pastoral charge of the refugees, soon discovered that the children had difficulty learning their catechism because they were unable to read French or English. The priest approached Lange, who had already begun operating her own day school, about establishing a teaching community consecrated to God in which the children could be taught to understand their catechism. Lange and another teacher, Marie Madeleine Balas, had already considered such an idea, and on July 2, 1829, it was realized with the establishment of the Oblate Sisters of Providence.

The beginnings of most religious communities are difficult, but this was particularly true for the four original Ob-

lates, Lange, the founder, and Balas, plus Rosine Boegue, and Almeide Duchemin Maxis. The white residents of Baltimore were sympathetic to Southern attitudes and did not peacefully accept the formation of these black women into a religious society, especially while some 400,000 of their brethren were enslaved in Maryland. One record reports that when the Oblate Sisters first appeared on the street they were stoned by angry white residents. With encouragement from Joubert, however, they were nonetheless able to combine the activities of teaching and devotional living into a religious community. In their habits of black dress, with a white collar and a large white bonnet for convent wear, they taught black children arithmetic, English, penmanship, religion, and housekeeping. In a black bonnet and cape for outside wear, they also tended to sick people outside the convent. The sisters had a great influence on their students, some of whom became Oblates, while others went on to establish their own schools.

When Joubert died on November 5, 1843, the order faced four desperate years. When it appeared that the church had deserted them, the sisters took in washing, sewing, and embroidery to support themselves. Believing that the order would be disbanded, some of the sisters withdrew in 1845. In 1847, however, when a Redemptorist priest named Thaddeus Anwander came to their assistance, the community began a resurgence, and the order began to grow and flourish. During the Civil War years, a Jesuit priest named Father Peter Miller carried them through. Still later, the Josephite fathers helped to solidify the struggling but determined order.

The Oblates proved that virtue and intelligence know no race, sanctity heeds no color, and determination has no end. They demonstrated courage and tenacity in perilous times and gave hope to their persecuted race. Most of all, they contributed to the history of black Catholics in America.

The Oblate Sisters of Providence is still in existence, and members of the order are at the forefront of leadership of black nuns in America. Saint Frances Academy, the original school, also continues to operate.

GLORIA MARROW

P

Phyllis Wheatley Homes and Clubs

Throughout their history, black American women have always celebrated the accomplishments of "one of their own," especially the "firsts" of their race and sex. Each accomplishment served to validate the worth of all black women. Therefore, it is no surprise that during the latter part of the nineteenth century and early in the twentieth century, when black women organized in large and small communities, the name most frequently given to their clubs and institutions was that of the slave poet, Phillis Wheatley. The story of Wheatley's rise from illiteracy and slavery to become the first published black woman in America served as inspiration to all, especially women who were suffering the trauma of separation from family and familiar surroundings. Thus, her name (originally spelled *Phillis*, but most often updated to *Phyllis*) became almost synonymous with residences for black women, young and old.

Although there is no record to establish the earliest Phyllis Wheatley Club, it appears as a popular nomenclature at the organization of the national black women's club movement. At the first meeting of the newly formed **National Association of Colored Women (NACW)** in 1896, Phyllis Wheatley clubs from New Orleans, Chicago, and Jacksonville, Florida, were represented. Also, delegates from the Phyllis Wheatley Club of Nashville, Tennessee, were noted in attendance at the 1895 Atlanta Congress of Colored Women. In later years, Phyllis Wheatley Club affiliates of the NACW were commonplace.

The first known Phyllis Wheatley Home was established in 1897 by black clubwomen as a home for aged women in Detroit. Originally, a small group of women pooled their own funds to rent a small building to house seven "inmates." By 1901, the group, which had expanded to twenty-four members, purchased a property that could accommodate twelve persons. A similar project of the Nashville Phyllis Wheatley Club evolved when, after years of charitable work with the needy, the group established a Phyllis Wheatley Room at Mercy Hospital and finally purchased a home for aged women in 1925.

More popularly, use of the name Phyllis Wheatley was associated with homes for young women. Of these, the first was a home in Chicago sponsored by the Chicago Phyllis Wheatley Club. The home was the third project of the group and seems to have evolved in tandem with the needs of black women in the city. During its first five years, for example, the group operated a sewing school for children of all nationalities. The school closed when the women shifted their focus to the needs of working women and opened a day nursery in a much-congested district. Finally, in 1906, the club purchased a home for black women migrants, which provided living accommodations, social facilities, and an employment bureau for single black women. It also offered classes and club activities for nonresident girls.

Exclusion of black women from all-white **Young Women's Christian Association** (YWCA) facilities prompted the establishment of Phillis Wheatley Homes in cities across the country. Most were created out of concern for the moral and social well-being of young black women during the period of the Great Migration. Typical of the young women's residences was the Phyllis Wheatley YWCA in Washington, D.C., which was organized as the Colored Women's Christian Association (CWCA) in 1905. The group struggled for years as a charitable organization that tried to minister to needy men and women while also trying to negotiate to affiliate with the national board of the YWCA. Finally, during World War I, through the YWCA War Work Council, the CWCA became the Phyllis Wheatley Branch of the YWCA. This pattern was repeated in at least thirty-three communities.

Through its "Colored Work" department, the YWCA's national board provided the best-known organizational model for Phyllis Wheatley residences for single women. These "colored branches" offered skills training, club activities, employment services, and industrial girls' organizations that mostly duplicated selected services of white associations on a smaller scale. In all cases, black members of a committee of management made decisions related to programs, classes, and activities, while fiscal

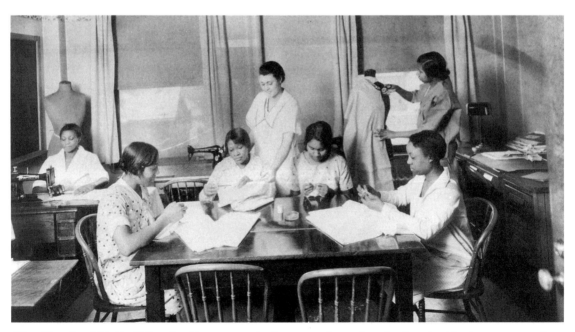

The Cleveland Phillis Wheatley Home was the largest independent facility for black women in the country, with an eleven-story building and several satellite centers. This is a sewing class in the 1930s. (PHILLIS WHEATLEY ASSOCIATION, CLEVELAND, OHIO)

Jane Edna Hunter was head of the Phillis Wheatley Home Department of the NACW. She was founder of the independent Phillis Wheatley Home in Cleveland, Ohio, and firmly believed in educating women for domestic work. This is a cooking class at her Sarah T. Hills Training School in Cleveland in 1937. (PHILLIS WHEATLEY ASSOCIATION, CLEVELAND, OHIO)

and personnel decisions were subject to the authority of white boards of directors of the central association. Altogether, at least seventeen segregated branches of the YWCA were named after Phillis Wheatley, including those in Indianapolis, Louisville, Little Rock, St. Louis, Charlotte, Harrisburg, Richmond, Chattanooga, and Atlanta.

Phyllis Wheatley branches of the YWCA were the best-known residences for young black women, but the YWCA did not have facilities in all the cities where there was a need. Moreover, the paternalistic governance structure of the YWCA was considered by some as an inappropriate model for black self-determination. In response to these and other concerns, the NACW formed the Phillis Wheatley Home Department in 1931 to coordinate and promote work among young women in cities where the YWCA did not have branches.

The head of the department for the NACW was **Jane Edna Hunter**, founder of the independent Phillis Wheatley Home in Cleveland, Ohio. The Cleveland home was the largest independent facility for black women in the country, with an eleven-story building and several satellite centers. Hunter consistently resisted efforts to have her institution become affiliated with the YWCA and instead established the Phillis Wheatley Department of the NACW. In her 1940 autobiography, *A Nickel and a Prayer*, she boasted that since the Cleveland association was founded, "the National Association of Colored Women has established like-named institutions in nine cities of the United States." Although each of these homes was locally funded and governance was left to independent boards of directors, Hunter provided materials with suggestions for programs and services.

There were also Phyllis Wheatley clubs and clubhouses affiliated with the NACW. For example, the Phyllis Wheatley House in Oberlin, Ohio, sponsored by the local Women's Progressive Club, served as a meeting center for black youth in the city. Phyllis Wheatley clubs in cities such as Billings, Montana, Jackson, Mississippi, Middlesboro, Kentucky, and New Orleans carried out a variety of activities including temperance and suffrage work.

ADRIENNE LASH JONES

Porter, Diane M. (1941–)

In September 1992, Diane M. Porter became the first black woman to hold one of the highest positions in the Episcopal Church in the United States. She is Senior Executive for Program for the Domestic and Foreign Mis-

In 1992, Diane M. Porter became the first black woman to hold a high position in the Episcopal Church, Senior Executive for Program for the Domestic and Foreign Mission Society. (DIANE M. PORTER)

sionary Society. Before joining the staff of the Episcopal Church in 1988, Porter was chief of staff to Congressman Edolphus Towns. She has also worked for the Department of Housing and Urban Development and as an urban planner for Roosevelt Island, New York, and Norwalk, Connecticut.

Born to Anna Marie Tompkins, a first-grade teacher, and James Porter, a high school principal, on July 25, 1941, Porter attended high school in East Chicago, Indiana. Of that experience she says, "I was able to stick it through, even when guidance counselors tried to put me in Home Ec." She attended Purdue University, where she received a bachelor's degree in American government and politics. She then moved on to the University of Illinois

in Champaign, where she earned a master's degree in urban planning. She has completed the senior managers in government program at Harvard's John F. Kennedy School of Government.

In 1994, Porter received a doctorate in humane letters (*honoris causa*) from St. Augustine's College. She is a member of the board of visitors for the Department of Urban and Regional Planning at the University of Illinois and is a member of the board of trustees for the General Theological Seminary. She also finds time to be a visiting professor for the Black Executive Exchange program of the National Urban League.

In her work, Porter, starting on the local level and moving to the international, has always involved herself in the betterment of the world. Managing all domestic and international programs and missions for the Episcopal Church, she promotes the church as an advocate for justice and peace worldwide. Of her work with the Episcopal Church she says, ". . . it has introduced me to the world stage as I never would have imagined in East Chicago."

HILARY MAC AUSTIN

Prout, Mary Ann   (c. 1800–1884)

"During the early days of Bethel [African Methodist Episcopal Church] when it was poor and in debt, she was constantly devising ways and means of relieving it. She lived to a great old age and was never married." These words, from Sylvia G. Dannett's *Profiles of Negro Womanhood, 1619–1900* (1964), sum up the life of Mary Ann Prout, reformer, educator, and church worker.

Prout was born in Baltimore, Maryland, in 1800 or 1801. According to Dannett she was born a slave, but documents indicate that she and her two older brothers, William A. and Jacob W., were born free and were of mixed African parents. Since William and Jacob immigrated to Liberia—a colony in West Africa for free Negroes—in 1824 and 1834, respectively, it is probable that the Prout siblings were indeed free persons.

While there is no evidence of where or how the Prouts were educated, all records that mention them refer to their intelligence and superior education. All three were noted teachers and lecturers and made their mark historically. William was for a time governor of Liberia, and Jacob's son, Samuel, was postmaster general of that country for many years.

Mary Ann Prout remained in Baltimore. In 1820 or 1830, depending on the source, she founded the Day School and taught there until 1867. It was presumably this school that kept her in the United States when her brothers immigrated to Africa.

The year the school closed, Prout founded a secret order from which evolved the Independent Order of St. Luke. Early in her life, Prout had recognized the need for a black organization that would administer financial aid to the sick and ensure proper burial for the dead. Later, there was a split in the order. The part that split off was headquartered in Richmond, Virginia, and was developed by **Maggie Lena Walker** into one of the most significant financial institutions in black American history. Walker always credited Prout as founder of the order.

That same year, 1867, the Gregory Aged Women's Home opened in Baltimore. Prout was president of the association in charge of the home and one of its two black trustees.

Throughout her life, Prout was a dedicated member of the Bethel AME Church, where she belonged to a group called the Daughters of Conference and appears to have been an active member of the choir. She died in 1884 in Baltimore.

MARGARET REID

R

Rankin, Marlene Owens (1939–)

Marlene Owens Rankin is executive director of the Jesse Owens Foundation, a not-for-profit organization dedicated to helping youth attain their fullest potential. The foundation honors her father, James Cleveland (Jesse) Owens, who was an Olympic track and field champion in 1936.

The daughter of a famous father, Marlene Owens Rankin has become a community leader in her own right. (GARLAND HALE)

Three years later, on April 14, 1939, Rankin was born to Jesse and Minnie Ruth Solomon Owens in Cleveland, Ohio. After moving to Chicago, which is still her home, she graduated from Parker High School in 1957, then earned a BS in social welfare from Ohio State University in 1961. Later, she would continue her education, receiving an MSW from the School of Social Service Administration at the University of Chicago in 1978. She married Stuart McLean Rankin in 1961, and they have a son, Stuart Owen.

Before joining the Owens Foundation in 1990, Rankin had acquired nearly thirty years of professional social work and management experience, all in Chicago, in positions such as director of human resources for the Museum of Science and Industry, director of personnel for United Charities of Chicago, social service planner for the Governor's Office of Human Resources, planning unit coordinator for the Chicago Committee of Urban Opportunity/Model Cities Program, and social work in youth programs such as Project Headstart and adoption/foster care.

Rankin's commitment to service has never stopped at her office door. For instance, she has been on the board of directors of the City of Chicago Board of Ethics, alumni associations of both the universities she attended, the Sporting Chance Foundation, and the Hyde Park Neighborhood Club, as well as the Owens Foundation. In 1992, the publication *Today's Chicago Woman* selected her as one of 100 women making a difference in the city.

The daughter of a famous father, Rankin is a significant achiever in her own right, and living proof that successful doesn't have to mean selfish.

INDIA COOPER

Ransom, Emma   (?–1941)

Emma Ransom was one of many women married to prominent African Methodist Episcopal ministers, who expanded the role of pastor's wife through careers in social and civic work. Born and educated in Selma, Ohio, Emma Conner married Reverdy C. Ransom in 1887. He would later become an influential bishop of the AME Church. Emma Ransom was the cofounder of the Ohio Conference Branch Missionary Society, and edited and published *Women's Light and Love*, the society's periodical. From 1896 to 1904, the couple founded and operated the Institutional Church and Social Settlement in Chicago, which forged an important link between the concerns of the church and issues facing African Americans in urban settings. As part of her work at the settlement, Ransom oversaw the day nursery, the kindergarten, domestic science classes, the women's club and the girl's club. Attention to both spiritual and material conditions facing African Americans would remain a focus of the work of both Emma and Reverdy Ransom throughout their lives.

The Ransoms moved to New York City in 1907, and from that time until 1924, Emma was an important figure in activist circles in the city. She served as president of the Committee of Management of the Har-

lem Branch of the New York City **Young Women's Christian Association** (YWCA) from 1909 to 1924. Ransom emerged as one of the central figures in helping the Harlem branch to establish itself as an important community institution, one that dealt with the range of issues facing young women in the city. The Harlem YWCA paid tribute to her great role in this when it named the branch residence the Emma Ransom House in 1926.

After Reverdy Ransom was named bishop, the family moved to Wilberforce, Ohio, where Emma Ransom continued to be an important figure in women's missionary work in the church, as well as an advisor to the YWCA, until her death in 1941. She lived to see her son, Reverdy C. Ransom, Jr., and her grandson, Reverdy C. Ransom, III, both AME ministers, continue her life's work of Christian activism.

JUDITH WEISENFELD

Roberts, Ruth Logan   (1891–1968)

"The basic cause of most problems in Harlem is segregation. Segregation makes ghettoes, which breed riots, unemployment, disease." With these words, Ruth Logan Roberts made known her views about the community in which she lived for over fifty years. One of Harlem's more renowned cultural salons, her home at 130 West 130th Street was known throughout New York City's elite black community as a place where aspiring young people could come to enjoy a warm welcome, excellent food, and stimulating conversation. Often called a Harlem society leader, Ruth Logan Roberts disliked such pretensions, and although she enjoyed international travel, elegant clothes, and the company of intellectuals, she often immersed herself in a wide variety of volunteer activities.

Ruth Logan Roberts, daughter of suffragist Adella Hunt Logan, was born in Tuskegee, Alabama, in 1891. She served on the national board of the **Young Women's Christian Association** (YWCA) as well as the board of directors of the Harlem YWCA, and Governor Thomas E. Dewey appointed her to the New York State Board of Social Welfare. Roberts' most significant contributions came, however, through her involvement with health-related organizations. She was the wife of one physician, Eugene Percy Roberts, and the sister of two others; a graduate of Sargeant School of Physical Education, where she was trained in physical therapy; and a director of physical education for girls at Tuskegee Institute. Roberts was a member of the boards of the New York Tuberculosis and Health Association, the Katy Ferguson Home for Unmarried Mothers, and, most significantly, the **National Association of Colored Graduate Nurses**. Her association with the latter organization centered on her unwavering efforts to desegregate training facilities and to equalize treatment of black nurses. She protested discrimination against black nurses in the military by writing directly to President Franklin Delano Roosevelt and other government officials during World War II. At Tuskegee, as early as 1913 she lobbied for woman's suffrage, and for many years she was active in Republican party politics.

She had no children of her own but raised her far-younger siblings, and worked with organizations dedicated to the youth of New York City, where she lived until her death in 1968.

ADELE LOGAN ALEXANDER

S

Saddler, Juanita (c. 1892–1970)

Speaking and writing against the evils of discrimination in the 1920s and 1930s was not a popular activity, but that is what Juanita Saddler did in her position as an employee of the national **Young Women's Christian Association** (YWCA). She was born and raised in Guthrie, Oklahoma, but seems to have regarded Tulsa, Oklahoma, as her hometown. She received her bachelor's degree from Fisk University in Nashville, Tennessee, in 1915 and her master's degree from the Teachers College at Columbia University.

Saddler was branch secretary for interracial education with the national YWCA from 1920 to 1935. In that capacity, she distinguished herself—and her employer—by developing a policy statement on the responsibility of the student YWCA in the struggle for integration. This statement formed the basis of the national YWCA's interracial charter, adopted in 1946. Saddler also established a program to integrate welfare programs for youth in Washington, D.C., as well as programs to help black girls in Boston. In addition, she helped organize church women to support ecumenical and interracial activity in New York City. She has been described as gracious, possessing a keen intellect and a good sense of humor, and an articulate public speaker.

Juanita Saddler was a woman of many firsts. She was the first black female dean at Fisk University and the first black woman to hold a position as deacon at Christ Chapel at the Riverside Church in New York City. Juanita Saddler died in 1970 in New York City. She was seventy-eight years old.

MILDRED PRATT

Saint Frances of Rome Academy, Baltimore

The year 1829 saw the simultaneous establishment of two historic black Roman Catholic institutions in Baltimore, the **Oblate Sisters of Providence** and the Saint Frances of Rome Academy. These two institutions were, and still are, inextricably woven together. The Oblates, the first order of black nuns, became the teachers at the new academy, which was the genius of Father Nicholas Joubert, a Sulpician priest who, because he understood the needs of Haitian refugees and the social climate of the time, believed that the school was necessary.

The academy was established to educate black girls in subjects that would be applicable to their social and economic environment. Under the guidance of the Oblates, students were taught religion, English, penmanship, geography, arithmetic, history, orthography, and art as well as washing, ironing, cleaning, care of children, and sewing.

The first school was located on Richmond Street. The facility was small, and this limited educational operations, but because the work of the Oblates pleased the Catholic leadership, they were able to initiate a move to larger quarters. In 1867, they purchased a lot on a hill between Greenmount Avenue and Jones Falls, facing Chase Street. In 1870, the cornerstone was laid for the new school, and by 1871 the new structure was completed. After forty-two years in cramped spaces, the Oblates, including their founder, **Sister Elizabeth Lange,** then ninety years old, moved into their new building. The site served as both the convent and the school. The school was well patronized, and wealthy white people often sponsored deserving students. Most of the girls who enrolled in the private institution came from the South, but some came from Washington, D.C., and Philadelphia, and still others came from the Caribbean. Although it was a Catholic school, non-Catholic girls were enrolled also, and the school was held in high regard by Catholics and non-Catholics alike.

Students were identified according to their class or tuition status as either boarders, the upper-class students, or pensionnaires, the day students. When the new school opened, there were twenty-three students—eleven boarders and twelve pensionnaires. Boarding students paid a fee of $4 a month, plus $1 for fuel during the winter months, whereas pensionnaires paid $2 a quarter, plus $.50 for fuel in the winter.

In its time, the school was an improvement over those institutions formerly open to black students. Indeed, the establishment of Saint Frances of Rome Academy marked the birth of a kind of social and educational elite within the black community. It forged scholastic achievement among black women who shared what they learned with others of their race. If length of continuance is any indicator of success, Saint Frances Academy has proven to be one of America's most successful and enduring institutions. It continues to operate. In 1993, the academy graduated 32 students, 86 percent of whom went on to college.

GLORIA MARROW

Sanctified Church

Sanctified Church is an indigenous term African Americans use to refer to Holiness, Pentecostal, Independent, Community, Spiritual, and Deliverance denominations and congregations collectively. Although there is a history of conflict with larger and older Baptist and Methodist denominations, Sanctified Church represents an alternative to more pejorative and hostile terms, and recognizes similarities in prayer, preaching, testimony, and music. Many denominations emerged during the late nineteenth and twentieth centuries emphasizing some aspect of sanctification and sharing ritual practices emphasizing the Holy Ghost (Spirit), and such activities as "shouting," the "holy dance," and speaking in tongues. Pentecostals highlight speaking in tongues in statements of doctrine and discipline.

Novelist and anthropologist **Zora Neale Hurston** pointed to the Sanctified Church as a song-making and cultural protest movement that preserved aspects of African-American worship considered primitive and unseemly by an emerging middle class. Usually classified as sects, cults, and storefronts because of their marginal status in northern urban ghettos, these churches often have their roots and hold their annual convocations in the South. Sanctified Church congregations tend to be around 90 percent female. Some denominations ordain women and were founded by women such as Bishop Ida Robinson. The

Church of God in Christ, the largest denomination, does not ordain women to be pastors, elders, or bishops, but women are central to the history and growth of the denomination as church founders, missionaries, evangelists, supervisors, and church mothers. Organization of a prominent, somewhat autonomous, powerful women's convention or department is a characteristic feature of these churches.

CHERYL TOWNSEND GILKES

Saunders, Cecelia Cabaniss (1883–1966)

The Harlem branch of the New York City **Young Women's Christian Association** (YWCA), founded in 1905, assumed a position of prominence in the Harlem community and among black New Yorkers in general largely through the efforts of Cecelia Cabaniss Saunders. Born Cecelia Holloway in Charleston, South Carolina, she grew up as a member of the nation's black aristocracy. The Holloways, a free family of color, had produced many educators, business people, and politicians in the eighteenth and nineteenth centuries. Cecelia's father, James H. Holloway, served as principal of the Timmonsville School in Charleston during Reconstruction, and she would follow in his footsteps through her lifelong commitment to education. Cecelia Holloway graduated from Fisk University in 1909 and worked for the national board of the Young Women's Christian Association before becoming executive secretary of the Harlem branch in 1914. She married Dr. James E. Cabaniss in 1912, was widowed, and was remarried in 1915 to John D. Saunders, a real estate agent in New York City.

Cecelia Cabaniss Saunders was tireless in her work with the Harlem YWCA, guiding it from a small organization in a make-shift rented building to an established community institution with an imposing physical plant. By the late 1930s, Saunders' Harlem YWCA consisted of a main building with offices and meeting rooms, a thriving trade school, the Emma Ransom Home residence, and summer camp facilities. Saunders dedicated herself, through the YWCA, to assisting young African-American women in entering into fields of work from which they were previously barred because of racism. Her philosophy was that industry would not reject women who were well trained. Over the years, the branch was successful in opening up new fields of work for black women in New York City. Saunders was also involved in many other organizations, but her love and life's work went to the Harlem YWCA.

JUDITH WEISENFELD

Sigma Gamma Rho Sorority

"Greater Service, Greater Progress" was to become the slogan and call of the organization that made November 12, 1922, a significant date in the history of the black Greek system. This date marked the establishment of the first sorority of black women—Sigma Gamma Rho—on a predominantly white campus, Butler University in Indianapolis, Indiana. Three other sororities of black women, all established at **Howard University,** and four fraternities of black men, two at Howard, one at Cornell, and one at Indiana University, had already been established in the early 1900s. Because black students could not join the all-white Greek sororities at Butler, a tough and determined black female, Mary Allison Little, envisioned the need to pull black women together into the bonds of sisterhood. Six other Butler students who had chosen teaching as their profession joined Mary Little in laying the foundation for a new sorority and further advancing the black fraternal movement.

Originally, the new sorority was to be composed of teachers and was to provide support and opportunities for networking to young people, with a focus on professional development. Soon, however, the members recognized that teaching went far beyond the walls of the classroom and that community service and interaction were needed in order to educate the whole child. Education was to be the mainstay of the sorority, but the organization also wanted to develop broad horizons with diverse dimensions in order to reach into communities and serve all people. Thus, Sigma Gamma Rho membership had to be expanded; it could not be restricted to teachers.

National conventions were not called in the early years because too many other issues needed to be addressed. Under the leadership of Mary Little, who was to become the first grand basileus (national president), members became immersed in developing unity and broad-based goals. After the first national meeting (Boule) in 1925, it was evident that an education-focused legacy was evolving, but it was during the fifth Boule, in 1929, that the sorority mandated an aggressive scholarship program that required alumnae chapters to maintain a scholarship fund. This led to the establishment of the Sigma Gamma Rho National Education Fund, which focuses on education, research, health, and the awarding of scholarships and grants to students regardless of race, gender, or nationality.

The torch of leadership passed through several hands during the 1920s, and the goal of involving women from various regions of the country was reflected in the selection of leaders from coast to coast. The Roaring Twenties ended with the sorority poising itself and moving aggressively to charter more chapters on black college campuses, particularly the land grant colleges that were experiencing considerable growth in enrollment. The first West Coast chapter was established in Los Angeles. A charter member of that chapter, **Hattie McDaniel**, became the first black Academy Award winner in 1939 when she received an Oscar for her performance in *Gone With the Wind*.

In response to the dire economic conditions of the times, the sorority established Sigma Gamma Rho's Employment Aid Bureau. In further pursuing its agenda, programs to assist in community education and uplift also were established; for example, circulating libraries on wheels, national literary contests, book exhibits, and book showers for black colleges were adopted as national programs. The African Book Shower Project, designed to send books to Wilberforce Institute in South Africa, was the sorority's first international involvement. It later expanded into the Linens for Africa Drive and other international projects.

During World War II, the sorority suspended its national conventions so that members could support the war effort at home and on foreign soil. Sigma Gamma Rhos were visible in the military, the Red Cross, the USO, and similar organizations.

Against the backdrop of the war, and with an upswing of juvenile delinquency, the sorority was stirred to develop programs to address this problem. Sigma "Teen Towns," centered around art, music, literature, games, and other forms of wholesome recreation, became a thrust of the organization, and was carried over into the 1950s. Sigma Gamma Rho was fully involved in the Mid-Century

Conference on Children, and its leaders were summoned to White House conferences that dealt with many pertinent issues.

The 1960s and 1970s were a time of great social, political, and moral change. In response to these changes, Sigma Gamma Rho intensified its support for the United Negro College Fund, the **National Association for the Advancement of Colored People** (NAACP), the Urban League, and other national organizations that offered service to the community and furthered in every possible way the dignity and worth of all people. Academic excellence, moral responsibility, political involvement, social awareness, and community outreach were built into the ongoing thrust of the sorority as it concerned itself with civil rights, human dignity, moral decency, and the strengthening of a new breed of poised and informed women.

As the number of black students increased on predominantly white campuses in subsequent decades, there was a noticeable expansion of the black Greek system. During these years, Sigma Gamma Rho modified its agenda to better address this expansion and the resulting societal changes. A national program called Project Reassurance was designed to deal with teenage pregnancy. Also, after the publication of Alex Haley's book *Roots*, and with heightened concern for Africa, the sorority established Project Africa, Project Mwanamugimu, and related programs to give assistance to the people of Africa and to help young African Americans understand and appreciate their ancestral history.

From that cold November day in 1922 when Alpha chapter sank its roots into the campus of Butler University, Sigma Gamma Rho has progressively evolved into a thriving sisterhood that comprises more than 70,000 college-trained women across the United States, and in Bermuda, Africa, the Virgin Islands, and the Bahamas.

KATIE KINNARD WHITE

Sisters of the Holy Family

The Sisters of the Holy Family is the second oldest Catholic congregation for women of color organized in the United States. Despite racial prejudice and discrimination, the order, founded in 1842, has a long history of providing services for black people. These services have included religious education for slaves and, after the Civil War, academic training for African Americans in Louisiana, Texas, California, Oklahoma, and Belize, Central America. In addition, the sisters have provided a home for the aged, orphanages, and a day-care center for the working poor.

Henriette Delille (1813–1862), the founder of the congregation, was an educated free woman of African descent born in New Orleans. A feminist, social worker, and educator, she rebelled against the convention of the quadroon women of her family who became concubines of wealthy white men during the era of slavery. She and the women who joined with her to organize their religious order challenged the prevailing belief that women of color were not capable of practicing celibacy or being nuns. Among the Catholics of New Orleans during the early nineteenth century, it was believed that only white women were called to religious congregations. As a result, it took three attempts in the seventeen years from 1825, the year their charitable work began, to 1842 for the congregation to be recognized and officially founded.

The African-American women were inspired by two French women who worked with black Catholics in New Orleans, Sister St. Marthe Fontier of the Ursuline Sisters, and Marie Jeanne Aliquot. As a result, Delille and a friend, Cuban-born Juliette Gaudin (1808–1888), began to teach religion to the slaves. The young women soon became interested in dedicating their lives to this work and sought to become the black branch of the Ursuline Sisters. Unfortunately, their plans were not well received by the all-white order.

Throughout the 1830s, Delille and Gaudin worked in the slave communities of New Orleans. In 1835, when Delille was declared of legal age, she sold all her property with hopes of founding a community of black nuns, separate from the Ursulines, to teach in a school for free girls of color. A campaign waged by civil authorities against those who sought to educate black people thwarted the effort. In the meantime, Delille and Gaudin began a campaign to encourage free quadroon women to select men of their own class, and to marry in the church. In addition, they encouraged slave couples to have their unions blessed by the church.

Finally, in November 1842, Delille and Gaudin received permission from the diocese to begin their new order in St. Augustine's Church, property earlier donated to the diocese by the Ursulines. A year later, the novices were joined by Josephine Charles, another quadroon.

Despite the barriers, their philosophy made a mark on other men and women of the quadroon class. When, in 1847, the state legislature passed an incorporation act that required the sisters to form an association, several prominent quadroons came to their rescue. The Association of the Holy Family was organized with Delille as president. Financial and moral support made it possible for the association to build a home in 1849 for the sick, aged, and poor black residents of the city. The home was called the Hospice of the Holy Family.

The first three novices led the order throughout much of the nineteenth century—Delille, 1842–62; Gaudin, 1862–67; and Charles, 1867–82. The three are considered the founders of the congregation. The primary work of the sisters in the nineteenth century was in the area of education. Between 1852 and 1898, they opened six schools in New Orleans. These various schools met the needs of middle-class families as well as the poor. St. Mary's School, for example, was founded as a night school in 1867 for freed slaves who could not attend classes in the day. Outside New Orleans, the sisters opened six additional schools in Louisiana, Texas, and Belize. Sacred Heart School was founded in Belize in 1898.

In addition to schools, the sisters administered other institutions during the nineteenth and twentieth centuries. In 1876, the Louisiana Asylum for Negro Girls was placed under their supervision by the state. In 1896, the sisters organized Lafon, the first black home for orphan boys in the city of New Orleans. Continuing their mission to meet the needs of black Americans into the twentieth century, in 1920 the sisters reorganized the former boys' home into the Lafon Home for the Aged. Fifty years later, they were using one of their former convents as a day-care center, which they operated across the street from the historically black Dillard University. Nonetheless, primary and secondary religious and academic training continue to be a major goal of the Sisters of the Holy Family.

ROSALYN TERBORG-PENN

Smith, Amanda Berry (1837–1915)

Called "the singing pilgrim" and "God's image carved in ebony" by the newspapers of her time and those at the various camp meetings she attended, nineteenth-century evangelist Amanda Berry Smith won international acclaim as a leader of the holiness revival that inspired widespread social and religious reform across racial lines. During a forty-five-year missionary career of arduous travel on four continents, this self-educated former slave and washerwoman became a highly visible and well-respected leader despite intense opposition to women in public ministry, a crescendo of white racist violence, and the tightening grip of segregation. Her leadership and devotion to her ministry also earned her recognition as "one of the most powerful missionaries of the nineteenth century."

Smith led revivals throughout the United States, Europe, and India; spent eight years as an independent missionary in West Africa; wrote an autobiography that has become a classic in women's literature; and founded and operated an orphanage and industrial school while continuing to speak at camp meetings and revivals throughout the country.

Although an active member of the African Methodist Episcopal (AME) Church, she spent most of her public ministry before mainly white congregations, and rose to prominence through her riveting spiritual singing and stirring testimonies at national camp meetings that attracted wealthy white worshipers to summer seaside and mountain resorts. Although some AME Church leaders accused her of neglecting her own people, her example and effectiveness helped win a more prominent role for

At the end of her successful career as an evangelist who appeared mainly before white audiences, Amanda Berry Smith used her entire life's savings to open an orphan home and industrial school for black children. (SCHOMBURG CENTER)

women in the AME Church, helped lay the foundations of the Sanctified Church, and bridged the gap that has divided the races in the Christian church well into the twentieth century.

Born a slave January 23, 1837, in Long Green, Maryland, she was the second child of Samuel and Miriam Berry. By 1840, her father had bought his family's freedom, and by 1850, he had moved them to York county in southeastern Pennsylvania. Inspired by her parents' efforts to help fugitives escape from slavery and their many references to her duty to aid her African homeland, Smith grew up with a missionary reformer's zeal.

Denied an education because of local prejudice, she learned to read and write at home, and at thirteen, as the eldest daughter in a family of eleven children, went to work as a domestic. At seventeen, she married Calvin Devine and moved with him to Lancaster County, where she experienced a religious conversion two years later. Her first baby died, but the second one, Mary, survived. Her husband's drinking led to marital problems and they separated. He later died fighting in the South for the Union Army. Amanda moved to Philadelphia after his death and married local AME Church deacon James Henry Smith, who was twenty years her senior.

In 1865, they moved to New York and settled in Greenwich Village. Their unhappy marriage produced three children, all of whom died in infancy, two of them from tuberculosis contracted in the dank rear apartment dwelling where Amanda Berry Smith stood long hours over a washtub and ironing board trying to eke out a living. One Sunday morning in 1868, she bypassed the Sullivan Street AME Church where she was a regular member to attend Greene Street Methodist Church and hear the Reverend John Inskip preach on the second blessing of sanctification, an experience that contemporary holiness revivalists were urging for all Christians. That morning, Smith received the second blessing, which she said empowered her to launch the preaching ministry that transformed her from a washerwoman to an evangelist. In 1869, the same month her husband died of stomach cancer, she began conducting revivals at AME churches in New Jersey and New York, branched out to white Methodist churches, and began

attending the popular national camp meetings convened by Inskip.

In 1872, she took part in the first AME Church general conference in the South, mounting the platform with the **Fisk Jubilee Singers** in Nashville, Tennessee. In 1875, she became a charter member of the Women's Christian Temperance Union (WCTU) by joining the Brooklyn branch, and in 1878, Mary Coffin Johnson, long-time WCTU national secretary, invited Smith to join her in England for a series of temperance revivals. Leaving her daughter behind with friends, Smith left for what would become a twelve-year mission to England, Scotland, India, and West Africa. She spent eight of those years in Liberia promoting Western education for women and children and preaching holiness and temperance reform.

Slowed by debilitating arthritis and frequent bouts with malaria, a weakened Smith returned to the United States in 1890 and almost immediately resumed her missionary work. She wrote her autobiography, continued conducting revivals, testified before a congressional committee on the liquor traffic, returned to England for treatment at a sanatorium, and, in 1893, settled in Chicago where her autobiography was published. Despite advancing age, she then began raising funds to open an orphan home and industrial school for black children in Harvey, Illinois, a new temperance settlement south of Chicago. In 1899, she opened the school in a building she purchased on Jefferson Street. She subsequently bought eighteen adjoining lots. Through a wide-ranging network of supporters, including women's club organizers **Ida B. Wells** and **Hallie Q. Brown**, Wells' attorney-husband Ferdinand Barnett, local realtors, philanthropists, and church leaders, Smith managed to operate the home without an endowment or government help. She published a newsletter and continued her desperate attempts to raise funds until 1913, when failing health forced her to retire to Sebring, Florida, where a wealthy Ohio businessman, George Sebring, had built a new town with a cottage for Smith near a lake. After a series of strokes, she died February 24, 1915. Sebring shipped her body back to Chicago for an impressive funeral at Quinn Chapel, AME Church. She was buried in Homewood, Illinois. The ill-fated industrial home, wracked by debt and decaying facilities, burned down in 1918, and the surviving orphans were placed in private homes.

ADRIENNE ISRAEL

Smith, Celestine Louise (1903–1975)

Celestine Louise Smith's lifelong quest to understand the intricacies of human relationships, together with her efforts on behalf of justice and human dignity for all, took her on many different paths during her seventy-two years. The quest for answers to her personal identity began shortly after her birth in Macon, Georgia, in 1903, the daughter of Fletcher Carrol Smith (Schmitzen), a German Jew, and Viola Jane Smith, an African American. When she was a child, people asked Celestine's mother why she gave her daughter the name Celestine, and her mother said it came from a Spanish novel. This mixing of cultural consciousness engendered in Smith a desire to heal the divisions between races and peoples, but it also confused her. As a Jungian analyst later in life, she searched for the knowledge that would help her understand the ancestral fusion that she represented.

Celestine Smith earned a bachelor's degree from Talladega College in Talladega, Alabama, in 1925, a certificate in social work from the University of Southern California in 1942, and a doctor of education degree in marriage and family counseling from Columbia University in 1952. Later in life, she received psychological analysis training at Union Theological Seminary in New York and the divinity school at the University of Chicago.

She taught for two years in a private high school in Florence, Alabama, before becoming involved with the **Young Women's Christian Association** (YWCA). She served the YWCA from 1929 to 1968 as national student secretary in the Southwest, director of counseling and casework, specialist in human relations, and, for one year, director of the Lagos, Nigeria, YWCA. As a YWCA employee, she worked to desegregate public schools and institutions of higher learning. She also was an administrative director of Morningside Mental Hygiene Clinic in New York City and, in her later life, a private practitioner of Jungian psychoanalysis.

Celestine Louise Smith was highly intelligent, jovial, aggressive, and articulate. She died on December 19, 1975, in Mount Holly, New Jersey.

MILDRED PRATT

Southeastern Association of Colored Women's Clubs

The Southeastern Association of Colored Women's Clubs (SACWC) originated as the Southeastern Federation of Colored Women's Clubs through the efforts of **Mary McLeod Bethune**. By 1919, in the midst of the Great Migration and shortly following their heroic efforts on the homefront during World War I, Southern African-American clubwomen realized the need for a regional organization within the National Federation of Colored Women's Clubs. Representing the concerns of black women in the politically repressive Jim Crow South, SACWC united state federation leaders and plotted common strategy on important issues.

At its first conference, held at Tuskegee Institute in January 1920, SACWC announced its intention to forge a stronger organization of Southern women. Bethune of Florida was elected president, **Charlotte Hawkins Brown** of North Carolina was named chairperson of the executive board, and Marion B. Wilkerson of South Carolina was elected vice-president-at-large. State presidents from eight states—Alabama, Florida, Georgia, North Carolina, South Carolina, Tennessee, Mississippi, and Virginia—served as vice presidents. Rebecca Stiles Taylor of the Georgia federation assumed the position of corresponding secretary, with Floridians Emma J. Colyer and Frances R. Keyser serving as parliamentarian and auditor, respectively.

Founding a regional organization enabled Southern African-American women to respond to white clubwomen's expressed interest in interracial work with a coordinated plan and united leadership; SACWC officers were among the representatives who went to Memphis in 1920 to meet with white clubwomen in order to develop an agenda for interracial cooperation. The groups worked together to issue a position paper to delineate interracial problems and propose mutual action. Controversy over its content soon erupted, however. When the white women moved to strike the plank calling for African-

American suffrage in the South, SACWC issued a pamphlet titled *Southern Negro Women and Race Co-operation,* which included their demand for voting rights. When women gained the right to vote a few months later, SACWC helped coordinate black women's efforts to register and vote in the South.

The association also planned regional campaigns on a variety of issues conducted by the several state federations. One of the leading causes from the 1920s onward was the effort to establish homes in each state for delinquent and dependent African-American girls as an alternative to their being incarcerated with adults. The strategy, which succeeded in North Carolina and Virginia but failed repeatedly in Mississippi, involved gaining the support of the state federation of white women's clubs in order to lobby state legislatures for annual appropriations. The size of these state appropriations varied, and they were sporadic, so the primary financial burden for maintaining the homes often fell on the state federations.

Rebecca Stiles Taylor of Savannah, Georgia, followed Bethune as president, serving from 1923 until 1927, when **Ora Brown Stokes** assumed the post for a few months. The official history of SACWC notes that from 1927 until 1940 the organization was inactive, yet others have reported that Bethune actively promoted the work of the Southeastern federations during the 1930s by encouraging citizenship departments despite political repression, urging state delegates to attend national conventions, and providing important connections to government agencies. Perhaps during the difficult years of the Great Depression, members were unable to pay dues to support the regional association, which forced a cutback in the official structure and led Bethune to continue its activities unofficially. Alternatively, perhaps the collapse of the Southeastern regional structure during this period reflects the national association's shift away from political involvement to middle-class domesticity and Bethune's interest in her new project, the **National Council of Negro Women** (NCNW).

In a 1940 meeting at Tuskegee Institute, birthplace of the organization, a group of women, including original founders Brown and Taylor, revived the association. Under the leadership of President Bertha L. Johnson of Mississippi, SACWC restored biennial meetings in 1946. Continuing the tradition it began in 1920 as the representative for Southern African-American women who wanted to work with white women for the cause of racial justice, in the 1960s SACWC promoted meetings between black and white women during the decade of integration. From its inception on the eve of woman's suffrage, throughout most of the twentieth century, SACWC provided a united front that encouraged Southern African-American women to work to solve social problems and to participate in political activities in the face of odds that might have overwhelmed individuals working alone.

GLENDA ELIZABETH GILMORE

Sprague, Fredericka and Rosabelle Jones

"A race can rise no higher than its women" was the belief expressed by Frederick Douglass' granddaughter, Fredericka Douglass Sprague Perry, when she advocated the membership of all young girls in the Missouri Association of Colored Girls, an organization she founded in Kansas City, Missouri. Fredericka Douglass Sprague Perry and Rosabelle Douglass Sprague Jones were community activists in Kansas City, Missouri. Active in the local and state chapters of the **National Association of Colored Women** (NACW), Fredericka and her sister, Rosabelle, developed child welfare and other initiatives to respond to the needs of the African-American community, especially young girls, in Kansas City. The activities of both Fredericka and Rosabelle are best characterized as community caregiving activities that were an outgrowth of the voluntarism so prevalent among middle- and upper-class black women during the first three decades of the twentieth century.

Both Fredericka and Rosabelle, like many women in the women's club movement, were married to educated, well-to-do African-American men. Fredericka was married to Dr. J. Edward Perry, who founded the Perry Sanitarium (later, Wheatley Provident Hospital) in 1910. The couple had one son, Dr. E. B. Perry, who practiced medicine in Houston, Texas. Rosabelle was married to physician Thomas A. Jones.

Before moving to Kansas City, Missouri, and marrying J. E. Perry, Fredericka was an instructor in cooking at the Lincoln Institute in Jefferson City. Before and for a short time after her marriage, she worked with her husband at the Wheatley Provident Hospital. In the early days of the hospital, she provided nursing-care-related services. Later, she organized the women's auxiliary and developed various fund-raising activities to support ongoing and expanded services at the medical facility. She consistently supported and encouraged her spouse's medical ambitions.

The extent of Rosabelle Mary Sprague Jones' contributions in Kansas City is difficult to determine. Recorded biographical materials on Rosabelle provide more details about her sister Fredericka's contributions to the Kansas City community than her own. Rosabelle was the younger of the two women and the youngest of the seven children in the family. Although she seemed to walk in Fredericka's shadow, she was a leader in her own right and active in civic and voluntary associations in Kansas City. For two years, she served as president of the Kansas City Federation of Colored Women's Clubs. Her second annual message on May 9, 1930, described the Kansas City "race" women as a "group of women who are earnestly endeavoring to do things for humanity."

Fredericka Douglass Sprague Perry's voluntary association activities were more extensive than those of her sister. Her focus on systematic child-oriented services through the Colored Big Sister Association of Kansas City founded in 1934 is particularly noteworthy. Fredericka's leadership in the National Association for Colored Girls, the Missouri Association for Colored Girls, and the local Colored Big Sister Association led to concrete services for dependent black girls who were not eligible for state-supported foster home services in Kansas City during the 1930s. The Colored Big Sister Home for Girls opened in April 1934, and continued as a private charity until 1943. Fredericka's concern for delinquent girls and her employment in the local court system led to broad-based community support for her pioneering efforts in child welfare reform in Kansas City. Her philosophy is reflected in the titles of the state song and the motto she composed for

the girls' association—"Show Me" and "Learning as We Climb."

WILMA PEEBLES-WILKINS

Stewart, Ella Phillips (1893–1987)

The child of sharecroppers, Ella Phillips Stewart rose to remarkable heights of accomplishment and honor in service of both the black women's club movement and the United States government.

Born in 1893 in Berryville, Virginia, Ella Phillips attended a local grade school, where she was an outstanding student. From there, she went to Storer College, winning five major scholarship awards and marrying fellow student Charles Myers. After the death of a child, she and Myers were divorced and she moved to Pittsburgh, Pennsylvania. While working as a bookkeeper at a drug store, she became acquainted with a local physician, who persuaded her to become a pharmacist. The first black woman to attend the pharmacy school at Pittsburgh University, she became friendly with two white classmates who, after graduation, hired her to work as a pharmacist at the drugstore they opened.

Ella Phillips owned her own drugstore when she met William Wyatt Stewart and married him. The Stewarts moved to Ohio, where they settled in Toledo, opened a pharmacy, and became important members of their community. Their store became a center of community activity, and their home, above the store, offered lodgings to visiting black celebrities such as **Mary McLeod Bethune** and W. E. B. DuBois.

Ella Phillips Stewart was active in club work, becoming president in 1948 of the **National Association of Colored Women** (NACW). She updated **Elizabeth Davis'**

Lifting as They Climb (1933), a history of the NACW, and, after traveling throughout the world for a number of groups, including the Education Exchange Service of the U.S. State Department, was appointed by Dean Rusk to the executive board of the U.S. Commission of the United Nations Educational, Scientific, and Cultural Organization (UNESCO). A lifetime of honors was capped when the city of Toledo named a new $3 million elementary building the Ella P. Stewart Elementary School.

KATHLEEN THOMPSON

Stewart, Sallie Wyatt (1881–1951)

Sallie Wyatt Stewart was a prominent figure in the flourishing black women's club movement in Indiana during the early decades of the twentieth century. A statewide network of scores of individual clubs provided space for black women to socialize and develop leadership skills. Such clubs were useful in galvanizing support for the establishment of an impressive array of welfare and service institutions designed to fulfill the distinct social, health care, and recreational needs of black Indianians.

By the 1920s, black women's clubs were found in every major city in Indiana. For example, in Terre Haute, black women organized the Phyllis Wheatley Association, which served as a recreational center and boardinghouse for young black girls; and Anna B. Barton, a beautician, organized the St. Pierre Ruffin Club in South Bend in 1900, where, as she asserted, black women "could learn the finer things of life: Literature, Art and Music." Other clubwomen founded and maintained retirement homes, settlement houses, hospitals and sanitariums, and gym-

nasiums, and raised money for scholarships for black youths across the state.

The woman who best epitomizes the contributions of black women in Indiana is Sallie Wyatt Stewart. Sallie migrated with her family from Ensle, Tennessee, to Evansville in the 1880s, joining the roughly 2,600 African Americans in the border city who shared a common inheritance of illiteracy, propertylessness, and powerlessness. Like their counterparts in cities throughout the Midwest, black migrants to Evansville suf-

Among the many organizations founded by clubwoman Sallie Wyatt Stewart was the National Association of Colored Girls, which was affiliated with the National Association of Colored Women, of which she was the fourth president. (SCHOMBURG CENTER)

fered low job status, poor living conditions, residential segregation, and white hostility.

When her father became disabled, Sallie shared with her mother the responsibility for raising her seven younger sisters and brothers. Through sheer will, Sallie was able to complete her education in spite of overwhelming demands at home. She graduated from the Evansville High School as valedictorian of her class and subsequently took courses at Evansville Normal School, the University of Chicago, and Indiana University. Sallie proved to be intelligent, resourceful, hard working, ambitious, and highly motivated. She completely subscribed to the ideals of self-help. After securing a teaching certificate, Sallie commenced a fifty-year career as a teacher in the Evansville school system. From 1924 to 1928, she was dean of girls at Douglass High School. She held a similar position at the all-black Lincoln High School from 1929 to 1951, where she introduced the first courses in domestic science, stenography, and mental hygiene.

An energetic and imposing woman, she became involved in many diverse ventures. In 1912, she became the catalyst for generating much of the black social service work in Evansville, which benefited the entire community. In 1915, she was secretary of the Evansville chapter of the **National Association for the Advancement of Colored People** (NAACP). She was selected chairperson of the black auxiliary of the county tuberculosis association in 1928. In the late 1920s, she founded a black women's newspaper entitled *Hoosier Women*. This was the first, if not the only, publication devoted exclusively to black women's concerns in Indiana. Other affiliations included president of the **National Association of Colored Women** (NACW) in 1930, fourth vice president of the National Council of Women (NCW), member of the Executive Committee of the National Negro Business League, member of the Executive Committee of the National Colored Merchant's Association, secretary of the Inter-Racial Commission of Evansville, trustee of the Eastern Star and Masonic Home of Indiana, and president of the Tuberculosis Auxiliary and the Lincoln Alumni Association. She was the founder of the Evansville Federation of Colored Women, the Day Nursery Association for Colored Children, the Phyllis Wheatley Association in Evansville, and the National Association of Colored Girls, which was affiliated with the NACW. In 1942, Stewart organized a Colored Women's War Work Committee to sell war bonds and stamps.

After her marriage to Logan Stewart, the two joined forces to develop a very lucrative real estate business, which she continued to manage after his death in 1928. When she died in 1951, Stewart left an estate valued at over $100,000, all of which she stipulated in her will was to be used to help young black girls.

DARLENE CLARK HINE

Stokes, Ora Brown   (1882–1957)

Only seven of the 240 biographies included in the Virginia volume of A. B. Caldwell's *History of the American Negro* (1921) chronicle the lives of African-American women. Among this select group is Ora Brown Stokes, whom Caldwell described as "a rare leader whose brilliant intellect and charming personality have been put upon the altar for her people." By 1921, when Caldwell's volume appeared, Stokes had completed nearly twenty years of service to church, temperance, education, suffrage, and civic reform organizations in Virginia, and had begun to acquire a national reputation as one of her state's most active and influential black leaders.

Ora M. Brown was born on June 11, 1882, in Chesterfield County, Virginia, the second daughter of the Reverend James E. Brown, a Baptist minister, and his second wife, Olivia Quarles Brown, a schoolteacher. In 1887, the Reverend Brown accepted a call to the pastorate of Shiloh (Old Site) Baptist Church in Fredericksburg, where young Ora Brown was raised and educated. Possessing a quick mind and a zest for learning that her parents encouraged, she excelled in Fredericksburg's segregated public school system, winning her class medal each year in high school and graduating at the age of thirteen. She then enrolled in the Virginia Normal and Collegiate Institute in Petersburg, where she earned her bachelor's degree with a major in economics. Ora Brown taught school in Milford, Virginia, for two years following graduation. On September 9, 1902, she married thirty-year-old William H. Stokes, the dynamic new pastor of Richmond's Ebenezer Baptist Church.

Ora Brown Stokes continued her education after marriage, studying at Hartshorn Memorial College, in Richmond, and at the University of Chicago's School of Civics and Social Administration. She also took an active part in the life of her husband's congregation, teaching Sunday school, singing in the choir, organizing a missionary society, and leading the Baptist Young People's Union. Within a few years, she had also become an officer in the statewide Women's Baptist Missionary and Educational Association. The Stokeses had no natural children, but during the early years of their marriage, Ora Stokes helped care for her husband's young sister and an adopted son, Earnest Morton. From 1909 to 1911, Stokes operated a millinery shop but abandoned this effort in favor of a career in civic and social work.

In 1912, Stokes founded the Richmond Neighborhood Association, a general relief and self-help organization dedicated to the needs of working women and girls. The association, with Stokes as president and superintendent, quickly grew in membership and scope to become one of Richmond's most important African-American community institutions. The association supported a day nursery and a home for young girls, sponsored satellite organizations such as the Camp Fire Girls, the Protective League for Negro Girls, and a chapter of the Council of Negro Women, held public lectures featuring black and white community leaders, and conducted discussion groups on topics ranging from "The Home Beautiful" to "Neglected Children." Members of the association also participated in community-wide activities, providing relief to flood victims, contributing to the care of tubercular patients, and sponsoring a city-wide cleanup campaign. By 1919, the association estimated that it had assisted more than 6,000 persons and had accumulated property valued at $10,000. Stokes' work on behalf of the Richmond Neighborhood Association brought her into contact with city and state welfare officials, who sought and relied upon her advice. Both the State Board of Charities and Corrections and the Richmond City Juvenile Court employed her as a probation officer, work she continued to do for the next twenty years.

Stokes' warm personality and gift for public speaking brought her many opportunities and invitations that placed great demands upon her time. She traveled extensively during the 1920s and 1930s, addressing community groups and college audiences, and participated actively in a host of influential organizations. She served on the executive committee of the Hampton University Conference and the Negro Organization Society of Virginia and was a trustee of Hartshorn College. She was staunchly committed to the cause of woman suffrage and after 1920 served as president of the Virginia Negro Woman's League of Voters. During World War I, she served as chair of the Colored Women's Section of the Council of National Defense in Virginia, and after the war served several terms as president of the Improved Order of Shepherds and Daughters of Bethlehem and of the Southeastern section of the **National Association of Colored Women (NACW)**, as well as vice president of the National Race Congress, the National Conference of Social Workers, and the Virginia Federation of Colored Women's Clubs. Ora Stokes curtailed her activities somewhat in the early 1930s because of her husband's failing health but resumed her hectic schedule following his death in 1936. She was serving as director of a receiving home for black youth operated by the Virginia Department of Public Welfare when she was asked by **Mary McLeod Bethune** to join the staff of the National Youth Administration in Washington, D.C.

Ora Brown Stokes continued to maintain a Richmond address until the end of World War II, when she accepted a position as a field director of the Women's Christian Temperance Union (WCTU), the only black member of the WCTU's national staff. While working for the WCTU in Houston, Texas, Stokes met physician John Edward Perry, whom she married on March 4, 1948. The couple moved to Kansas City, Missouri, where Ora Stokes continued her work on behalf of black women's organizations. She became ill in the spring of 1957 while in Washington, D.C., on an assignment for the National Association of Colored Women. She returned to Kansas City and died there on December 19, 1957.

Nearly a generation younger than **Maggie Lena Walker** and **Janie Porter Barrett**, Ora Stokes' contributions to African-American life in Virginia were on a par with those of her more famous contemporaries. Well educated and deeply committed to the advancement of her gender and race, she worked tirelessly in the areas of social reform that she believed to be most pressing. Typical of college-trained Southern black women of her day, Stokes contributed to the activist tradition of black women's organizations that later energized the men and women of the mid-twentieth-century civil rights movement.

SANDRA GIOIA TREADWAY

T

Tanneyhill, Ann (1906–)

Ann Tanneyhill has dedicated her professional life to serving others through the National Urban League. Her career with the league began in 1928 when she worked for the Springfield, Massachusetts, affiliate office as a secretary to the executive director. Between 1947 and 1961, Tanneyhill was the director of vocational services for the league's national office in New York. As director of vocational services, Tanneyhill organized vocational opportunity campaigns to provide vocational guidance and counseling to black youth at predominantly black high schools and historically black colleges and universities (HBCUs) throughout the South.

Ann Tanneyhill was born in Norwood, Massachusetts, on January 19, 1906. She is the daughter of Alfred Weems Tanneyhill and Adelaide (Grandison) Tanneyhill. In 1928, Tanneyhill earned her B.S. from Simmons College in Boston. Ten years later, she received her M.A. in vocational guidance and personnel administration from Teachers College of Columbia University in New York City. In addition, Tanneyhill was awarded a certificate from the Radio Workshop of New York University.

Tanneyhill's career within the league was particularly full. After she left the league's affiliate office in Springfield in 1930, she moved to New York City where she contin-

A longtime executive of the National Urban League, Ann Tanneyhill has had an extraordinary commitment to black youth and a flair for distinctive methods of reaching those youth. She was a pioneer in the use of radio and television to inspire pride in black heritage. (SCHOMBURG CENTER)

ued working for the league at its national headquarters. Between 1930 and 1940, Tanneyhill was the secretary to the director of industrial relations. The following year, she became the assistant in charge of guidance and personnel. From 1941 through 1981, the year she retired, Tanneyhill served in a number of professional posts at the league, including secretary, Bureau of Guidance and Placement (1941–45); Executive Assistant (1946); Director of Vocational Services (1947–61); Assistant Director of Public Relations (1961–63); Associate Director of Public Relations (1964–68); Director of Conferences (1969–70); Consultant to the Executive Director of the League (1971–79); and Director of the George Edmund Haynes Fellowship Program (1979–81).

In addition to holding several key positions within the league, Tanneyhill served on the boards of many associations, including the Advisory Committee on Young Workers of the Bureau of Standards, U.S. Department of Labor; the National Vocational Guidance Association; the New York Personnel and Guidance Association; the Advisory Commission of the New York Vocational High School in New York City; and the New York Citizens Committee for Nursing Education. Tanneyhill is a charter member of the Urban League's Quarter-Century Club, which is composed of those who have been in service to the league for twenty-five years or longer.

Tanneyhill's commitment to black youth is extraordinary. She once wrote that one of the most serious problems facing the nation was the "high rate of unemployment among black and other minority youth. . . . There is great need to place more attention on basic education, and on the guidance, counseling, and preparation of youth for jobs and careers." Tanneyhill has emphasized the need for a "massive upgrading" of inner-city schools to better prepare the students for postsecondary education and employment. She has ardently supported voter registration efforts, declaring that "the need for a massive 'voter education' program . . . is

essential," and that minority youth need to understand the "privilege of the ballot box."

The career conferences on HBCUs in the 1950s were the brainchild of Tanneyhill. Between 1950 and 1955, these conferences established the practice of inviting major companies to recruit on black college campuses, thereby providing black students with professional opportunities and providing employers who had records of discriminatory practices with opportunities to improve their records by hiring black talent. Tanneyhill also established the "Tomorrow's Scientists and Technicians Project," a national effort to encourage black youth to explore their vocational talents and interests.

Tanneyhill is the recipient of several awards and honors. In 1963, she was presented with two awards, the Merit Award of the New York Personnel and Guidance Association and the National Vocational Guidance Association Award. In 1970, the Ann Tanneyhill Award was established and named in her honor by the National Urban League. The award is presented annually to a league staff member "for excellence and extraordinary commitment to the Urban League Movement." In 1971, Tanneyhill was honored by her alma mater, Simmons College, with its Alumnae Achievement Award.

Tanneyhill authored several articles, vocational guidance aids, radio program scripts, and a number of other publications, including *From School to Job: Guidance for Minority Youth* (1953), *Program Aids for the Vocational Opportunity Campaign* (many editions), and *Whitney M. Young Jr.: "The Voice of the Voiceless"* (1977). Tanneyhill used a variety of resources to promote her work among minority youth. In the 1940s, she arranged two radio programs for CBS. In 1941, Tanneyhill supervised the radio program *The Negro and National Defense.* In 1943, Tanneyhill also promoted the *Heroines in Bronze* radio program, "which was an appeal for the inclusion of black women in the war effort." In 1960, Tanneyhill was the primary consultant to the television documentary film *A Morning for Jimmy,* sponsored by the National Urban League.

Tanneyhill is affectionately called "Miss 'T' " by Urban League staff members who have worked with her. Her life and work testify to her dedication to the black community and her unswerving devotion to promoting the talents of minority youth in America.

LISA BETH HILL

Thomas, Cora Ann Pair (1875–1952)

The Lott Carey Baptist Home and Foreign Mission Convention of the United States opened its first mission in 1897 in Brewerville, Liberia, fifteen miles from Monrovia. In 1909, the convention sent the Reverend William Henry Thomas, a Jamaican, and his wife, Cora Ann Pair Thomas, to work at the mission station.

Cora Ann Pair was born in Knightdale, Wake County, North Carolina on September 8, 1875. In 1895, she graduated from Shaw University (Raleigh, North Carolina) with a higher English diploma. Between 1904 and 1906, she took missionary training courses in the theological school of Fisk University (Nashville, Tennessee). Before traveling to Africa, Pair acted as principal of the orphanage for black children in Oxford, North Carolina.

In November 1908, Cora Pair married William Henry Thomas, who had been born in Jamaica but came to the United States to complete his higher education. The couple met at Shaw University, where William Thomas earned A.B. and B.Th. degrees. The following month, the pair traveled to Liberia, arriving at Monrovia in January 1909. The salary and transportation expenses for Cora Thomas were paid by the Lott Carey Women's Baptist Missionary Convention of North Carolina.

At Brewerville, Cora Thomas successfully persuaded the Lott Carey mission board to establish a school, which was later named the Lott Carey Mission School. Hundreds of girls and boys and young men and women attended the school where Cora Thomas taught.

After the Reverend Thomas' death in September 1942, Cora Thomas was appointed superintendent of the mission, succeeding her husband. She served in that capacity for four years. In 1946, she left Liberia because of failing health.

Cora Thomas returned to Liberia in November 1951 with the Lott Carey Pilgrimage Group. After a severe attack of malaria, she died at Brewerville on May 10, 1952. She was buried next to her husband on the Lott Carey Mission School campus.

SYLVIA M. JACOBS

W

Waddles, Charleszetta (1912–)

Charleszetta Lina Campbell Waddles, founder of the Perpetual Mission for Saving Souls of All Nations, was born on October 7, 1912, in St. Louis, Missouri, the first of seven children of Henry and Ella (Brown) Campbell. Only three of the seven children lived to adulthood. Henry Campbell was a barber for many years and later did construction work until his health failed; he died in 1924 when Charleszetta was twelve. Ella Campbell was also in frail health, so Charleszetta left school when she was in eighth grade to work to support the family. Her numerous jobs included work as a maid, sorting in a rag factory, restaurant cook, day work, and dishwashing. Ella found it necessary to receive Aid to Families with Dependent Children (AFDC) as did Charleszetta, when later she was a single parent of several children. As an adult, she read to educate herself but never had the opportunity to return to school.

Charleszetta has been married several times, been divorced and widowed, and is the mother of ten children. The longest of her marital relationships was with Le Roy Wash, a truck driver for a coal company, to whom she was married from 1933 until their divorce in the late 1940s, and with Payton Waddles, an employee of the Ford Motor Co., from 1957 until his death in 1980. In 1936, Charleszetta and Le Roy Wash migrated to Detroit, seeking better job opportunities. Except for a short time in the 1940s when she and her children returned to St. Louis to care for her ailing mother, she has remained in Detroit.

Her own experiences with poverty motivated Charleszetta Waddles and a small group of neighborhood women who were members of a prayer group to think creatively about how to aid others. Charleszetta had started the prayer band, continued as its leader, and began to develop the skills and practices that led to her starting her mission church. She was ordained a pentecostal minister in 1956 and reordained by Bishop M. J. Moore of the International Association of Universal Truth in 1961. In September 1957, the prayer band decided to become an organized group, and developed into the Perpetual Mission for Saving Souls of All Nations, Inc. Aid is available to persons of all races and creeds. In 1980, Mother Waddles estimated that black people constituted 75 percent of those receiving help.

The mission is best known for providing immediate relief to the needy with a minimum of red tape and qualification barriers. Those in need of food, clothing, furniture, and small amounts of money can usually get help quickly. Mother Waddles also tries to solve problems and run interference for her clients with various agencies. Receiving no governmental funds, the mission is entirely dependent for its success on voluntary donations of time, materials, and money. The mission has often moved from one location to another and increased or decreased its program due to availability of resources. At various times, the mission has offered free or inexpensive restaurant meals, shelter, legal aid, assistance with housing, job placement for the unemployed, medical services, and transportation. The work of the mission has had a wide influence: governmental agencies have adopted some of Waddles' ideas and, in the 1970s, branches of the mission were established in ten African countries.

Mother Waddles has written two cookbooks, a training manual for missionaries, and two autobiographies. Wide publicity has been given to her efforts and numerous awards and honors have been extended to her. Mother Waddles' work is guided by a practical application of Christian principles rather than a concern for formal theology. In her lifetime, she has aided thousands and set an example for all.

DE WITT S. DYKES, JR.

Walker, A'Lelia (1885–1931)

Called "queenly," "lavish," and the "Mahogany Heiress" by some of her contemporaries, A'Lelia Walker was one of the foremost promoters of black arts in Harlem during the 1920s. Writer/poet Langston Hughes called her "the joy goddess of Harlem's 1920s. "Born Lelia McWilliams, she changed her name to A'Lelia when she was about thirty-five years old. She had long before started using her stepfather's last name—Walker.

Walker was born to Sarah Breedlove and her husband, Moses McWilliams, in Vicksburg, Mississippi, on June 6, 1885.

After her husband's death in 1887, Sarah and her daughter moved to St. Louis. There, Sarah worked as a washerwoman until 1905, when she began to develop hair-care products and techniques for black consumers that would make her America's first self-made woman millionaire. In July 1905, Sarah Breedlove moved to Denver, Colorado, where she married newspaperman Charles Walker and became Madam C. J. Walker. A'Lelia was probably attending Knoxville College in Knoxville, Tennessee,

One of the foremost promoters of black artists in Harlem during the 1920s, A'Lelia Walker was rejected by some members of the Harlem community because of her fast-paced social life and her unusual style of dress. (A'LELIA BUNDLES)

when her mother moved initially, but she was living in Denver, Colorado by 1907–08. Madam Walker began to sell her products door to door in Denver, then trained agents to sell them, expanding her business. In 1908, they moved to Pittsburgh, Pennsylvania, closing down the Denver office and opening one in Pittsburgh, managed by twenty-three-year-old A'Lelia. In 1910, Madam Walker set up office in Indianapolis, Indiana. A'Lelia continued to work for her mother in the Pittsburgh office and at Lelia College, a school Madam Walker opened to train Walker hair culturists and agents. In 1914, Madam Walker moved to a townhouse at 108-110 West 136th Street in New York City, becoming one of the first black people to own property there.

That same year, A'Lelia divorced her first husband and moved to New York to manage the headquarters of the Walker College of Hair Culture. She adopted a daughter named Mae Bryant in 1912.

In 1917, Madam Walker began building an Italianate country home in Irvington-on-Hudson, New York, at a cost of $250,000. One account states that the home was designed by black architect Vertner Tandy and called "Villa Lewaro" by singer Enrico Caruso, who took the syllables from A'Lelia Walker Robinson's name.

While on a business trip to South America in spring 1919, A'Lelia wrote to her mother that she intended to marry Dr. James Arthur Kennedy, as Madam Walker wished. On May 25, 1919, Madam Walker died while A'Lelia and Mae were in Panama. Returning to New York, A'Lelia canceled her engagement to Kennedy, buried her mother privately on June 3, and married Dr. Wiley Wilson on June 6. Soon after, however, she divorced Wilson, then reconciled with and married Kennedy.

Following Madam Walker's death, A'Lelia Walker became president of her mother's company and inherited an estate estimated to have been worth about $1 million. In 1923, she gave Mae a lavish and expensive wedding at Saint Philip's Episcopal Church in Harlem.

In the mid-1920s, A'Lelia Walker, purposefully setting out to encourage the literary and artistic renaissance in Harlem, welcomed young writers and artists into her home and provided them with food and moral support. In 1927, she cemented her intentions by creating in her 136th Street home a salon where artists could exhibit their paintings, writers could discuss their work, and all could enjoy food and drink. Richard Bruce Nugent named the salon Dark Tower after Countee Cullen's column of the same name in *Opportunity: A Journal of Negro Life*. Manhattan designer Paul Frankel decorated the salon, placing on opposite walls texts of Cullen's "The Dark Tower" and Langston Hughes' "The Weary Blues," which were either painted directly on the wall by a local sign painter or were framed pieces.

Walker organized a planning committee and had a grand opening, but in October 1928, after only a year, Dark Tower closed. Walker went to live in her apartment on Edgecombe Avenue in Harlem's West End, but still maintained her townhouse. In October 1929, a redecorated Dark Tower reopened as an expensive restaurant, eventually moving even further away from A'Lelia Walker's vision of a hangout for well-to-do cafe society. The club had a hat checker and formal tea room.

During the Harlem Renaissance, A'Lelia Walker became notorious for elaborate gatherings and expensive parties at both Dark Tower and Villa Lewaro. Her guests included European royalty, influential white Americans, and black artists such as James Weldon Johnson, **Zora Neale Hurston**, Langston Hughes, Countee Cullen, **Florence Mills**, Rudolph Fisher, Charles Gilpin, Bruce Nugent, Aaron Douglas, and Jean Toomer. Society writer Geraldyn Dismond colorfully described the nightly excitement at Dark Tower in the *Inter-State Tattler*, a publication covering black social life in both small and large cities.

A'Lelia Walker was not accepted by everyone in the Harlem community, however. Some begrudged her the fact that she was the daughter of a washerwoman. Some also objected to her fast-paced social life and unusual style of dress, which included turbans and jewelry. Some of her contemporaries called her the "De-kink Heiress." James Weldon Johnson's wife, Grace Nail Johnson, who was known as the social dictator of Harlem, refused to attend Walker's parties.

The Great Depression took its toll on A'Lelia Walker. In 1930, she closed her restaurant and auctioned off some contents from Villa Lewaro. In 1931, she divorced Dr. Kennedy. On August 16, 1931, while visiting friends in New Jersey, A'Lelia Walker died at the age of forty-six.

At her funeral, the Reverend Adam Clayton Powell gave the eulogy, **Mary McLeod Bethune** spoke, Edward Perry read Langston Hughes' poem "To A'Lelia," and the Bon Bons, who had often entertained at her parties, performed for her one last time.

TIYA MILES

Walker, Maggie Lena   (c. 1867–1934)

Maggie Lena Walker was always crystal clear about what she was trying to accomplish as executive head of the Independent Order of St. Luke, the organization she ran for thirty-five years and built to a membership of 85,000 in nineteen states and Washington, D.C. She wanted to create businesses that would provide employment for black Americans, particularly black women, through cooperative effort and mutual support. As a vehicle for community education, the order had, she said in 1913, "devoted itself to the teaching of the power

The daughter of a laundress who had at one time worked for Elizabeth Van Lew, Richmond, Virginia's famous Union spy, Maggie Lena Walker once said, "I was not born with a silver spoon in my mouth, but with a laundry basket practically on my head." (NATIONAL PARK SERVICE)

Taking over the meager assets of the Independent Order of St. Luke in 1899, Maggie Lena Walker transformed the society into a highly successful financial complex that greatly bolstered the black community of Richmond, Virginia. (NATIONAL PARK SERVICE)

of organization and the lesson of confidence." This spirit animated her career of public service, explains much about her personal style, and suggests why St. Luke's business enterprises, with one exception, enjoyed quiet, steady success while so many similar ones failed.

There is no official record of Maggie Walker's birth. Standard sources state that she was born in Richmond, Virginia, on July 15, 1867. There is no reason to doubt the month and day, which is still celebrated in Richmond, but several lines of evidence suggest she was born two or three years before the date she used. In any case, she was a member of that remarkable generation born during or just after the Civil War. Her mother, Elizabeth Draper, worked for Elizabeth Van Lew, Richmond's famous spy for the Union. Her father, Eccles Cuthbert, was an Irish-born newspaperman who was a correspondent for the *New York Herald* for many years.

Elizabeth Draper married William Mitchell, the butler in the Van Lew house, on May 27, 1868. The little family moved to a house in College Alley just off Broad Street, close to William Mitchell's new job as a waiter in the St. Charles Hotel, at that time the city's most luxurious. Maggie's brother, John B., called Johnnie, was born in 1870. William Mitchell disappeared in February 1876, and after an intensive five-day search, his body was recovered from the James River. The coroner's report specifies suicide by drowning, but all other reports, including Maggie Walker's own, assume he was murdered.

The widowed Elizabeth Mitchell worked from her home as a laundress; of the few occupations available to black women, this one was preferred by women with young children. The children, especially Maggie, picked up and delivered the clothes. As she later put it, "I was not born with a silver spoon in my mouth, but with a laundry basket practically on my head." Participation in her mother's work was itself an education because laundresses worked in groups rotating between houses and discussed possible solutions to community problems.

Maggie Mitchell and the Richmond public school system virtually grew up together. She attended a grammar school that had no bathrooms of any kind, but had, almost from the beginning, an all-black faculty who were outstanding community leaders. She completed her education at the Normal School, graduating in 1883, a member of a class of ten that made its mark locally, and through the black press nationally, by demanding to use a public facility other than the black church they were usually relegated to for their graduation ceremony. While they were unsuccessful in forcing desegregation of the Richmond Theater, where white high school graduations were held (they refused the balcony), they were considered heroic to face expulsion and their exercises were held at the school.

Right around the corner from the Mitchell home was the First African Baptist Church, the oldest and largest black Baptist congregation in Richmond. Maggie Mitchell joined the Sunday school and was baptized during the Great Richmond Revival in the summer of 1878. The church, both in particular and in general, remained central to her life. Her speeches and diaries illustrate the depth of her religious commitment, and her wide-ranging knowledge of the Bible is a tribute to the thoroughness of her training. She was active in Baptist affairs, served on the boards of Hartshorn College, Virginia Union University, and the **National Training School for Girls** in Washington, D.C., and was an early member of **Nannie Helen Burroughs**' Women's Auxiliary of the National Baptist Convention.

After graduation, Maggie Mitchell became a teacher in the year the Readjuster political victory opened unprecedented, long overdue opportunities for black professionals in the school system. Not only was there an influx of black teachers, but there were some black principals, all of whom were fired at the end of the year. She was assigned to Valley, her old elementary school, where she taught both primary and grammar grades for three years, starting at thirty-five dollars a month.

Her career ended, as was the rule, when she married Armstead Walker on September 14, 1886. Walker had graduated from Normal School in 1875, and worked in his father's prosperous bricklaying and construction business, later forming a partnership with his brother. For ten years, he also was a mail carrier, a coveted job. Although he was active in St. Luke affairs for some years, his participation beyond membership lessened when his wife became the Right Worthy Grand Secretary.

The Walkers had three sons: Russell Eccles Talmage in 1890, Armstead Mitchell in 1893 (who died in infancy, the same year her brother Johnnie died at age 23), and Melvin DeWitt in 1897. Another child, Margaret (Polly) Anderson, known after her marriage as Polly Payne, was adopted into the Walker household from a connection in Armstead's family in the early 1890s. She became the anchor who ran the house, cared for the Walker children as well as those of other St. Luke families while their mothers traveled, and in the end devoted herself to a severely disabled Maggie Walker. Elizabeth Mitchell, an active St. Luke member, lived with them until her death in 1922, working for many years as a midwife and "doctress."

While in Normal School, Maggie Mitchell had joined Good Idea Council No. 16 of the Independent Order of St. Luke, one of the myriad mutual aid societies in Richmond. These multipurpose organizations were so important in the life of the black community for networking and insurance reasons that people typically belonged to several, but usually concentrated their energies in one. Officers came and went annually, but despite periodic elections, the executive headship was typically for life. At this time, the head of St. Luke was more interested in his other job as head of the Odd Fellows.

The nature of some societies was changing in the 1880s. One argument was over shifting the responsibility for caring for the sick and burying the dead from the local councils to a centrally administered system supported by special assessments from all the society members. Ultimately, over the years, the industrial insurance principle of forwarding a small amount every week or month to a central office as a purchase of life insurance was adopted by almost all societies, and black insurance companies formed in the 1890s. Richmond was at the forefront of these controversies and developments.

Centralization, membership drives, increased income, and quickly accumulated capital to finance programs and investments transformed some societies into diversified businesses. The first organization to tread this path was Richmond's own True Reformers, who put their insurance policies in place in 1884, started their Rosebud children's division in 1885, founded what was arguably the first black bank in 1888, and organized a regalia department, a real estate division, newspaper, hotel, and grocery store in quick succession in the 1890s.

Maggie Walker had been Chief of Good Idea Council, and had held all the ritual positions in the order, culminating as Right Worthy Grand Chief in 1890. While she taught, she worked as a fraternal collection agent and received some business training. When she found that home and the social whirl were not enough for her talents, it was natural for her to turn to St. Luke. She started her professional career at the 1895 convention, when she submitted a resolution for the formation of a Juvenile Division

with Circles, headed by Matrons, to be formed by each local council. With one stroke, women achieved a formal, innovative, commanding position. They created the Juvenile Department and a Council of Matrons. She was shortly elected Grand Matron, which she remained for life. A powerful vehicle of socialization into race pride, thrift, responsibility, and mutual caring, St. Luke's youth organization touched the lives of tens of thousands of children.

The next move was taken outside the formal St. Luke structure. Twenty-five Richmond councils formed a joint stock company called the St. Luke Association for the purpose of purchasing property on which to build a headquarters. Maggie Walker was secretary of the board. The association accomplished all its goals, raising money with bazaars and entertainments, and in 1903 built a three-story brick hall that it rented to the central organization, the Right Worthy Grand (RWG) Council. The building was important, not only as an office and headquarters for regalia and printing enterprises but also to provide meeting rooms, an auditorium, and as a tremendous source of pride.

In addition to her organizational and leadership skills, Maggie Walker's dramatic talents and her love of ritual kept her in demand to run ceremonies. By the time it became obvious that St. Luke would not progress under its then executive head, who was more interested in his other job as head of the Odd Fellows, Walker was the 1899 convention's obvious choice as RWG secretary. Taking over the meager assets, she and her associates went to work. They used charm, persuasion, and an emphasis on building good will, harmony, and optimism to enforce a compulsory insurance plan, which meant added income. A big membership drive, the first of many that spread St. Luke into nineteen states and Washington, D.C., got under way. She spoke everywhere, moving audiences to tears over disfranchisement, electrifying them with hope for cooperative enterprise, urging economic independence of the black community from the white community and women from men, exhorting women to enter the business world, and urging black consumers to support black enterprise. Her low, rich voice and storytelling style captivated people whether they agreed with her or not. Despite her emphasis on women, she always said St. Luke was a women's organization that gave equal opportunity to men, and many men were prominent activists. The development plan started with a newspaper, moved to a bank, then a store, and fantasized a factory.

Very few copies of the *St. Luke Herald* (founded 1902) survive. Under the guidance of Lillian Payne, in the early years its editorials were written by the fiery lawyer James Hayes, an arch rival of John Mitchell, the editor of the *Richmond Planet*. The *Herald* was considerably more than a fraternal bulletin; it was outspoken on lynching, the position of black women, the situation in Haiti, whatever the outrage of the day. The paper also gave rise to a profitable printing business.

Maggie Walker prepared to be a banker by spending a few hours a day for several months in the Merchants' National Bank of Richmond. When the St. Luke Penny Savings Bank opened in St. Luke Hall in 1903, she became arguably the first woman bank president in the United States, running the fourth black bank in Richmond. The bank grew slowly, and the constant selling job necessary to convince the St. Luke family

and Richmond's black community to trust the institution began.

About this time, she bought a large house on Leigh Street that became the home for her extended family. Her sons brought their brides there, and all the Walker grandchildren were born there. This house has been restored by the National Park Service as a national historic site, which gives the public an opportunity to experience something of her world. The library is particularly evocative. It holds over a thousand books, and the walls are covered with photographs of family, St. Luke notables, and other race leaders of all political persuasions. The last St. Luke project, the department store called the Emporium (1905–11), was the most symbolically crucial because it was to provide substantial employment for women, both in the store and on the board. Situated on Broad Street, Richmond's main thoroughfare, in a three-story building with an elevator, it struggled against overt white merchant pressure, and black consumers' preference for the labels of Richmond's traditional stores. After a promising start, it lost more and more money each year, made up from St. Luke general revenues. Even after the insurance commissioner said the Emporium had to close, the St. Luke women were reluctant to surrender their dream.

Regulation drastically changed both the insurance and banking businesses. Too late to save True Reformers (whose empire collapsed in 1910), it forced St. Luke to restructure. Insurance policies had to be guaranteed by reserves, in each state, which meant capital had to be invested in secure bonds, not risky business enterprises. Every aspect of their activity was inspected. As Maggie Walker said, "The only secret we have left is our password." Insurance became the order's major, very complex, business, and it did provide employment for many women clerks. In Walker's lifetime, St. Luke never missed a death payment.

To comply with the new law, the bank was separated from the order, although the order remained the major stock holder. Other black banks failed in Richmond and two more were founded. When the latter weakened at the beginning of the Great Depression, St. Luke Bank and Trust was senior partner in two mergers that resulted in the Consolidated Bank and Trust Company headed by Emmett Burke, the original St. Luke cashier, with Maggie Walker as chairman of the board. As the sole black bank in Richmond, the bank made a smooth transition after her death and flourishes today.

She entered the **National Association of Colored Women** (NACW) late (1912) but as a well-known achiever with the fascinating status of bank president. As chairman consecutively of the business, finance, and budget committees, she was a member of the executive committee until her death. She was part of **Margaret Murray Washington**'s small group of prominent women who were invited to start the **International Council of Women of the Darker Races**. She served on the board of trustees of the Frederick Douglass Home. On the local level, she was an active member of **Janie Porter Barrett**'s Virginia Federation of Colored Women's Clubs (founded 1907) and a staunch supporter of its primary activity, founding and running an Industrial School for Colored Girls, with Barrett as superintendent, as an alternative to putting delinquent children in jail and thus onto chain gangs. She founded in 1912 and was lifelong president of Richmond's Council of Colored Women (CCW). The council raised $5,000 for the Industrial School and continued to support it and many other social service projects. When

the school was taken over by the state, she continued on the board as the appointee of the governor.

Other activities of the CCW centered around the house it purchased at 00 Clay Street. It was a well-decorated facility where club affairs were held. It was rented to other groups, served as an office for an embattled **National Association for the Advancement of Colored People** (NAACP), was a canteen for black servicemen during World War I, and was the site of a gala reception for the NACW at the Richmond convention in 1922. When the Depression hit, and the council could not keep up the payments, the St. Luke Bank auctioned it, bought it, and sold it to the city (at a profit) to house Richmond's black library. This illustrates the levers of power Maggie Walker had accumulated. Today, 00 Clay Street is the site of the Black History Museum that opened in 1991.

She was one of the founders of Virginia's Negro Organization Society, which tried to bring every black organization in the state into the fight for better health and education. As the interracial movement gained strength following World War I, she was on the board of the Community House for Colored People, which evolved into the Richmond branch of the Urban League. She was put on the State Interracial Commission. As always, her style was direct, confrontational when necessary, and impressively well informed. She and her associates formed the core of the local NAACP (founded 1917), but segregated Southern branches found it difficult to be active except as fund-raisers. Her heart lay with the national organization, for which she served as a board member from 1923 until her death.

Other honors, in addition to those bestowed by St. Luke, were a master's degree from Virginia Union University, and honorable mention in the 1927 Harmon Award for Distinguished Achievement competition in the business category. In 1921, she was chosen to run as Superintendent of Public Instruction on Virginia's Republican ticket.

Her personal life was shattered in 1915 when her son, Russell, shot and killed his father while mistaking him for a burglar. He was indicted for murder and, after a traumatic trial that polarized the community, was acquitted. This tragic situation caused a serious challenge to her leadership, but she faced it down with style. Russell died in 1924, having worked in his father's construction business, at the bank, and in the order. Melvin, who died a year after his mother, also spent his working life in St. Luke enterprises.

For reasons that are not clear, she began to lose the use of her legs in the late 1920s. In 1908, she had fractured her kneecap in a bad fall that left her with a limp, but the new condition was progressive. After several years of trips to Hot Springs, Arkansas, exercise regimens, and braces that constantly broke, one day, with characteristic decisiveness, she ordered an elevator for the house and sent her Packard to be customized to accommodate a wheelchair. During her last years of scarcely diminished activity, she was known as the Lame Lioness. She died of diabetic gangrene on December 15, 1934.

GERTRUDE W. MARLOWE

White Rose Mission, New York City

A teacher at the Baylan Home for Colored Youth in Jacksonville, Florida, wrote to the superintendent of the White Rose Mission, asking her to meet one of her students who was traveling to New York to seek employment. The superintendent, **Victoria Earle Matthews**, arrived at the Old Dominion pier at the expected time but could not find the student. Three days later, the extremely upset young woman appeared and told of having been lured away by employment agents.

The White Rose Mission filled special needs for black women migrating from the South. It was established by Matthews and a small group of black women. Its principal purpose was "to protect self-supporting Colored girls, to direct and help them amid the dangers and temptations of New York City." Matthews organized committees to study the living and working conditions of black women, to contact teachers, and to locate a suitable place for the meetings.

On February 11, 1897, the White Rose Mission became a reality when it opened on East 97th Street. The White Rose Mission was nondenominational and conducted as a settlement house. It provided a social center for community women and children as well as shelter and protection to young women coming from the South in search of employment. In addition to mothers' meetings, there were vocational courses in cooking, sewing, dressmaking, woodcarving, cobbling, chair caning, basketry, and clay modeling. There were separate boys' and girls' clubs. The children ranged in age from three to fifteen. A kindergarten class was organized and taught by **Alice Ruth Moore (Dunbar-Nelson)**. Cultural events featured Booker T. Washington, Paul Laurence Dunbar, and other distinguished speakers and musicians.

The first travelers' aid service was formed by the White Rose Mission in 1898. Victoria

Matthews and a few volunteers took turns meeting docking boats. The mission hired two agents who were Sunday school teachers, and placed Dorothy J. Boyd at the Old Dominion pier in New York City and Hattie Proctor at the same line in Norfolk, Virginia. Matthews' sister, Anna Rich, later became the New York dock agent.

In 1905, Matthews established the White Rose Travelers' Aid Society. Within approximately ten years, the society met 50,000 women. At least 5,000 were sheltered at the White Rose Mission.

The White Rose Home and Industrial Association for Working Girls was supported through contributions and fund-raising activities. The patrons included the Reverend Adam Clayton Powell, Sr., and Booker T. Washington. Reformers such as Frances Kellor and Mary White Ovington joined the White Rose Home Association.

Victoria Matthews was superintendent of the White Rose Home until her death in 1907. Her successor, Frances Reynolds Keyser, and other black women assumed the leadership of the home. Its location changed several times, moving from 97th Street to 1760 Third Avenue, and later to East 95th Street. It remained at 217 East 86th Street for seventeen years. In 1918, the White Rose Home Association established permanent quarters on West 136th Street.

After 1924, financial support for the White Rose Home came from both the Empire State Federation of Women's Clubs and the Northeastern Federation of Colored Women's Clubs. As the need for separate housing facilities for black women declined, the White Rose Home was used as a center for forums, club programs, and other community activities.

FLORIS BARNETT CASH

Williams, Fannie Barrier (1855–1944)

Fannie Barrier Williams recognized that racism was a central problem in the United States, but she believed that sexism played an even greater role in inequality. For "to be a colored woman," she asserted, "is to be discredited, mistrusted, and often meanly hated." She worked tirelessly, quietly, and sometimes successfully to eradicate discrimination against black women.

Fannie Barrier grew up in the North in a sheltered and affluent environment. She was born on February 12, 1855, in Brockport, New York, to Anthony J. Barrier and Harriet Prince Barrier. Anthony Barrier, a barber, coal merchant, and homeowner, was an active leader in the predominantly white community. As one of three children (two daughters and one son) of this middle-class black family, Fannie often attended parties and socialized with others, regardless of race, and felt on equal terms with her white acquaintances. She attended the local schools and the State Normal School at Brockport, from which she graduated in 1870.

Fannie Barrier's innocence of racism and discrimination ended abruptly, however, when she joined other black and white Northern teachers who ventured South during the 1870s to teach freed black Southerners. White Southerners taught her that social equality was not a right extended to black Americans. Jim Crow laws prevailed, and white Southerners expected her to strictly adhere to a racist and segregationist code. This racial etiquette, she discovered, intimated that because of her blackness, she belonged to an inferior race.

Quickly leaving the Deep South, Fanny Barrier found a teaching post in Washington, D.C. While teaching in the public schools, she explored her artistic talents. She became an art student of several Washington artists and developed her skills as a portrait painter. She also spent some time extending her studies at the New England Conservatory of Music and in private studios in Boston.

While in Washington, D.C., she met a promising young law student, S. Laing Williams. He was a native of Georgia, an 1881 graduate of the University of Michigan, and a former Alabama schoolteacher. Upon completion of his law degree in 1887, the couple married and moved to Chicago. In Chicago, S. Laing Williams worked as one of eleven assistant attorneys in northern Illinois. With a recommendation from Booker T. Washington, he later became an assistant district attorney in Chicago.

Fannie Barrier Williams gained notoriety at the Chicago World's Fair in May 1893 when she addressed the Departmental Congress of the National Association of Loyal Women of American Liberty at the World's Congress of Representative Women. In her speech "The Intellectual Progress and Present Status of the Colored Women of the United States since the Emancipation Proclamation," she told the audience that black women "are the only women in the country for whom real ability, virtue, and special talents count for nothing when they become applicants for respectable employment." A few months later, she told the World's Parliament of Religions that "it should be the province of religion to unite, and not to separate, men and women according to superficial differences of race line." Within the year, Williams was deluged with speaking engagements.

In 1894, Williams was nominated for membership in the elite white Chicago Women's Club. For fourteen months, the club deliberated on admitting a black woman. Her controversial admission caused some members to withdraw from the club and forced the General Federation of Women's Clubs to confront the issue of black female membership.

She was an active social welfare reformer in Chicago and took a leading role in several initiatives to create new institutions. Williams was a consultant and fund-raiser for a training school for black nurses at Provident

Fannie Barrier Williams became famous after speaking at the 1893 Chicago World's Fair, but her greatest contributions were probably her work with Provident Hospital—a training hospital for black staff that served both black and white patients—and with the women's club movement. (MOORLAND-SPINGARN)

Hospital, established in 1891. Even though Provident served black and white patients, Williams argued that a segregated training school for black women was imperative because "there are other training schools for white women, but none at all for colored women. Why let white women take any of the few places we'll have open."

In 1905, the Frederick Douglass Center opened as a settlement project under the auspices of white Unitarian minister Celia Parker Woolley, with the aid of several prominent black families, including the Williamses. The center, located on the fringes of the predominantly black Second Ward, was an interracial experiment dedicated to promoting amicable race relations.

Williams was the Chicago reporter for the *Woman's Era*, a monthly newspaper published by **Josephine St. Pierre Ruffin** and her daughter, **Florida Ruffin Ridley**. The newspaper disseminated news about and by black women throughout the country. Williams supported the *Era*'s call for a national black female organization in the mid-1890s. By 1896, the **National Association of Colored Women** (NACW) was established.

In addition, Williams was chairperson of the committee on state schools for dependent children for the Illinois Woman's Alliance. She was corresponding secretary of the board of directors of the **Phyllis Wheatley Home Association**, and belonged to the Prudence Crandall Study Club. The club, an exclusive twenty-five-member elite organization, was primarily a literary society. Williams headed the art and music department. From 1924 to 1926, Williams served on the Chicago Library Board. As the first black woman to hold that position, she was a trailblazer.

Williams championed Booker T. Washington's industrial education and the need for white philanthropy. She blamed white employers for high unemployment among black workers and was successful in persuading some white employers to hire black women. She also abhorred housing segregation, which, she argued, led to demoralizing lifestyles steeped in poverty and crime.

In 1926, Williams returned to her home in Brockport to live with her sister. She died of arteriosclerosis in 1944 at the age of eighty-nine.

WANDA HENDRICKS

Williamson, Sarah (1899–1986)

Sarah Williamson liked to tell how she always came back to the United States from Liberia C.O.D. (cash on delivery) until her passage could be paid by the National Baptist Convention U.S.A., Inc. During her eight years in Africa, she took several furloughs in the United States, where she campaigned to raise funds for mission work.

Sarah Williamson, her parents' second child, was born in Norfolk, Virginia, on December 8, 1899. She was sent to boarding school at Hampton Normal School (now Hampton University) in Hampton, Virginia, where she completed four years of high school and two years of normal school. Upon graduation from Hampton, she attended the University of Rochester (New York) through her sophomore year, training in preparation for missionary work in Africa.

Williamson sailed to Liberia in November 1924, arriving six weeks later. She was stationed at Suehn Industrial Academy, becoming its third principal. It was through her efforts that Suehn became such a vital force in the National Baptist Convention's

Through the untiring efforts of Sarah Williamson, Suehn Industrial Academy in Liberia became a vital force in the National Baptist Convention's mission program. (SYLVIA JACOBS)

mission program. Many of the buildings on campus were erected under her supervision.

Early in her missionary experience in Liberia, Williamson became very discouraged when she learned that her African translator was not interpreting her religious messages correctly. She decided to work with the children, believing that they could learn English more easily than their parents and that they could teach her their language. She would teach them to read and she hoped that they, in turn, would teach their parents to read the Bible.

In 1932, Williamson returned to the United States. She was married and widowed twice. In 1954, she was appointed as

a missionary-at-large in West Africa, returned to Suehn Industrial Academy as dean of girls, and worked there until 1957. She died in Washington, D.C., in December 1986.

SYLVIA M. JACOBS

Woman's Loyal Union of New York and Brooklyn

The Woman's Loyal Union was founded in October 1892 by two active reformers who would later be associated with the **National Association of Colored Women** (NACW), **Victoria Earle Matthews** (1861–1907) and **Maritcha Lyons** (1848–1929). This black women's club acted as an information clearinghouse for the black communities of New York and Brooklyn, a center for disbursal of funds for reform work, and a locus of "race work" and community "uplift."

The Woman's Loyal Union, like many black women's clubs in the Progressive Era, supported a variety of reforms. For example, the Union encouraged and often monetarily aided black-initiated, black-run self-help organizations and institutions such as the Home for Aged Colored People in Brooklyn and the New Bedford Home for the Aged. The Union also nurtured ties to suffrage organizations such as the Brooklyn Equal Suffrage Club. Since many women who were members of the Loyal Union were also members of other clubs and/or active in social reform organizations such as the Urban League and the **National Association for the Advancement of Colored People** (NAACP), fund-raising events, efforts to lobby Congress, and public demonstrations were often performed in concert with these other groups.

Matthews, not only the cofounder of the Loyal Union but also its first president, established the White Rose Home and Industrial Association in 1897 in an attempt to address the growing problem of unscrupulous men advising or employing newly arrived black migrants from the South. The association's **White Rose Mission** acted much as a settlement house for these women. It offered employment advice, a library, a kindergarten, classes in "Negro history," and courses in sewing and cooking. The Loyal Union and the White Rose Mission often shared resources. The Loyal Union, for example, contributed to Matthews' extensive collection of books and reference materials housed within the White Rose Mission's building. The Loyal Union also disseminated information (in the form of pamphlets) on the White Rose Mission both to the general public and to government agencies.

THEA ARNOLD

Y

York, Consuella (1923–1995)

"You know what Mother Teresa [means] to people all over the world?" asked the Reverend Clay Evans in the *Chicago Sun-Times*. "[Mother York] meant the same thing to us. She was a saint."

Consuella York was born in Chicago in 1923. Her father was a Baptist minister. She attended Phillips High School and then the Chicago Baptist Institute, on a scholarship. Even before graduating in 1953, she began her community service work by forming Consuella's Public Service and Christ Way Enterprise. The organization was hired by local churches to print flyers and bulletins or to type business letters. Consuella's Public Service provided employment to teenagers, senior citizens, young mothers (who could bring their children to work), homeless people, and drug addicts from 1950 until it closed in 1970.

Mother York was ordained as a Baptist minister in 1954 and immediately opened Christ Way Church on the south side of Chicago. She was the first woman to be ordained in the Baptist Church in Chicago and was the first African American to become the assistant pastor at Fellowship Baptist Church. She also served as the announcer for the church's sermons on local radio.

In 1952, Mother York visited the Cook County jail and, as she said, "I've been a jailbird ever since, serving a life sentence for the Lord." She became the senior chaplain at the jail, the first woman in that position. Her work for the inmates included holding services every weekend. Also, during the week she would take around "Mother York's Goodie Wagon," which provided inmates with not only baked treats but also many of the necessities, such as toiletries, that they would not have otherwise received. Nor did she forget Cook County jail at Christmas. Every year she provided both the staff and the inmates with Christmas dinner.

Sheriff Michael F. Sheahan summed up her work this way, "She has been a missionary, motivator, disciplinarian, mother and cheerleader . . ." A fine epitaph for a fine woman.

HILARY MAC AUSTIN

Young Women's Christian Association

One Imperative: To Thrust Our Collective Power to Eliminate Racism Wherever It Exists and by Any Means Necessary.

YWCA, 1970

When the above declaration was approved by the national convention of the Young Women's Christian Association (YWCA) in 1970, it signaled a dramatic climax to the organization's century-long struggle to fulfill its social mission. At that juncture in its history, the YWCA was giving voice to its experience as the oldest and largest women's multiracial association in the world, and yet, in all its work with, and for, women, the most overwhelming obstacle to social progress continued to be relations between the races. At the height of the civil rights and Black Power movements, and in the early stages of the modern women's movement, YWCA members asserted that by focusing on racism, women of all races could identify their positions as oppressors as well as oppressed persons and could then work more effectively to combat the ills of society.

The multiracial membership of the YWCA resulted both from incidental and deliberate actions by its membership. As early as 1870, only four years after the formation of the Boston YWCA, and only nineteen years since the first association was begun in England, black churchwomen in Philadelphia represented a Colored Women's Christian Association at the second annual national convention of Women's Christian Associations. During the remainder of the nineteenth century, as black women migrated in large numbers to industrial centers, similar associations were begun in an effort to meet the increasing need for social services and lodging. These early city associations were founded and operated by black women because their race excluded them from organizations established to serve white women. However, in spite of their adoption of the name Young

One of the many activities of the Young Women's Christian Association was to set up local canteens for black servicemen during World War I (they were excluded from all other canteens). One of the earliest (and a model for others) was the Camp Upton Hostess House, led by Lugenia Burns Hope (center). (YWCA OF THE USA, NATIONAL BOARD ARCHIVES)

Women's Christian Association, and despite their unceasing efforts to affiliate with their white counterparts, these black associations were not accepted as part of the growing national movement of women's associations that combined to form the International Board of Women's and Young Women's Christian Associations.

By contrast, as part of a separate movement of students organizing YWCAs, black students at predominantly white colleges as well as on black college campuses were welcomed as members. This group's national umbrella organization was known as the American Committee of Young Women's Christian Associations. There were cordial relations between the two national bodies, but they worked as independent organizations. The American Committee associations were most often led by white students and teachers. With much emphasis on the task of evangelizing the world, this group believed that part of their Christian mission included ministering to black and Native American students as well as working as foreign missionaries. Affiliates of the American Committee were closely aligned with the world and the international committees of the Young Men's Christian Association (YMCA), which pioneered work among minority students. Stressing prayer and Bible study in preparation for a life of service, the women's student associations grew rapidly among young black women at the turn of the century.

When the two national organizations merged in 1906 to form one national board, fourteen black student associations formally affiliated with the American Committee and four black city associations were recommended for affiliation. Although these associations by no means represented all the work being done by black women under the name Young Women's Christian Association, Addie W. Hunton, a black social worker hired by the new national board to assess the work of these groups, believed they held the most promise.

However, true to the segregationist policies of the era, white women were reluctant to accept black affiliates, especially in city associations. Their concern centered on two main issues. First, they did not want to assume fiscal responsibility for the struggling black associations. The second issue was equally compelling. White Southern women were especially worried that "any parallel work among colored people would mean attendance by both at conferences," and they were not willing to suffer the embarrassment of being seated at regional and national meetings alongside black women from their own cities.

The early solution was to affiliate already established black associations directly with the national board in a separate category, independent of the white associations. This arrangement was not satisfactory in most cases, however, for a variety of reasons, not the least of which was the fact that, without financial support from the larger white associations, the small black operations could not afford professional leadership or provide quality services. It soon became apparent that the more expedient arrangement, especially in fast-growing Northern cities, was to have a central association, which usually was all white, and so-called colored branches. Moreover, "no work was to be undertaken . . . to promote Association work among colored people in the cities in the South."

Under this arrangement, branch committees of management were mostly free to design their own programs, and a few were responsible for raising operating funds. Prior to World War I, the central association designated members of its board of directors to serve on a subcommittee for colored work. This committee, which reported back to the board, acted as liaison to maintain control over personnel and major capital decisions. Black women tolerated this structure as a trade off for fiscal support, leadership training, and credibility as part of the powerful national organization. Moreover, affiliation provided access to a national network of white Christian leaders who sometimes could influence the quality of local race relations. During this same period, according to association records, black student association work grew to include 150 institutions. At white colleges where there were representative groups of black students, some organized separate associations.

The benefit of affiliation was dramatically illustrated when, during World War I, the national board received $4 million from the government to supervise war-work activities for women; of this amount, $400,000 was set aside for work among black women. During the war period, **Eva Bowles**, secretary for colored work for the national board, supervised the expansion of service to black women—from sixteen affiliates to association work in forty-nine communities covering twenty-one states and Washington, D.C. In the South Atlantic region alone, at least 4,000 black women and girls were enrolled. In a two-year period, Bowles also expanded the opportunity for hundreds of competent black women to become employees and volunteer leaders in the association. At the end of the war, the association allocated $200,000 of its remaining funds to

build the **Phyllis Wheatley** branch in Washington, D.C.

Association work expanded to include two principal groups of women. The first emphasis was on providing recreation and housing services for young women migrating to urban centers in search of employment. Because many of these cities were in the South, association work for this group had been almost nonexistent. YWCA workers mobilized black leaders, and with their help organized activities, some skills development, and employment and residence registries. This work, which began as a supplement to government-sponsored "hostess houses" for the families of soldiers near army camps, formed the nucleus of postwar center development. The second thrust was incorporating the large number of young women who had been organized into Girl Reserve clubs, originally formed as so-called Patriotic Leagues to support the war. These clubs contained girls between the ages of ten and eighteen in schools all over the nation.

From their beginning activities as founders, members, and participants in the YWCA, black women petitioned in various ways to be recognized and represented in the organization's decision-making bodies. As early as 1915, black and white women met to try and resolve racial relations between central and colored branches in Southern cities where associations existed prior to the 1907 agreement and to demand black representation on regional field committees. After World War I, having greatly increased their number as members in the association, black women began to demand more control of the work of their own branches and to insist that their committee chairs become members of the local central committees;

moreover, they pressed for representation on the national board. In 1924, **Elizabeth Ross Haynes**, the national board's first full-time black staff member, was elected as the first black member of the board. Thereafter, black women also were represented on regional field committees. Further, in response to protests by black members, the national board resolved to hold national conventions only in cities that would assure accommodations to all members in attendance. Although black women were critical of the slow rate of progress, the so-called biracial policies of the organization were considered quite advanced for the time.

In 1931, the national board phased out its colored work subcommittee and assigned headquarters-based black workers to mainstream departments. Initially this plan was greeted by the black staff as a step toward interracial work. However, not long after it was put into place, Bowles resigned in protest, charging that in reality, "the plan would diminish the participation of Negroes in decision making." In response to her allegations, as well as to the mounting complaints of black association leaders, the national board formed a committee on interracial policies that functioned for ten years. During this period, the board also commissioned a national study of race relations in the association.

After a careful review of local associations, the national organization adopted an interracial charter in 1946, which served as an internal sanction against all forms of segregation in instances where there were no legal restrictions. This action was preceded in 1942 by a decision by black association leaders to disband their Negro Leadership Conference. (The conference dated back to the immediate post-war period when black

Dorothy Height (center of photo) was appointed in 1963 to be the director of the Office of Racial Justice of the YWCA, reflecting a more aggressive approach to integration. She is shown here at an awards ceremony with Mary McLeod Bethune. (SCHOMBURG CENTER)

residents of the South Atlantic region had no opportunity to function as part of normal association life; from their meetings had grown a national gathering of black YWCA representatives.) The unanimous 1946 vote was recorded as the recognition "that in the YWCA, the high value is its interrelatedness—its process of togetherness in working on the common concerns of humanity."

Adoption of the interracial charter was a watershed in the life of the organization. It meant that associations were expected to actively integrate black women into programs, facilities, and governing bodies. Eventually, it meant dismantling all segregated branches. In spite of strong resistance in many Southern cities, including a few court battles against the national board, and more subtle resistance in other parts of the country, the YWCA desegregation effort was fairly successful. To help local associations prepare for the change, the board assigned **Dorothy Height** to the position of interracial education secretary. In 1963, her position was changed to director of the Office of Racial Justice, reflecting a more aggressive approach. The new office was in charge of planning strategies to overcome internal segregation and to assist in the desegregation of all facilities.

The 1970 convention that voted in favor of the association's "one imperative" to eliminate racism was preceded by a series of interracial awareness gatherings for local members and a national board-sponsored retreat for 500 black leaders in the organization. During a period when black members had become disillusioned with the slow rate of progress and the high emotional cost of integration, the issue had become whether to remain part of the association or separate in order to be in complete charge of services to black women. After much agonizing, and with the thoughtful leadership of Helen Jackson Wilkins Claytor, the first black president of the national board, the group concluded that the organization represented a historic investment for black women as well as white women, and that they would present their "imperative" to the total convention.

Although the Young Women's Christian Association remains an organization with a predominantly white membership, its leadership has mirrored the organization's commitment to integration. Between 1973 and 1990, the organization chose two black women as national executive director, and two black women have served as president of the national board. Also, the programs and projects of local associations are scrutinized to ensure the inclusion of women of all races represented in the population.

ADRIENNE LASH JONES

Z

Zeta Phi Beta Sorority

The successful growth of Zeta Phi Beta sorority is perhaps best captured in a speech by its founder, first president, and grand basileus-emeritus, Arizona Cleaver Stemons, who said, "The lamp of learning is passed from hand to hand, the seed maturing becomes the many seeds of future plantings."

Zeta Phi Beta was founded on January 16, 1920, at **Howard University** in Washington, D.C. The period after World War I was a paradoxical time for black Americans. Tremendous strides had been made in creating greater opportunities for higher education and in acquiring personal property, and yet, the economic and political gains seemed minuscule because of the country's segregationist policies. There was no intermingling of the races, no engaging in interracial community and social activities. In addition, women had very limited roles to play. Women were chaperoned, they did not smoke or use profanity, and their primary pursuits were getting an education and exhibiting the finest qualities of womanhood. Thus, Zeta was founded at a time when there was a tremendous need for women to expand their roles in order to address many of the problematic issues confronting society.

Recognizing the need for an organization that would assume a leadership position in making the world a better place, Charles Robert Samuel Taylor, a member of Phi Beta Sigma fraternity (founded in January 1914), began to sow the seeds of a sister organization while escorting his friend, Arizona Cleaver Stemons, across the campus of Howard University in Washington, D.C. In 1919, Taylor and his brother, A. Langston Taylor, took Stemons' request to establish a sister organization to the Sigma conclave. After the request was approved, Stemons arranged a meeting in her dormitory room at Miner Hall with fourteen other women to determine whether there was interest in establishing a new sorority. Five of the women decided to establish a new organization, which subscribed to some of the basic tenets of the two other black sororities on campus. Thus, the first Greek sister and brother organizations were born—Phi Beta Sigma fraternity and Zeta Phi Beta sorority.

The five founders, called the five pearls, were Myrtle Tyler Faithful and Viola Tyler Goings, both education majors from Flushing, Ohio; Pearl Neal, a music major from Charlotte, North Carolina; Fannie Pettie Watts, an education/social work major from Perry, Georgia; and Arizona Cleaver Stemons, a social work major from Pike County, Missouri. The sorority, a private nonprofit organization, was incorporated in Washington, D.C., in 1923 and in Illinois in 1939.

The Taylor brothers formally introduced the sorority to the community by holding a reception at the Whitelaw Hotel in Washington, D.C. The Zetas also were welcomed in Miner Hall by members of the other two sororities, **Alpha Kappa Alpha** and **Delta Sigma Theta**. During the organization's first year, a Zeta, Pauline Phillips, earned top academic honors at Howard by graduating *summa cum laude*.

Taking blue and white as its colors, basing its constitution on that of the Sigmas, and borrowing part of its name from Phi Beta Sigma, Zeta Phi Beta sorority was chartered for the specific purpose of developing the ideals of service, educational and scholastic achievement, civic and cultural involvement, sisterhood, finer womanhood, and charity and compassion for all human beings. Cofounder Myrtle Faithful, the daughter of a former slave, emphasized that the sorority must distinguish itself by stressing its founding principles. Following the Greek alphabet, the first chapters were: Alpha at Howard; Beta at Morris Brown University in Atlanta; Gamma at Morgan State College in Baltimore; Delta at Pittsburg State College of Pittsburg (Kansas); and Epsilon in New York City.

Zeta Phi Beta's 75,000 members are primarily college-educated, black women professionals in medicine, law, dentistry, business, engineering, and education. Many prominent Americans have been Zetas, including **Violette Anderson**, the first black woman admitted to practice law before the U.S. Supreme Court; Deborah Wolfe, president of the New Jersey Higher Education Commission; and **Elizabeth Koontz**, first black president of the National Education Association.

There are 500 collegiate and graduate chapters in thirty-nine states, Washington, D.C., the Caribbean Islands, West Africa, and West Germany. In 1933, the sorority

was decentralized, and regions, to be supervised by regional directors, were designated. Local chapters are organized and administered in these nine regions: Atlantic, Eastern, Great Lakes, Midwestern, Pacific, South Central, South Eastern, Southern, and West Africa. Since its inception, when Arizona Stemons served as grand basileus (president), nineteen grand basileis have been elected, including current international grand basileus Eunice S. Thomas. The sorority is governed by a nationally elected board of directors and administered by an executive director at its national headquarters in Washington, D.C.

Zeta Phi Beta sorority has established a phenomenal track record as the first sorority constitutionally bound to a fraternity; as a charter member of the National Pan Hellenic Council, Inc.; as the first to organize international chapters in 1948 in West Africa and West Germany; the first to organize auxiliary groups for youths (Archonettes) and adults (Amicae); and the first to establish a centralized administrative office with a paid staff. Zetas opened the Domestic Science Center in Monrovia, Liberia, in October 1965.

Prior to 1965, the sorority's program thrust was housing and juvenile delinquency projects, including the sponsorship of vocational guidance clinics, youth clubs and camps, Operation Bootstrap (a parent-child training program), and debutante cotillions. In 1965, these projects were expanded under a new program called Welfare, Education, and Health Services, with the primary emphasis being the implementation of projects designed to address the issues of poverty, education, and health care. In 1975, the sorority established a tax-exempt private corporation, the National Educational Foundation, in an effort to facilitate educational scholarship, research, and community education projects. The sorority continues to implement innovative community service projects; among them Stork's Nest, a cooperative prenatal project with the March of Dimes; Illiteracy Eradication 2000, which includes tutorial partnerships; Project Zeta, designed to fight substance abuse; Just Say No clubs for youth; Project Z.I.P. (Zetas Investing in People); the Latch Key Children's Program; Zeta Leadership Academy; Zeta child care centers; and legislative initiatives for social and political change.

Seventy-one years after its inception, the seeds of Zeta Phi Beta Sorority, Inc., are still germinating, and the lamp of learning is still being passed from hand to hand. Perhaps the spirit of the organization is best captured in these thoughts: "Yesterday is gone. Use it as a guide, but don't dwell on it. Make the best of today by planting seeds and being agents of change. Make tomorrow better than today by cultivating and serving as living legacies."

ALGEANIA FREEMAN

Chronology

1619

A ship carrying twenty Africans into slavery lands at Jamestown, Virginia. Three are women.

1692

Tituba, a West Indian slave, is accused of witchcraft in the town of Salem, Massachusetts.

1758

The Bluestone African Baptist Church is formed on the Byrd plantation in Mecklenburg, Virginia.

1773

The Silver Bluff Baptist Church is founded in Silver Bluff, South Carolina.

1784

The first black Catholic community in the United States is founded in St. Augustine, Florida, by escaped slaves.

1787

The Free African Society, a mutual assistance organization, is founded by the free black citizens of Philadelphia to provide for their community.

1793

The welfare functions of the Free African Society are absorbed by the Female Benevolent Society of St. Thomas, one of hundreds of such societies organized by free black women in antebellum cities.

A former slave, **Catherine Ferguson**, enrolls forty-eight children, both black and white, in her school, called Katy Ferguson's School for the Poor, in New York City.

1794

The Bethel African Methodist Church, first known black church in the North, is founded in Philadelphia.

1796

The Benevolent Daughters is founded in Philadelphia.

1805

The Joy Street Baptist Church, first Northern Baptist church, is founded in Boston.

1809

Jarena Lee first asks to be allowed to preach, at the Bethel African Methodist Church of Philadelphia. Her request is refused.

The African Female Benevolent Society of Newport, Rhode Island, sponsors that city's school for black children until 1842, when Newport finally opens a public school.

1812

The Daughters of Africa is founded in Philadelphia.

1816

The African Methodist Episcopal (AME) Church, first black denomination, is founded.

1817

Jarena Lee is authorized by African Methodist Episcopal Bishop Richard Allen to lead prayer meetings in her house. She is, in this limited sense, the first woman minister in the AME.

Zilpha Elaw begins to preach, or "exhort" in the area around Burlington, New Jersey.

The American Female Bond Benevolent Society of Bethel is founded in Philadelphia.

1818

The Female Benezet is founded in Philadelphia.

1819

The Daughters of Aaron is founded in Philadelphia.

1821

The African Methodist Episcopal Zion (AMEZ) Church is founded.

Two hundred working-class women form the Daughters of Africa mutual benefit society.

1825

Zilpha Elaw becomes a traveling preacher, speaking against slavery and racism while speaking for God and traveling the South, as well as Washington, D.C., and Maryland.

1827

The African Dorcas Association is founded in New York to provide clothing for black schoolchildren.

The AME Daughters of Conference groups are officially sanctioned to offer clothing and other assistance to ministers.

1828

The St. Thomas Episcopal Church in Philadelphia hires a young black woman, Ann Appo, as church organist.

The Colored Female Roman Catholic Beneficial Society of Washington, D.C., is founded.

1829

One of the world's oldest black Catholic churches is founded in St. Augustine, Florida.

The **Oblate Sisters of Providence** is founded in Baltimore, Maryland. It is the first Roman Catholic religious community of black women.

1830

Women make up 49 percent of the American Protestant missionary force overseas. By 1880, that number had increased to 57 percent.

1830s and 1840s

Rebecca Cox Jackson travels from town to town preaching her own personal vision of God and speaking of the importance of unity among black people.

1831

Nat Turner's rebellion triggers laws in the South forbidding black Christians to worship without the presence of "respectable" whites.

The Female Literary Association of Philadelphia and the Afric-American Female Intelligence Society of Boston are founded.

1832

The Colored Female Charitable Society of Boston pledges itself to "mitigate [the] sufferings" of widows and orphans.

The Female Anti-Slavery Society of Salem, Massachusetts, is founded by black women.

1833

The interracial **Philadelphia Female Anti-Slavery Society** is founded with nine black women among the charter members. These women include Margaret Bowser, Grace Bustill Douglass, **Charlotte Forten [Grimké]**, **Sarah Louisa Forten**, **Margaretta Forten**, Sarah McCrummell, Harriet D. Purvis, Lydia White, and Mary Woods.

1837

When the first Antislavery Convention of American Women meets in New York, at least one-tenth of the members are African Americans. Grace Bustill Douglass is elected a vice president.

1838

There are 119 mutual aid societies in Philadelphia alone, more than half of which are female associations. Women make up nearly two-thirds of the membership of all benefit societies.

1842

Henriette Delille founds the second black Roman Catholic religious community in the United States, the **Sisters of the Holy Family**, in Louisiana.

1844

The first petition to the AME Church General Conference asking to license women to preach is defeated.

1846

The New Orleans Colored Female Benevolent Society of Louisiana, in addition to providing insurance benefits, calls for the "suppression of vice and inculcation of virtue among the colored class."

Zilpha Elaw publishes *Memoirs of the Life, Religious Experiences, Ministerial Travels and Labors of Mrs. Zilpha Elaw.*

1849

Jarena Lee publishes a "spiritual autobiography" that tells of her more than three decades of traveling and preaching the Christian gospel.

1859

Rebecca Cox Jackson founds the first black Shaker community, in Philadelphia.

1861

The Civil War begins.

1865

The Thirteenth Amendment to the Constitution, abolishing slavery, is adopted.

1867

The Independent Order of St. Luke is founded in Baltimore by a former slave, **Mary Prout.**

1868

The AME Church creates the position of stewardess. These women, chosen by the minister of each church, are officially allowed to render service to the church.

1869

Amanda Berry Smith begins conducting revivals. She spends most of her preaching career "exhorting" white audiences, particularly in the National Camp Meeting Movement, a Holiness crusade within the Methodist Episcopal Church.

1870

The Fifteenth Amendment is adopted and interpreted to provide black men with the right to vote. It does not extend the same right to black and white women, nor does it protect the voting rights of black men.

The Colored Methodist Episcopal (CME) Church is founded.

The Philadelphia Colored Women's Christian Association is founded. It is probably the first black **Young Women's Christian Association** (YWCA).

1876

Harriet Purvis is the first black woman to be elected vice president of the National Woman Suffrage Association.

1878

Amanda Berry Smith begins a twelve-year tour, preaching in England, Scotland, India, and West Africa.

1881

Atlanta Baptist Female Seminary is founded in Atlanta, Georgia. It will become Spelman Seminary in 1884.

1884

The General Conference of the AME agrees to license women preachers. These preachers are not ordained ministers of the gospel and can neither administer sacraments nor have churches.

1886

Louise "Lulu" Fleming is the first black woman to be commissioned for career missionary service by the Women's Baptist Foreign Missionary Society of the West.

1888

The General Conference of the AME Church reprimands Bishop Henry McNeal Turner for ordaining a woman, Sarah A. H. of North Carolina, without the sanction of the church.

Sarah E. Gorham, at the age of fifty-six, wins the right to serve as a missionary in Africa. She is the first woman appointed by the AME Church to serve in a foreign field.

Nancy Jones is the first unmarried black woman to be commissioned by the Congregational American Board as a missionary to Africa.

1890

Clarence and Corinne or God's Way, by Amelia E. Johnson, is the first book by a woman to be published by the American Baptist Publication Society and the first Sunday school book published by an African American.

1892

Members of the Bethel Literary and Historical Society come together with others in Washington to form the Colored Woman's League of Washington, D.C.

New York women, including **Victoria Earle Matthews** and Maritcha Lyons, form the Woman's Loyal Union.

Boston women, including **Josephine St. Pierre Ruffin**, her daughter **Florida Ruffin**

Ridley, and **Maria Baldwin**, form the Woman's Era Club.

1893

The Woman's Home and Missionary Society of the AME Church is founded.

Anna Julia Cooper, **Fanny Jackson Coppin**, and **Fannie Barrier Williams** address the Women's Congress at the **World's Columbian Exposition** in Chicago.

1894

The *Woman's Era*, later to become the official newspaper of the **National Association of Colored Women** (NACW), begins publication.

1895

The Colored Women's League of Washington, D.C., makes the first attempt to form a national black women's organization, at the National Council of Women convention. The result is the National Colored Women's League (NCWL).

One hundred and four women from twenty clubs come together at a conference in Boston and form the National Federation of Afro-American Women (NFAW).

The National Baptist Convention (NBC) is formed.

The Church of God in Christ (COGIC) is founded.

1896

The NCWL and the NFAW merge to form the **National Association of Colored Women** (NACW).

1897

Sara J. Hatcher Duncan becomes general superintendent of the Women's Home and Foreign Missionary Society of the AME, making her one of the most influential women to that date in the black church.

Victoria Earle Matthews founds the **White Rose Mission** in New York City to serve as a community center, with special emphasis on assistance to black women migrating from the South.

1899

The Richmond branch of the Independent Order of St. Luke comes under the leadership of **Maggie Lena Walker**.

1900

The General Conference of the AME creates the position of deaconess.

Nannie Helen Burroughs delivers the speech entitled "How the Women Are Hindered from Helping" at the National Baptist Convention annual meeting. Under her leadership, the Women's Convention of the National Baptist Convention (NBC) is formed.

1903

The Women's Convention of the National Baptist Convention has almost one million members.

1904

Mary Church Terrell represents the **National Association of Colored Women** (NACW) at the International Council of Women congress in Berlin, Germany.

1905

Eva del Vakia Bowles becomes the first black woman on the **Young Women's Christian Association** (YWCA) staff.

In service to the black community, the Woman's Improvement Club of Indianapolis opens an outdoor tuberculosis camp.

1906
The National League for the Protection of Colored Women is founded.

1908
Alpha Kappa Alpha Sorority, the first black Greek letter society for women, is founded at **Howard University.**

The Empire Federation of Colored Women's Clubs is founded.

The Atlanta **Neighborhood Union** is founded, under the leadership of **Lugenia Burns Hope.**

1909
The **National Association for the Advancement of Colored People** (NAACP) is founded.

1910
Sara Winifred Brown, Mary Church Terrell, and others establish the College Alumnae Club.

1911
The National Urban League is founded.

1913
Delta Sigma Theta Sorority, the second Greek letter society for black women, is founded.

1915
Mary Burnett Talbert becomes president of the **National Association of Colored Women** (NACW), serving until 1920 and representing the NACW at the meeting of the International Council of Women in Norway.

1916
The first black students' conference of **the Young Women's Christian Association** (YWCA) is held at Spelman Seminary in Atlanta, Georgia.

1917
Black women develop the Circle for Negro War Relief to provide medical, recreational, and other services to black soldiers.

1918
Juliette Derricotte becomes secretary of the national student council of the **Young Women's Christian Association** (YWCA).

1920
Zeta Phi Beta Sorority is founded. It is the third Greek letter society for African-American women.

The **Southeastern Association of Colored Women's Clubs** holds its first conference at Tuskegee Institute, where **Mary McLeod Bethune** is elected its first president and **Charlotte Hawkins Brown** is elected chairperson of the executive board.

1921
Mary Talbert's invitation to speak at a National Woman's Party (NWP) meeting is rescinded after Alice Paul, NWP president, rules that, as a representative of the **National Association for the Advancement of Colored People** (NAACP), Talbert represents an organization related to race, not sex.

1922

The Anti-Lynching Crusaders is organized under Mary Talbert's leadership.

The first Greek letter society for black woman on a predominantly white campus is founded. It is **Sigma Gamma Rho**, at Butler University in Indianapolis.

1924

The Methodist Episcopal (later United Methodist) Church approves limited ordination for women.

Mary McLeod Bethune becomes president of the **National Association of Colored Women** (NACW).

Elizabeth Ross Haynes is the first black woman elected to the National Board of the **Young Women's Christian Association** (YWCA).

1925

Black delegates are seated at a conference of the International Council of Women after a protest by Mary McLeod Bethune.

1926

An interracial charter is adopted by the Young Women's Christian Association (YWCA), committing the organization to the involvement of black women.

1927

Girl Friends, Inc., a national social, civic, charitable, and cultural organization, is formed in New York City.

1928

The **National Association of Colored Women** (NACW) opens its national headquarters in Washington, D.C.

1935

The **National Council of Negro Women** (NCNW) is founded.

Mary McLeod Bethune is appointed by President Franklin Delano Roosevelt to the Advisory Board of the National Youth Administration (NYA) and in December, begins her tenure as director of the newly created Division of Negro Affairs of the NYA.

1938

The National Council of Negro Women (NCNW) sponsors a national Conference on Governmental Cooperation in the Approach to the Problems of Negro Women and Children, held at the Department of the Interior and the White House.

Jack and Jill of America, Inc., is founded to sponsor cultural events and opportunities for black children.

1946

The Links, Inc., is founded in Philadelphia by Margaret Roselle Hawkins and Sarah Strickland Scott.

1948

The AME Church agrees to ordain women, making official the position of traveling evangelists and teachers.

1950s

Early in this decade, the **Women's Political Council (WPC) of Montgomery, Alabama** decides to make the issue of discrimination on buses its prime concern.

1955

On December 1, **Rosa Parks** triggers the Montgomery, Alabama, bus boycott by refusing to give up her seat.

1956

Women attain full status as ministers in the Methodist Episcopal Church and the United Presbyterian Church.

1957

Dorothy I. Height becomes the fourth president of **the** National Council of Negro Women (NCNW).

Ebony Fashion Fair stages its first tour. It will grow into the world's largest traveling fashion show, raising millions of dollars for black churches, schools, and charitable institutions.

1967

Helen Natalie Jackson Clayton becomes the first African American to serve as national president of the Young Women's Christian Association (YWCA).

1976

Every major Protestant denomination in the United States has approved the ordination of women. The Church of God in Christ (COGIC) still has not done so.

1984

Leontine T. C. Kelly is named bishop in the United Methodist Church. She is the first African-American woman to become a bishop in any major denomination in the United States.

1989

Barbara Harris is consecrated a bishop of the Episcopal Church. She is the first woman of any race to fill that position.

Joan Salmon Campell is elected moderator of the Presbyterian Church, U. S. A. She is the first black woman and the sixth woman to head the church.

1990

Sister Cora Billings is installed as a pastor in Richmond, Virginia, becoming the first black nun to head a parish in the United States.

1991

Edith Guffey is named Secretary of the United Church of Christ, making her an administrator in one of the largest religious organizations in the country.

1992

Diane M. Porter is named Senior Executive for Program for the Domestic and Foreign Missionary Society of the Episcopal Church, one of the highest positions in that denomination.

Bibliography

GENERAL BOOKS USEFUL TO THE STUDY OF BLACK WOMEN IN AMERICA

Reference Books

African-Americans: Voices of Triumph. Three volume set: *Perseverance, Leadership,* and *Creative Fire.* By the editors of Time-Life Books, Alexandria, Virginia, 1993.

Estell, Kenneth, ed. *The African-American Almanac.* Detroit, Michigan, 1994.

Harley, Sharon. *The Timetables of African-American History: A Chronology of the Most Important People and Events in African-American History.* New York, 1995.

Hine, Darlene Clark. *Hine Sight: Black Women and The Re-Construction of American History.* Brooklyn, New York, 1994.

Hine, Darlene Clark, ed., Elsa Barkley Brown and Rosalyn Terborg-Penn, associate eds. *Black Women in America: An Historical Encyclopedia.* Brooklyn, New York, 1993.

Hornsby, Alton, Jr. *Chronology of African-American History: Significant Events and People from 1619 to the Present.* Detroit, Michigan, 1991.

Kranz, Rachel. *Biographical Dictionary of Black Americans.* New York, 1992.

Lanker, Brian. *I Dream a World: Portraits of Black Women Who Changed America.* New York, 1989.

Logan, Rayford W., and Michael R. Winston, eds. *Dictionary of American Negro Biography.* New York, 1982.

Low, W. Augustus, and Virgil A. Clift, eds. *Encyclopedia of Black America.* New York, 1981.

Salem, Dorothy C., ed. *African American Women: A Biographical Dictionary.* New York, 1993.

Salzman, Jack, David Lionel Smith, and Cornel West. *Encyclopedia of African-American Culture and History.* Five Volumes. New York, 1996.

Smith, Jessie Carney, ed., *Notable Black American Women.* Two Volumes. Detroit, Michigan, Book I, 1993; Book II, 1996.

General Books about Black Women

Giddings, Paula. *When and Where I Enter: The Impact of Black Women on Race and Sex in America.* New York, 1984.

Guy-Sheftall, Beverly. *Words of Fire: An Anthology of African-American Feminist Thought.* New York, 1995.

Hine, Darlene Clark, Wilma King, and Linda Reed, eds. *"We Specialize in the Wholly Impossible": A Reader in Black Women's History.* Brooklyn, New York, 1995.

Jones, Jacqueline. *Labor of Love, Labor of Sorrow: Black Women, Work, and the Family from Slavery to the Present.* New York, 1985.

Lerner, Gerda, ed. *Black Women in White America: A Documentary History.* New York, 1972.

BOOKS ABOUT BLACK WOMEN IN RELIGION AND COMMUNITY

Giddings, Paula. *In Search of Sisterhood: Delta Sigma Theta and the Challenge of the Black Sorority Movement.* New York, 1988.

Higginbotham, Evelyn Brooks. *Righteous Discontent: The Women's Movement in the Black Baptist Church, 1880–1920.* Cambridge, Massachusetts, 1993.

Neverdon-Morton, Cynthia. *Afro-American Women of the South and the Advancement of the Race, 1985–1925.* Knoxville, Tennessee, 1989.

Salem, Dorothy. *To Better Our World: Black Women in Organized Reform, 1890–1920.* Brooklyn, New York, 1990.

Contents of the Set

(ORGANIZED BY VOLUME)

Dance, Sports, and Visual Arts

Dance

Sports

Visual Arts

Jackson-Jarvis, Martha
Jones, Lois Mailou
Lewis, Mary Edmonia
Maynard, Valerie
McCullough, Geraldine
Moutoussamy-Ashe, Jeanne
Owens-Hart, Winnie
Pindell, Howardena
Piper, Adrian
Pogue, Stephanie
Powers, Harriet
Prophet, Nancy Elizabeth
Ringgold, Faith
Roberts, Malkia
Saar, Alison
Saar, Betye
Savage, Augusta
Sklarek, Norma Merrick
Thomas, Alma
Waring, Laura Wheeler
Woodard, Beulah Ecton

Business and Professions

Andrews, Rosalyn
Avant, Angela
Baker, Augusta
Beasley, Delilah
Bowen, Ruth
Bowser, Yvette Lee
Bradford, Martina
Bragg, Janet Harmon
Bricktop (Ada Smith)
Britton, Mary E.
Brooks, Hallie
Brown, Willa Beatrice
Brunson, Dorothy
Cadoria, Sheridan Grace
Cardozo Sisters
Clayton, Xernona
Coleman, Bessie
Coston, Julia Ringwood
Day, Carolyn Bond
Delaney, Sara "Sadie"
de Passe, Suzanne
Diggs, Ellen Irene
Dunnigan, Alice

Early, Charity Adams
Fisher, Ruth Anna
Florence, Virginia
Fudge, Ann
Gillespie, Marcia Ann
Gleason, Eliza Atkins
Hare, Maud Cuney
Harris, Marcelite
Harsh, Vivian Gordon
Haynes, Elizabeth Ross
Houston, Drusilla Dunjee
Hunter-Gault, Charlayne
Hutson, Jean Blackwell
Jefferson, Lucy
Jemison, Mae C.
Jenkins, Carol
Johnson, Eunice Walker
Jones, Clara Stanton
Jones, Virginia Lacy
Julian, Anna Johnson
King, Reatha Clark
Latimer, Catherine Allen
Lewis, Ida Elizabeth
Major, Gerri
Malone, Annie Turnbo
Malveaux, Julianne
Matthews, Miriam
McClain, Leanita
Morgan, Rose
Murray, Joan
Nelson, Jill
Oglesby, Mary
Payne, Ethel L.
Phinazee, Alethia
Pleasant, Mary Ellen
Procope, Ernesta G.
Proctor, Barbara Gardner
Quarles, Norma R.
Randolph, Lucille
Rhone, Sylvia
Rollins, Charlemae Hill
Saunders, Doris
Simmons, Judy
Simpson, Carole
Sims, Naomi
Smith, Ida Van
Smith, Jessie Carney
Stewart, Pearl
Taylor, Susan

Thompson, Era Bell
Villarosa, Linda
Walker, Madam C. J.
Washington, Sarah Spencer
Wattleton, Faye
Wesley, Dorothy Porter
White, Eartha Mary
Willis, Gertrude

Music

Addison, Adele
Akers, Doris
Allen, Geri
Anderson, Ernestine
Anderson, Marian
Armstrong, Lillian "Lil"
Arroyo, Martina
Ashby, Dorothy Jeanne
Austin, Lovie
Bailey, Pearl
Baiocchi, Regina Harris
Baker, Anita
Baker, LaVern
Barnett, Etta Moten
Barrett, "Sweet Emma"
Barton, Willene
Battle, Kathleen
Blige, Mary J.
Bonds, Margaret
Braxton, Toni
Brice, Carol
Brown, Anne Wiggins
Brown, Cleo Patra
Brown, Ruth
Bryant, Clora
Bryant, Hazel Joan
Bumbry, Grace
Caesar, Shirley
Calloway, Blanche
Campbell, Lucie E.
Capers, Valerie
Cara, Irene
Carlisle, Una Mae
Carter, Betty
Chapman, Tracy
Chiffons, The
Coates, Dorothy

Education

Religion and Community

Science, Health, and Medicine

Contents of the Set

(LISTED ALPHABETICALLY BY ENTRY)

Index

Page numbers in **boldface** indicate main entries. *Italic* page numbers indicate illustrations.